DISCA

ZOAR

ZOAR

The Story of an Intentional Community

KATHLEEN M. FERNANDEZ

THE KENT STATE UNIVERSITY PRESS

Kent, Ohio

To my late husband, Jim Hillibish.

I wish we could have written this together.

© 2019 by The Kent State University Press, Kent, Ohio 44242
ALL RIGHTS RESERVED
Library of Congress Catalog Card Number 2018052569
ISBN 978-1-60635-374-5
Manufactured in the United States of America

Parts of chapter 9, "Zoar and the Courts," were first published as "The Society of Separatists of Zoar v . . . " in *Communal Societies* 26, no. 1 (2006).

Parts of chapters 1–3 were first published as "A Separatist Song: A Newly Discovered Poem about Zoar's Beginnings" in *Communal Societies* 38, no. 1 (2018).

LIBRARY OF CONGRESS CATALOGING-IN-PUBLICATION DATA
Names: Fernandez, Kathleen M., 1949- author.
Title: Zoar : the story of an intentional community / Kathleen M. Fernandez.
Description: Kent, Ohio : Kent State University Press, 2019. | Includes bibliographical references and index.
Identifiers: LCCN 2018052569 | ISBN 9781606353745 (cloth)
Subjects: LCSH: Society of Separatists of Zoar. | Collective settlements--Ohio--History--19th century. | Zoar (Tuscarawas County, Ohio)--History.
Classification: LCC HX656.Z8 F47 2019 | DDC 307.7709771/66--dc23
LC record available at https://lccn.loc.gov/2018052569

23 22 21 20 19   5 4 3 2 1

Contents

Introduction

Eine güter Gemeinschaft. In German, it means "a community of goods," or "a communal society," but in another context, it can also mean "a good community."[1] And it was. For seventy-nine years, this group of German emigrants and their descendants were part of one of the most successful communal societies in the United States. They called their town "Zoar," named for Lot's place of refuge in the Bible, and it was a refuge indeed.

It was not to form a communal group that a band of close to three hundred German Radical Pietist dissenters left their homes in Württemberg in 1817. They only wanted to worship their God the way they wanted, without interference from the government or church authorities, which in Württemberg were one and the same.

Sharing everything was not their initial aim—worshipping together was. But when economic conditions and a hard winter would have forced them apart, they instead bound themselves together into this *güter Gemeinschaft,* a community of goods, where all shared their work, their wealth, and their future.

With luck, pluck, and a lot of hard work they became so successful in America that by the 1860s both their neighbors and the local Tuscarawas County government were borrowing money from them, exceeding anything they had dreamed of in Germany. All because they worked together, men and women alike, in community.

It was crucial that they had a person to lead them who could translate their mystical religious beliefs into such spellbinding sermons that they were published after his death. This same person, Joseph Michael Bäumler (later Bimeler), went from being a simple weaver in Ulm, Germany, to influencing the State of Ohio to bring the Ohio & Erie Canal through their land, paving the way for the community's success.

Sheer economic desperation drove them to become communal. If they had not banded together, shared the work and the sacrifice, they could not have become this "singular people," as one outsider called them. But it was not easy. They suffered from bad weather, disaffected members leaving and filing lawsuits, an epidemic of cholera that wiped out a third of the village in 1834, and, after Bimeler's death in 1853, a leadership void that no one could truly fill.

If they had not had the memories of the floggings, hard labor, and jail time in Württemberg to spur them on and the solace of their religion and the longed-for Resurrection to comfort them, these immigrants, like so many, may have gone their different ways in America. Instead, they persevered—together.

Despite its success, the Society of Separatists of Zoar, so called because the members had separated themselves from the established state Lutheran Church in Württemberg, eventually came to an end in 1898. The admiration (and curiosity) of outsiders toward them caused problems in the community. Travelers brought not only money to the Society coffers but also envy and an underground cash economy, both factors in the Society's eventual demise. Other reasons for the dissolution included a decline in religious fervor, the death of those who could remember the persecutions in Germany, some bad investments, lack of outlay in technology, and the young leaving to seek their fortunes outside.

But for almost four score years, the community flourished, creating a little piece of Germany in east-central Ohio, which even today showcases its German heritage and the legacy of how a group of foreign religious dissenters can persevere in America to create *eine güter Gemeinschaft.*

It is their story I hope to tell in this volume.

Author's Note

This book has been many years in the making. As site manager of Zoar Village State Memorial for fifteen years (1989-2004), it's a book I myself wanted to use to interpret the village to visitors. A book compiling all of the myriad sources of information about Zoar was not available; the closest thing was Edgar Nixon's dissertation (thank goodness for that!), but it was not published and has only recently been available online, so was not accessible to either scholars or the public. Several manuscript collections have been acquired by the Ohio History Connection since Nixon's work, most notably the Jack and Pat Adamson Collection, purchased by the Ohio Historical Society in 2000 and used extensively in this work.

In the book, I have standardized the spelling of German names, especially that of Zoar's leader, Joseph Bimeler. Although his name in German is "Bäumler," he changed it to "Bimeler" in America, so I've used that spelling throughout the book, including correspondence in which he is addressed in the German form. And, although it's not scholarly convention, the names of Zoar buildings, (Number One House, the Bakery, etc.) are capitalized, as they are the official designations of these buildings, both then and now. Except for Number One House ("Nummer Eins"), the other numbered Zoar homes are indicated with an Arabic number ("Number 9 House"). Primary source material containing underlining is shown with italics.

As you see in the bibliography, there has not been a lot of scholarly research on Zoar. Unlike Harmonist scholars, who have Karl J. R. Arndt to thank for his books of translated documents, the Zoar Papers have not been translated into English until recently, and there has been no basic history widely available to spur scholarly research. I hope this book will help eliminate Zoar's perceived position as the "stepchild" of historic communal research.

I wish to thank everyone who has helped me learn more about Zoar. First of all, thank you to my Otterbein history professor, Dr. Thomas Kerr, who introduced me to the joys of research. Thanks also to Dr. Amos Loveday, formerly of the Ohio Historical Society, who hired me at Zoar and who was my supervisor there for many years; thanks for your belief in me. Thank you to the Communal Studies Association and its first director, Dr. Donald E. Pitzer, for showing me that there are many parallels in the history of communal societies, that they come in all shapes and sizes, and for giving me a platform to present my early Zoar research.

Thank you to the people of Zoar and the Zoar Community Association for their commitment to the preservation of this unique town. Thanks also to the Ohio Historical Society, now the Ohio History Connection, and the State of Ohio for their dedication to maintaining the historic fabric of Zoar, its physical buildings, collections, and records. I invite all scholars to delve into the various collections of Zoar Papers to find even more treasures than I have discovered.

My thanks go to the many scholars who have helped with this work, by reading chapters, translating documents, and providing insights. A grateful thank you to Dr. Eberhard Fritz, archivist to the Duke of Württemberg, whose research on the early Separatists has been invaluable to my understanding of why the Separatists emigrated. Little did I know when I answered that long-ago phone call from Germany how much help you would give me. Thanks also to Dr. Hermann Ehmer, University of Tübingen, for locating a key document and for reading chapters. As I am not a German speaker (oh, how I wish I were!), I have depended on my good friend Dr. Philip Webber, retired German professor at Central College in Pella, Iowa, and a Zoar scholar in his own right, for translations and chapter readings. Thank you to another good friend and colleague (and former intern!) Susan Colpetzer Goehring for reading the chapter on tourism. Thanks also to my Communal Studies Association friends Lanny Haldy of Amana and Carol Medlicott of Northern Kentucky University for locating Amana and Shaker documents for me. Additional thanks go to Dr. Donald Pitzer of the University of Southern Indiana for his comments on the book.

Thank you to the staff of Kent State University Press for their help in editing and production and for their commitment to publishing material on Zoar.

And, finally, thank you to my friends and family for their support, and to Judi for keeping my doxie, Lilly, while I was away on researching trips. I appreciate your faith in me.

Kathleen Fernandez
North Canton, Ohio
November 2018

CHAPTER 1

"And Speak the Truth Freely"

Zoar Separatists in Germany

Even as the Separatists
Perceived the tyranny,
And wished to live as Christians
And speak the truth freely,
The war and battle raged
Far and wide throughout the land.
   —Daniel Huber, untitled poem, 1833

In 1833, just two years after his arrival in Zoar, Daniel Ulrich Huber penned a forty-one-verse poem describing the Separatists' travails in Germany and their emigration to America.[1] Huber (1768-1840) was a shoemaker, and, although he waited until 1831 to emigrate, he had witnessed their persecution in Germany firsthand—he was one of the ringleaders of the fledgling Separatist movement in his hometown of Rottenacker, a village in the district of Alb-Donau (on the Danube) in southeastern Württemberg. Historian Eberhard Fritz has called the Huber family "the nucleus of the Rottenacker Separatists' movement."[2] Daniel, his brother Stephan, their father Stephan, cousin Johannes, and their families broke away from the established state-run Lutheran Church as early as 1792.[3] Daniel, something of a martyr, actively disobeyed the church ministers by not attending Sunday services, keeping his children from the church-run schools, and refusing to doff his cap in front of the authorities. For this, soldiers were quartered in his home, and he spent jail time in the Fortress Asperg, as did many other Separatists.[4]

Why did he rebel? Let's let Daniel tell his story:

Verse 4
Noble freedom, noble fortune
Here in the liberated land,
Yes, when I think back now,
To the sorrowful condition
Where the countryman's goods and blood
Belonged to the brood of tyrants.[5]

One "tyrant" referred to was Duke Friedrich II of Württemberg (who became elector in 1803 and King Friedrich I in 1805). The Peace of Augsburg treaty in 1555 allowed the rulers of the many territories now making up today's Germany to decide how their subjects would worship. The Peace of Westphalia (1648) at the conclusion of the Thirty Years' War confirmed this policy: the religion of the ruler in 1624 became that of his subjects. For the most part, the inhabitants were not allowed to choose their own religion. The country in southwest Germany ruled by the Duke of Württemberg became Lutheran, with state and church rules intermingled. Church attendance was mandatory, all children were required to be baptized, schools were run by the church, and citizens were forced to pay for a minister they could not choose.

In 1800 the French Empire under Napoleon Bonaparte occupied Württemberg, causing Duke Friedrich and his wife to flee. In 1803, after annexing the west bank of the Rhine, Napoleon elevated the now-returned Friedrich to the office of elector. With the Confederation of the Rhine, Friedrich became king, allowing him to take over the lands of many smaller nearby principalities.

During this period, the uncomfortable tensions between the church and some of Württemberg's residents became even worse. The people were suffering: men were drafted into the state's army, battles were fought in the area, and the government was spending money on the war, not on its citizens. The state-run Lutheran Church wasn't sufficiently responding to the spiritual needs of its congregations—it seemed to care only about its formal rituals and making sure that the people attended church and paid tithes (taxes that supported the church and clergy). It did not help that church attendance

Called a "tyrant" by the Separatists, Württemberg's King Friedrich considered the Separatists to be lawbreakers and forbade them to emigrate. He sentenced many to jail for long periods. (King Friedrich I of Württemberg, early nineteenth century, painter unknown. Private collection.)

was mandatory; this suggested some congregation members were cynical unbelievers just going through the motions because they had to, while others had a sincere desire to be better Christians.

PIETISM

As a remedy, around 1800, at the start of Napoleon's campaign, some people turned to a reformist movement called Pietism that had energized the church more than a century before. Pietists believed in a direct, personal relationship with God. Pietist assemblies had coexisted with the state church since the 1700s, but attendance now increased. For others, however, becoming Pietist wasn't enough. They thought the church was too corrupt, too ritualistic, and not personal enough to meet their spiritual needs. These folks became *Radical Pietists,* focusing on a deep, individually felt devotion to God. Eberhard Fritz observed that Separatism "has always risen in times of crisis" within the Lutheran Church.[6] Pietism was called "the religion of the heart." Its hallmarks were individual prayer, hymns, Bible study, and personal conversion, or *Wiedergeburt* (born again), in which a once-sinful life was begun anew. Because these practices largely bypassed the clergy and laws regarding church attendance, Pietism was inherently heretical. Most Pietists wished to reform from within the church; others, including those who eventually came to Zoar, wished to leave a church that could not be reformed.[7]

Seventeenth-century Pietism, originally a derisive term given to adherents by their opponents, has been called "the most significant religious movement in Protestant Christianity since the Reformation." Whereas the Reformation begun by Luther in 1517 was a reformation of church *practices,* Pietism was a reformation of church *life.*[8] After the Thirty Years' War (1618-1648), where Germany was a battleground, everyday life was difficult, but the populace found the Lutheran Church more concerned with dogma than solace.

Pietism is said to have begun around 1675 with the publication of *Pia Desideria* ("Pious Desires") by a Lutheran minister named Philip Jakob Spener (1635-1705). The book's subtitle, "Heartfelt Longing for a God Pleasing Convalescence," illustrates Spener's desire for a more responsive church. He accused the church of "ceremonialism and arrogance" and wished for the laity to be more educated about the Scriptures, to be more involved in all functions of the church, and to practice their faith in their daily lives.[9] Adherents met in "conventicles," small prayer groups held in private homes or churches. This movement gained considerable influence within the Lutheran Church until the advent of "rationalism" in the early eighteenth century. Religious rationalism rejected symbolism and was highly logical. This new rational perspective, plus the adoption of a new hymnbook (1791) and a new liturgy (1805) in Württemberg,[10] caused many congregants to "separate" from an established church they viewed as Babel.

A large part of what became the Zoar religion was based on mysticism, with the shoemaker Jakob Böhme (1575-1624) as one of the greatest visionaries. His book *Aurora,* ("Die Morgenröte im Aufgang" ["Rising Dawn"], 1612), was the result of a dream, or "central vision" (*Zentralschau*), he had in 1600. He urged man to prepare for a "new dawn" or new way of life. Böhme was pantheistic, seeing "everything in God and God in everything."[11] In *Aurora* he described his vision of the "Heavenly Sophia," the personification of divine wisdom, the female aspect of God. After his book was judged heretical even by his own pastor, Böhme did not put pen to paper again until 1618, when he began a flurry of writing, including *Mysterium Magnum* (1623) and *Weg zu Christo* (1624), both of which were in Zoar leader Joseph Bimeler's library. Böhme believed in "dualism": light/dark, good/evil, life/death. He also was a chiliast, or millennialist, believing the world would soon end with

Christ's return to reign in a "Golden Paradise" for a thousand years prior to the final judgment, a belief derived from Revelation 20:1-6, that man should be prepared for the Second Coming by living an exemplary life, to welcome his Savior at any time.[12]

All this—the philosophers, the conventicles, and the controversies of the Pietist movement—took place well over a hundred years before those who came to Zoar were even born. Why did they choose the beliefs of Radical Pietism to call their own?

The political circumstances were similar—war (the Thirty Years' War in the case of the earlier Pietists, and the Napoleonic wars in the case of the soon-to-be Zoarites) and the havoc, destruction, and upheaval it caused drew many to the comfort of religion, but the church they turned to was not responsive, for it was too doctrinal earlier, too unfeeling in later years. To the latter group, there was nothing left to do but rebel, to refuse to attend church, to worship on their own in secret, and to refuse to send their children to church-run schools: in other words, to break the law.

Jacob Sylvan, one of the group's leaders, described the situation in the preface of *Die Wahre Separation oder die Wiedergeburt* ("The True Separation or the Rebirth"), the first book of Bimeler's Sunday *Discourses,* or sermons, printed after his death: "Just as the kingdom of darkness was making its cruel impact felt most intensely (through the French Revolution, terrible wars, and a highly depraved humanity with its spirit for vices and all their

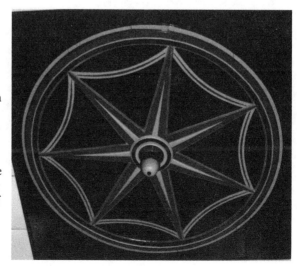

The seven-pointed star, representing the Star of Bethlehem and the light of God in us all, was the symbol of the Separatists. In Germany, stars made of cloth were worn as badges, with wearers punished by the authorities. In America, the star became Zoar's emblem and is shown here on the ceiling of Zoar's Number One House. (Courtesy of the Ohio History Connection, David Barker, photographer.)

consequences), God prepared an instrument [*Werkzeug*] to counter all this,[13] and raised a light that should shine among the peoples, and it did shine and spread its beams. In the souls of those who allowed themselves to be illuminated by this light, a bright signal star [*ein heller Signalstern*] arose, and seeing this very light, they could be glad and rejoice in it. This light showed them clearly and convincingly what God proposed to do at that time with humanity, and how He now intended to set up His kingdom."[14]

ROTTENACKER

According to extant records, Separatist activity began in Rottenacker, home to poet Daniel Ulrich Huber.

> *Verse 8*
> The officials and the priests,
> Came forth in total anger.
> It was decreed that [the Separatists] should be punished
> Until they took off their cap and hat.
> Troops would be sent to them
> Until they gave [the authorities] honor.[15]

Although the town of Rottenacker may not be typical of the approximately thirty-six villages from which the Zoar Separatists came, we know the most about it, thanks to the research of German historian Eberhard Fritz.[16] It was the home to two early Separatist leaders, Stephan Huber and Johannes Breymaier (also Breimaier), and the town had the distinction of being occupied by the king's troops in 1804 to quell the rebellious Separatists. It was also here where a Swiss visionary, Barbara Grubermann (also Grubenmann) came to live, preach, and greatly influence their beliefs.

Rottenacker, in southern Württemberg, a Protestant enclave surrounded by Catholic villages, was originally property of the Abbey at Blaubeuren. Because of its isolation, its inhabitants intermarried and were all closely related. Unlike most villages, the highest official was not its mayor, but a governor/bailiff. A committee composed of the governor, mayor, town council, and leading citizens chose the minister. As in all Württemberg villages, everyone was required to attend church and send their children to the church-run schools.[17]

It is said that underground secret religious assemblies began in Rotte-nacker sometime around 1790, with itinerant preachers helping to spread Pietist teachings.[18] First to be influenced were the Huber family, shoemaker Stephan, his sons—Stephan (1759-1838) and Daniel Ulrich, the poet, whom you have met—and his cousin Johannes (1747-1807). Johannes, a tailor, had traveled to nearby Switzerland on business and heard the visionary Barbara Grubermann preach.

Grubermann was born in 1767 in Niederteufen, near the larger town of Teufen in Canton Appenzell-Ausserrhoden, Switzerland. She was reported to be a stubborn child, chided for not staying in her seat during church services. Little is known of her religious education, but she apparently read the Berleburg Bible (printed 1736-42), an annotated version used by many Separatists, and consulted the works of Konrad Dippel (1693-1734), another Pietist theologian; these influences seem to have inspired her to separate from the church.[19]

While preaching, she would deliver "prophetic sermons, ecstasies and visions" and enter trances that could last for days. According to Fritz: "Al-legedly she saw the spirits of heaven, and she was convinced that all things returned after the souls had been cleansed in heaven so anyone could be saved. She thought that even the devil would be saved some day and be-lieved that she knew which of those deceased were in heaven and which still stayed in hell. She encouraged people to do penance and dismissed the church, its ministers and catechism. When she experienced states of trance she did not feel any pain."[20]

After several years of preaching such borderline blasphemy, Grubermann fled from Teufen, hiding in several locations, and was briefly imprisoned. It was after escaping from prison in 1792—at the Zurich home of a promi-nent Swiss Pietist minister, Johann Kaspar Lavater (1741-1801), who was sympathetic to Radical Pietism—that the three Huber men met Barbara Grubermann and invited her to stay in Rottenacker.[21]

Barbara arrived in Rottenacker that same year. There, she lived with Stephan and Daniel's widowed mother, Dorothea, and worked as a maid for Johannes. At first, she preached to the underground conventicles but still attended church and took Holy Communion. She traveled back and forth to Switzerland during these years, even getting married to a fellow Swiss, Johann Ulrich Mohn, for a short time (she left her husband due to his "extravagance").[22]

More families began to join the Separatists. Any lawbreaking with regard to prayer groups or church attendance was ignored until about 1800,
with the advent of two new officials, Governor August Ludwig Friedrich
Schuster and Minister Christoph Ludwig Rau.

Village officials in Württemberg supervised the morals of the townspeople in the courtlike *Kirchenkonvent,* made up of the mayor, pastor, and
leading citizens. This body also directed the school, which was run by the
church. It was in the *Kirchenkonvent* that any complaints about the Separatists' conduct were raised.[23]

The Separatists began to get bolder and provoke the authorities. Male
followers were derisively called "Babele's Boys" or, worse, "Babele's Whore-
Boys." (Babele was a nickname for Barbara.) The atmosphere ebbed and
flowed until 1803, when the Separatists began to have daily meetings,
inviting Separatists from other villages. (It should be noted that overnight
visitation between villages had to be reported. Unlike today, a person could
not move freely from town to town.) They installed an organ in a member's
home, and their spritely songs, much happier than the usual hymns, were
also accompanied by a fiddle.[24]

One song by Stephan Huber ("Now Raise Your Head and See") was sung
at prayer meetings all around Württemberg, and contrasted the current
political situation with Huber's religious convictions. The political content
of this song, along with the Separatists' sympathies toward the French
Revolution (they wore blue trousers, red and white caps, and cockades,
or fabric rosettes, which resembled the French tricolor flag) has led some
German historians to consider the Zoar Separatists as more political than
religious dissenters. This may have been true in Germany, but after their
arrival in America, the Separatists were apolitical (see chapter 8).[25]

Also worn as a symbol of their beliefs was a small fabric and thread
representation of the Star of Bethlehem, that "bright signal star" referred
to by Jacob Sylvan. Men wore it on their lapels, women on their bonnet
strings. Such a badge indicated not only inner belief, but an outward show
of belonging; one knew at a glance if a person had similar convictions.
But this symbol was offensive to the authorities, and its wearers punished.
Records show Anna Maria Morlok of Mötzingen (1776-1851) spent time
in the Tower "because she wore a star." Later, to avoid punishment, the
stars were hidden under clothing. After their arrival in America, the Zoar
Separatists made the seven-pointed Zoar Star their symbol, adding an acorn
to its center to indicate their success.[26]

It may have been around this time that the Separatists formulated the ideas that underlay their twelve principles (*Grundsätze*), although they were not written down until around 1816. (See appendix 2 for the principles in their entirety.) After declaring belief in the Holy Trinity, the fall of man, the return of Christ, and "the Holy Scriptures as the rule of our lives" (Principles 1-4), they list the "chief cause of our separation" to be that "all ceremonies are banished from among us" and "are declared to be useless and harmful" (Principle 5). Other principles refer to cutting "ecclesiastical ties," civil marriages, recognition of temporal authority ("no one can prove us to be unfaithful to the state"), and, most controversial of all, that "intercourse between the sexes, except that which is necessary for perpetuation of the race, we hold to be sinful" (Principle 9). Although some married couples in Rottenacker lived apart, and some left spouses to emigrate,[27] this principle was not singled out by the German authorities. Celibacy did, however, become important after their arrival in America (see chapter 3).

The authorities were greatly insulted by Principle 6—the Separatists' refusal to doff their caps in the presence of officials and to not address them in the German third person, *Sie*.[28] "We render to no mortal honors due only to God, such as uncovering the head, bending the knee, and the like. We address everyone as 'thou' [*du*]."[29] In Rottenacker, this claim that "Christ was their king and he was the reason they would not lift their cap before the authorities" caused seven Separatists to be briefly jailed and their followers to create a "riot." In the capital Stuttgart, officials minimized the situation, wondering "just how 30 persons could become so dangerous in a community of about 1,000 inhabitants."[30] Events would prove just how "dangerous" these dissenters, fueled by religious zeal, could be.

Another Separatist practice, keeping their children away from the church-run schools, the "schools of Babylon,"[31] was also frowned upon by officials. When parents such as poet Daniel Huber refused to send their children to school, they were fined and the children were often sent to orphanages, where their parents were expected to pay for their upkeep or, if they were too poor, let them become wards of the state. Fritz reports that seven out of fifty children in the Ludwigsburg Orphanage at one point were from Rottenacker.[32]

Meanwhile, Barbara Grubermann disappeared from the scene, leaving behind only a few letters and memories of her apocalyptic visions.[33] No longer residing in Rottenacker, she vanished from the written record in 1806, but not before prophesizing that her followers would go to America where they would have freedom to worship as they chose, that they would recognize their leader when they saw him, and that they would band together in an organization that would become prosperous, which would "last only as many years as a man's age."[34] In time, all of these things came to pass, but not without a lot of anguish and hard work.

Despite the threat of jail, the Separatists continued to have their assemblies and ignore the threats of the authorities. Matters came to a head during Christmas 1803. Elector Friedrich II, "an energetic and authoritarian ruler who showed little tolerance against whatever opposition . . . be it political or religious,"[35] issued a series of decrees against the Rottenacker Separatists, which were read to the entire town. After the ringleaders were taken briefly to prison and initially agreed to stop holding assemblies, the Separatists broke their promises and began meeting again. Other non-Separatists felt free to imitate the Separatist lawbreakers. Finally, on May 6, 1804, military action was ordered.[36]

Fourteen male Separatists from Rottenacker were arrested, and twenty soldiers, led by a Lieutenant Seybold, were quartered in the homes of Separatists.[37] So generously were they treated by their hosts that the soldiers were told by Seybold not to accept extra food and drink, but the cost of quartering the soldiers for the four weeks of occupation cost many Separatist families dearly; some would have resorted to selling property if the authorities had not ended the occupation.

The military detachment left, taking the fourteen men with them to the Fortress Asperg for prison terms of three months to a year each. In addition, Stephan Huber was to be banished from Württemberg after serving his sentence. After a brief return in December 1804 to settle his affairs and incur another scuffle with the authorities, Huber appears in the records of the cities of Ulm (where he met Joseph Michael Bimeler) and Memmingen; in 1806 he traveled to Teufen, home of Barbara Grubermann, then he disappears from the records until he reappears in Zoar in 1817.[38]

The Fortress Asperg housed approximately sixty Separatists from all over Württemberg who were regarded as model prisoners. Often, they were entrusted to travel from place to place with large sums of money. They were forced to work on the royal estates, carving faux marble in the Stuttgart Palace's Marble State Room, where even the king himself was pleased with their work. They participated in backbreaking labor at the king's country home, Monrepos ("my rest"), where they hand dug an ornamental lake

Male Separatists were imprisoned at the Hohen Asperg in Württemberg, still used today as a minimum-security prison. As punishment, they labored on the king's estates, some for as long as twelve years. (Courtesy of the Archiv des Hauses Württemberg, Altshausen, Germany.)

under cover of darkness because the king did not wish to see the prisoners working. Two Separatists died after being severely beaten.[39]

At the end of their prison sentences, the Separatists were then asked if their attitudes had changed, if they would no longer rebel against the state. If they did not assent, they were imprisoned for another year. Some prisoners continually refused to recant, including Johannes Breymaier, who spent twelve years there.[40]

In 1811 a group of Rottenacker Separatists purchased the vacant home of the governor, whose office had been abolished when Württemberg became a kingdom in 1806. Their aim was to live together communally, but such arrangements were not recognized by the government, so they continued to hold their private property. It is interesting to note that Zoar was not the Separatists' first experience with communal living.[41]

Emigration might have been seen as the answer, to rid the country of these troublemakers, but in 1807, King Friedrich forbade emigration, ostensibly because the country needed its young men to serve in the army, now fighting with Bonaparte's Confederation of the Rhine. Serving in the military violated the Separatist principle of pacifism (Number 11, "a Christian cannot murder his enemy, much less his friend"). The Separatists refused to enter the draft lottery, and since they could not afford to pay for substitutes, they were jailed.

The wives and the families of those prisoners had to make do as best they could, keeping businesses and farms running and the children fed. Even with such hardship, many Separatist women continued to defy the authorities, withholding their children from school, despite the fines and imprisonments in the Tower and workhouse. Some marriages did not survive such stresses, with couples divorcing or leaving their partners behind when they emigrated. Stephan Huber, Barbara Schoch, and Christine Striebel from Rottenacker all left their spouses to travel to America.[42]

The imprisonment of the Separatist ringleaders tamped down much of the conflict with the authorities and had the desired effect of essentially stopping its growth, both in numbers and in philosophy.

In 1813, after the disastrous 1812 Russian invasion by Napoleon in which Württemberg lost 11,500 of 12,000 soldiers,[43] King Friedrich changed sides to fight with the allies and participated in the Congress of Vienna in 1815, which allowed him to keep the lands he had acquired during the years of war.

The year 1816 saw terrible crop failures due to the effects of Mount Tambora, an Indonesian volcano halfway around the world, which had erupted the year before, spreading ash and air pollution throughout the northern hemisphere, including America. During the so-called "Year without a Summer," the weather played havoc with agriculture. It snowed in June in Albany, New York, for instance. Württemberg was hit especially hard, with grain prices almost doubling. Returning soldiers seeking work added another drag on a fragile economy recovering from war. People thought the end times were upon them.[44] Faced with this disaster, King Friedrich lifted his ban on emigration in 1816. Many Separatists took advantage of low-cost land offered by Czar Alexander I of Russia and traveled down the Danube to settle in southern Russia, in what is today's Ukraine. Included in this group were some Separatists from Rottenacker.[45] Prisoners at the Fortress petitioned the king to be released so they could emigrate to America. But that didn't happen just yet—some Separatists had another idea.

To remain in Württemberg and not risk the voyage to America, the Separatists made another attempt to settle together. The estate of Brandenburg near the Bavarian border (not to be confused with the eastern German state of the same name) was being auctioned. It had belonged to Countess Caroline of Fugger-Blumenfeld, who had gone bankrupt. Prosecutor Christmann of Ulm bought the estate, probably as a "straw purchaser," allowing the Separatists to be anonymous, and offered it to them at the price he paid. Since the location was "in the most remote part of the country,"[46] it was hoped that the Separatists could live there in peace as a group, a "united fellowship." On April 28, 1816, they petitioned King Friedrich to allow them "to unite themselves into a community in that place . . . in industry and unity."[47] Anticipating their request would be granted, a deposit was made, and four Separatist families moved to the estate, which had three hundred acres of fields and one thousand acres of woodland, including the estate buildings, which were "wrecked . . . and now standing empty."[48]

Despite their efforts, Friedrich tore a subsequent petition (now lost) in half and returned it to the Separatists.[49] In October that year, the king died suddenly, which was looked on as "a sign from God that their worst enemy had perished."[50] He was succeeded by his son, Wilhelm I. Undeterred, the petitioners tried again, flattering the new king ("A day of common joy was received through the Kingdom by the accession to the throne of our much loved Crown Prince . . . on whose kind heart we lay our request"). Somewhat disingenuously, the Separatists claimed to have lived "peacefully & obediently" and they wished "to unite with each other more closely in a larger more spacious dwelling place." They asked that legal red tape be cleared up with the district court at Wiblingen "which opposed our religious principles," and "who had described the record of purchase erroneously" and had even gathered signatures from the surrounding community against their settlement. The Separatists asked that this latest petition be granted, as they were "loyal citizens."[51] This Wilhelm refused to do.

Verse 17
Yes, who could believe it?
You furtive band of robbers
First robbed us of all we had,
Then drove us from our fatherland.
They wanted nothing more
Than to rob us of God and honor.[52]

Not only God and honor, but they were robbed of their deposit to purchase the Brandenburg estate, which was never returned. Their only recourse was to go to America.

Verse 19
Previously, by God's order from above
Lot, the pious man
Also went out of Sodom
Before judgment began,
Fled to the village of Zoar
Where he, too, found his rest.

CHAPTER 2

"Remove the Whole in a Body to the West of the Ohio"

Emigration and Settlement in Zoar

The Committee began to entertain strong suspicions that [Joseph] Michael Baumler exercised an undue influence and command over the rest. . . . he stated his determination to remove the whole in a body to the west of the Ohio.
— Thomas Cope, Philadelphia, to Thomas Rotch, Kendal, Ohio,
   February 6, 1818

Even though he was not a participant, Daniel Huber's 1833 poem details the ocean voyage, the generosity of the Quakers, and traveling to Ohio:

Verse 22
And before arriving in this land,
Already at this time
The Quakers all together
Had prepared a house for them,
Where they could enter in,
Old, young, great and small.[1]

After getting permission to emigrate, this tiny group of German Separatists knew they needed help, in both monetary and physical terms, once they reached the United States. They turned to the Quakers. The Society of Friends has always been known for its benevolence and its "engagement in social reform and witness."[2] The Separatists came to know the Quakers through contacts in northern Germany and England. The Separatists received high praise from a German member of the Friends who related his experience with four Separatists he had employed as "the most trustworthy people he had under him."[3]

Johann Gottfried Banzhaff (also spelled Banzhoff and Banzhaf, b. 1780), a leader of the group, first contacted the English Quakers and received a warm reception to his plea for help. William Allen "a well-known Quaker philanthropist"[4] (1770-1843), took a leading role in gathering funds for their transport, raising three hundred pounds sterling. Banzhaff also wrote directly to the Philadelphia Friends, describing the Separatists' plight. The London Quakers, in turn, contacted Stephen Grellet, a well-known Quaker minister who had traveled extensively in Europe and who was now in New York. He then informed the Philadelphia Friends through an influential merchant there, Thomas Pym Cope.[5]

Allen considered the Separatists to be "co-religionists," having common beliefs. They did share some convictions, such as the presence of the Holy Spirit, an unpaid ministry, military nonresistance, simplicity of speech and dress, disregard for religious ceremonies, refusal to doff hats, and more. It was the "more," however, that became troublesome after the Separatists reached American shores.

Spurred by the warm reception from the Friends, the Separatists pooled their own meager resources and began to investigate immigration. Oral tradition states that two Separatist women, Katharina and Christina Zeller, with more means than the others, presented their money to the leaders in coins gathered in their aprons.[6] An advance party consisting of Banzhaff and a few others traveled through northern Germany and the Netherlands to Antwerp, Belgium, where they found passage on a Russian ship, the *Vaterlandsliebe* ("love of the fatherland"). While some of the advance party provisioned their quarters aboard ship and others traveled back to Württemberg to gather the group, Banzhaff went to England to see the Quakers and inform them of their impending passage.[7]

In mid-April 1817, upon their arrival in Antwerp, the Separatists, having sailed down the Neckar and Rhine Rivers to the sea coast, boarded the ship.[8] The *Vaterlandsliebe* remained in the harbor until sailing in mid-May. This delay, according to one account, depleted their stores of food, which became critically low. Illness, crowded conditions belowdecks, and the misery of seasickness tested the resolve of the Separatists. Scrofula, a

In April 1817 the Separatists finally obtained permission to leave Württemberg for America. This passport belonged to Anna Maria Notter and her three children. (Courtesy of the Ohio History Connection, MSS110, box 3, folder 1.)

bacterial infection of the lymph glands, probably caused by breathing the fetid air aboard ship, affected some of the passengers.[9]

The ship was buffeted by northerly winds that took it near the shores of Nova Scotia, where, according to the one account, they met fishermen off the Grand Banks and bought fish to supplement their dwindling supplies. The ship's captain went ashore by longboat to find food and failed to return. After waiting several days, the ship was driven by a strong wind to Halifax, where the governor there welcomed them and offered land to settle. Finding the land "somewhat barren," the Separatists declined his kind offer. Instead, they departed, still with no captain, and sailed with a favorable wind to Philadelphia.[10]

During this difficult voyage, the Separatists were comforted by their religious faith and in particular by one man, Joseph Michael Bäumler, his name later anglicized to "Bimeler." Not only was he well versed in their Radical Pietistic teachings, but he also had some homeopathic medical training.[11]

Bimeler was involved in ways unknown in gathering the group to emigrate. There is evidence he participated in the failed attempt to settle at the Brandenburg estate.[12] He does not emerge as their leader until this time onboard ship and in Philadelphia. Bimeler's role in the success of the Zoar Society will be examined in detail in chapter 4.

The Quakers received the Separatists at their August 14, 1817, arrival with efficient kindness, renting a wing of a hospital—"a more comfortable situation"—for their housing "as the weather [was] very warm." The Quakers cared for those who had become ill on the long voyage, found work for those who were able, and raised funds to provide food for them, at an estimated cost of three hundred dollars per week. The Separatists, impoverished by the need to purchase more food on their detour to Halifax, "could not even come up with funds to pay the duty to get themselves and their baggage off the ship. Philadelphia Friends intervened on their behalf at the customs house paying the tonnage duty so a baggage permit could be issued." This work was done by a committee of fifteen "weighty Friends," of which Thomas Cope was the secretary.[13]

The Friends took care of the sixty-seven males and seventy-eight females (plus many children), ministering to the sick and finding jobs for those who were able—as house servants, apprentices to tradesmen, and farm workers.[14] Some Friends bypassed the committee completely, visiting the city hospital directly and picking out those they wished to employ.[15] The committee also petitioned other Friends' meetings from as far away as New York and Baltimore for funds to support the refugees.[16] They assisted in the location of nearby land parcels upon which the group could settle, even accompanying those who were investigating the properties.[17] But the Separatists found nothing suitable nearby.[18]

The situation was complicated further by the Separatists' relationship with the Harmony Society, another Württemberg Radical Pietist group, living at this time in southern Indiana. They had emigrated in 1803, before the edict that forbade it. The two groups had corresponded over the years and some Separatists had relatives who were Harmonists. The Harmonist leader, George Rapp, even suggested the two groups might live together, but that was mostly wishful thinking on his part. Rapp's adopted son, Frederick, was in Philadelphia upon the Separatists' arrival there, and may have introduced them to Godfrey Haga, a German Moravian land dealer, who had five thousand five hundred acres in the Tuscarawas Valley of Ohio for sale. He had tried to sell this same land to Rapp upon the latter's arrival, but Rapp thought it was "too far west" and settled in western Pennsylvania instead.[19]

Bimeler, acting for the Separatists, decided to buy Haga's land, sight unseen. He did not tell the Quakers, causing a rift between the two groups. "These people appear to have dealt rather disingenuously with us & B[imeler] in particular is thought to be an artful man," said Cope in the minutes of the Committee.[20] The terms from Haga were generous: fifteen thousand dollars for the five thousand five hundred acres (less than three dollars per acre), with three yearly payments, the first not due until 1828, and no interest for three years. Bimeler signed the deed on behalf of the Separatists, but it was made out to him only.[21] Bimeler's lone signature on the document proved to be an obstacle, not only with dealings with the

Quakers, but for the rest of his lifetime. The land was transferred in trust to the Society of Separatists only on his deathbed in 1853.[22]

It wasn't only land for settlement that was troublesome. As the two groups got to know each other, the Quakers found that the Separatists were not so much alike religiously, either. Cope reported: "We found they entertained scruples respecting the eating of swines [*sic*] flesh, had notions on the subject of worship with which we could not accord and, we were informed, would not allow their members to marry" although "their leaders denied the fact."[23] Celibacy was not a tenet embraced by all Separatists at this time, although the eschewing of sexual relations was considered a higher ideal. The Separatists did become celibate for a period of eight years here in Ohio, from 1822 through 1828, but it was, as will be seen, mostly for economic reasons, and they resumed marital relations after the building of the Ohio & Erie Canal allowed them to become financially secure.[24]

Bimeler also wanted to control the funds the Friends had raised for the Separatists' welfare. "He seemed anxious & determined to get the people speedily away, & wished to have the money which had been raised in London, no part of which had been expended—& also such other sums as remained on hand, & had been collected for their use. The Committee had become so dissatisfied with this Individual, that they were not easy to pay to him alone the money which had been raised for the general benefit. The sum was therefore divided into equal portions for each and given to them separately." This amount worked out to be eighteen dollars per person for a total of two thousand two hundred dollars.[25]

Relations between the two groups became strained. Banzhaff tried to clarify the situation by saying the Separatists' guidance came only from "divine direction and appointments and that the same being who had hitherto ordered their trip and made provision for them would continue his aid and support for them in their present undertaking."[26]

However, "the Committee began to entertain strong suspicions that [Joseph] Michael Baumler exercised an undue influence and command over the rest. . . . he stated his determination to remove the whole in a body to the west of the Ohio," Cope reported. But it was now "so late in the season."[27]

Indeed it was late—it was by now October. By the end of October, 125 of the 250 Separatists had left Philadelphia; the rest made their way in the spring of 1818. The first winter was very hard. Sometime during that season, they were visited by Cope's correspondent, Quaker Thomas Rotch (1766-1823) of nearby Kendal, Ohio (now part of Massillon), a former New England whaler, land developer, and abolitionist. He was curious about the new settlement, had heard "some tales about Bimeler's character and policies, and that he was treating his former close associate J. G. Banzhoff very unfairly."[28] (Although he did sign the Articles of Agreement that created the communal society in 1819, Banzhoff later left the Society, and, in 1822, brought suit to recover what he had contributed to its welfare. He lost the case.)[29]

Although his letter has been lost, Rotch apparently wrote to Cope in Philadelphia about his findings. Cope replied on February 6, 1818, with a lengthy letter describing the circumstances of the Separatists' dealings with the Friends. Cope asks Rotch to keep an eye on the Germans: "As your opportunities of information and observation may be considerable, it would be acceptable & may be useful if you would write to us again, & state the facts . . . entirely close up."[30]

On June 4, 1818, Cope wrote again to see if Rotch could convince Bimeler to sign a Declaration of Trust for the land purchase. If he could persuade the Separatist leader to sign over the deed, the Quakers would forward six hundred dollars of the sum they were holding for them, presumably part of the unexpended money left over from what they had raised for their benefit, which the Separatists had requested from the committee to build a gristmill and sawmill.[31] In a letter to Bimeler, Quaker John James gave a report on the few Separatists still remaining in Philadelphia, while exhorting him to sign the declaration: "Our mutual friend Thomas Rotche informed me that you had a conference together and thou had signed the Declaration of Trust. It afforded me much consolation, but [I] was very sorry when I understood thy friends objected to its being put upon Record, which I consider a great mistake and hope they have come to see the impropriety of it but as thou assured me it shall be done. If not I hope you will [not] let one day pass over without having it finished as it be the means of quieting many minds and it will be of very great advantage of the company."[32] Other extant letters state that Bimeler was ready to sign, but that "at the alleged insistence of the members of the society, this declaration was torn up and never registered legally."[33]

In the last of the three Zoar/Cope/Rotch letters, Cope gives up. "I perceive that the Separatists are not disposed to accept the generous offer made them by the Committee." The minute book does not state what happened to the remaining funds. One historian presumes they were used to support individual Separatists when they came to Philadelphia on business, which they did frequently throughout their long seventy-nine-year history as a communal group.[34]

Less than a year after their arrival in Zoar, in a final missive to the Quakers, Bimeler defends the observation that he is acting "like a despot." Stressing that the Zoarites and the Friends are "very close to each other in their religious beliefs, closer than to any other [group]," he gives a detailed description of their land and its promise and, in his own way, thanks the Friends and asks for their blessing: "In short, there can't be any doubt that we are in the place where God will grant us happiness and dry our tears.—Now offer us your hand and we will in future times praise you as the fountain head of our happiness and say: The Lord has done that through the Friends."[35]

And, such has proven to be the case through the years. It speaks volumes for the "kind-hearted Quakers," as local historian Hilda Morhart called them, that they would render such aid and succor to a group of persecuted immigrants they hardly knew. Even Thomas Cope, for all his difficulties with the Separatists, finally admitted in a letter to Thomas Rotch that "most of them, while here, conducted [themselves] soberly & steadily—and we are of the opinion that there are among them many innocent & valuable people."[36]

Perhaps it's not unusual for a group like the Separatists to assert their independence from those who wished to help them. The Separatists can also be accused of manipulating the benevolence of the Quakers to their own ends. And it's common for those like the Quakers who render assistance to wish to control those to whom they extend the hand of charity. The German-English language barrier might have also played a part, as did the fact that, to the ordinary Separatist, "Baumlar their leader . . . was another Moses," and they would follow where he led.[37]

Verse 32
By group effort they began to build,
Laying out the little city of Zoar,
Gardens, grasslands, green meadows:
The promised Canaan
In which milk and honey flow
As promised by God to his people.[38]

Where Bimeler led them was into the wilderness of Ohio. In the late fall of 1817, Bimeler, some of the able-bodied men, their families, and their goods traveled by wagon from Philadelphia to Pittsburgh. A bill of lading states they brought with them 4,893 pounds of freight at a cost of $371.32.[39] It is presumed that other wagoners were hired for the trip from Pittsburgh to Ohio, but no documentation has been found. It was early November when the settlers arrived at Sandyville, the town nearest their lands. The remainder of the Separatists made the arduous trip from Philadelphia across the Allegheny Mountains in the spring of 1818, after some served out their indentures and others recovered from their illnesses.[40]

Rolling hills, with fertile plains that had originally been cultivated by the Delaware Indians marked the Tuscarawas Valley lands purchased by the Separatists. The hills contained thick forests of oak, hickory, chestnut, and maple trees. The Tuscarawas River, a branch of the Muskingum, ran diagonally across their lands, from northwest to southeast. The river plains, which the Indians had kept unwooded by periodic fires, allowed the Separatists to start cultivating their land that first year.

Alexander Gunn, a wealthy outsider who lived in Zoar during the last years of the Society, recorded the recollections of Michael Miller (1807-1893), who was age ten when he arrived in Zoar:

> Old Mike told me to-day of the time when he came to Zoar, among the first. His father was left behind sick, and his mother, with her two children—Mike, aged twelve, and a younger sister—came on through the woods alone. The wagoner who had carried them from Pittsburg left them, as agreed, at Sandyville, three miles from here, then a wretched settlement of log huts in the woods. It was a few days before Christmas, 1817. Mike tells me how his mother sat down on a log and burst into tears. Far from home, in a strange land, a trackless wilderness, and no place to shelter her children! No wonder Mike says "Men were kinder in those days"; for a man with bushy beard and butternut-colored homespun clothes came up and asked her what troubled her. She told him. And then he asked, "Can you spin'?" and she said, "Yes," and he offered her a home until she should get settled with her own people.[41]

Gunn relates the memories of another old Zoarite's experiences that first year: "Old Mr. Ruof [probably Georg Ruof, 1806-1891], who was with the first party of five families in 1817, says that the first night (it was the beginning of December) they slept under a large oak tree near where the log church is [present corner of East Third and Foltz Streets]. The next day they made a tent-like hut of poles, covered with leaves and earth, in which they burrowed. The weather during December was fine, and they built cabins of logs."[42]

Five of these log cabins still stand in Zoar today, albeit in modified condition. The Separatists decided to build their village on the European model, with the village and ancillary farm buildings in the center of their lands and the cultivated land on the outskirts, rather than each family living on a separate parcel, as was common to America. They founded their village about a half mile from the east side of the river, where several large springs ran from a hill, ensuring a supply of fresh water.

They named their town Zoar, after the place in the Bible where Lot fled after the destruction of Sodom in Genesis. In Hebrew, the name Zoar means both "a little one" and "a place of refuge," which indeed it was.

Work on the new town continued through January 1818, but the weather turned, with snow thick on the ground through April. Kindly neighbors provided flour and potatoes as food supplies dwindled. Gunn gives Ruof's further recollections of that first winter: "During February the snow lay four feet thick; the top, a frozen crust, made it easy to capture the deer. The hunters brained them with tomahawks, flayed them, and gave the carcasses away; this was a great relief to the new settlers. Wolves were very thick and troublesome; the south side of the river was avoided, owing to the multitude of wolves, whose howlings at night filled the new-comers with terror."[43] The hill where the wolves lived is still called *Der Wolfberg,* and its spring, *Der Wolfbrunnen.*

That spring, the Separatists who had remained in Philadelphia traveled west to Zoar, singly and in small groups.[44] Crops were planted. Bimeler and twenty-five others walked the thirteen miles to New Philadelphia, the county seat, to declare their intentions to become US citizens.[45]

The group worked diligently to make a home in the Ohio wilderness. In a letter to Frederick Rapp of the Harmonists, dated September 11, 1818, Bimeler paints an optimistic picture: "In the vicinity of where we live we have about 1000 acres of very good land, which produces everything we could only wish. . . . We believe that our God who has brought us thus far will continue to lead us as will be useful and wholesome for us."[46]

Despite Bimeler's rosy picture, the winter of 1818-19 tested the mettle of the party. Although they still acted in many ways as a unit with collective decision making, they had intended, in a somewhat hazy plan, for each family to obtain enough capital through its own farming to purchase a plot of the common land for itself. But at that point, just surviving was paramount. Jacob Sylvan, an original Separatist who led the group after Bimeler's death in 1853, described the situation: "Throughout this year of 1818, there was as yet no communal sharing of goods, and each individual lived for himself. But it was found that this would not work, since there were destitute old people who were too poor to buy a little piece of land, and too weak to feed themselves. Others capable of work were forced to work for the Americans in order to get by, and this impeded the work at home, which was not making headway."[47] Needing to work for others instead of for themselves on their own land, together with having a large group of elderly and infirm members, made it clear that something had to be done, and quickly. How could they keep themselves from starvation, care for everyone, save funds for their eventual land payment, and, most importantly, keep their distinctive faith—the very thing that impelled them to leave Württemberg and settle here? What was to be done?

We hear from Sylvan again: "Over the next winter, several members met together and considered whether it would not be better to take up a communal way of life. Bit by bit, this proposal gained support, and finally the decision and consensus was reached to begin and try it out."[48]

How the idea of a communal society came about is not well documented. Communalism was not an original stated goal of the group—freedom of worship was their aim. Obviously, the example of the successful Harmony Society played a part, due to their German nationality, common religious backgrounds, the contact with Frederick Rapp in Philadelphia, and the correspondence of Bimeler and other Separatists with the Harmonists. The mutually shared experiences of the common house in Rottenacker, the aborted land purchase in Brandenburg, the ocean voyage, the travel overland, and the past eighteen months of working as one allowed the Separatists to see that they were stronger together than apart. Perhaps most influential was the "true Christian love" of the early Christians in Acts 2:44-45 and 4:34-35, which is referenced in the preamble of their 1819 Articles of Agreement that stated that the Separatists were "induced to unite themselves, according to the Christian apostolic sense."[49]

Levi Bimeler, Joseph's great-grandson, who in 1896 campaigned for the Society's dissolution in his newsletter, *The Nugitna*, posited the thought it was "the old, infirm, feeble and others who were too lazy to work," that "they were the ones who began to agitate for the Communistic idea."[50] Of course, this was seventy-five years after the fact and was written by

In order to survive and keep its congregation together, the Separatists decided to form *eine güter Gemeinschaft,* or communal society. By signing its Articles of Agreement, all members of the new Society of Separatists of Zoar pledged to give up individual wealth, obey their elected trustees, and work together for the benefit of all. (Courtesy of the Ohio History Connection, First Class Membership Book, MSS110, box 1, folder 4.)

someone who was not an eyewitness and who was actively campaigning for the Society's end.

One of the first to suggest *eine güter Gemeinschaft,* a community of goods, was Johannes Breymeier (also Breimaier), who called Napoleon a devil (see page 251, note 28), who had been a Separatist since 1799, and had endured twelve years of imprisonment in the Hohen Asperg prison.[51] As both Joseph Georg Ackermann and August Huber also signed the first Articles of Association as directors (later to be called trustees), it is probable that they may have also promoted the notion.

Bimeler was reluctant to consider the idea; he thought the members might not be unselfish enough to work for the good of the group, nor want to remain as tied together as a communal society must be. In later years, he reconsidered his opinion: "Nevertheless, affairs progressed, and those who have lived according to these principles [the Articles of Association] have profited thereby, for they are the principles of justice, and, in truth, Godly principles."[52]

Bimeler did not himself sign these first Articles of Agreement, nor did he sign the second Articles of 1824, but he did sign the third Articles in 1833. Despite this, he gave the fledgling Society of Separatists of Zoar his wholehearted support and the benefit of his vision and leadership.

After a few weeks of discussion, and, undoubtedly, consultation with an attorney (although no documentation has been found for this), the following articles were submitted to the membership for their approval:

> The undersigned members of the Society of Separatists have, from a true Christian love toward God and their fellow-men, found themselves convinced and induced to unite themselves, according to the Christian apostolic sense, under the following rules, through a communion of property, and they do hereby determine and declare that from the day of this date the following rules shall be valid and in effect:

(1) Each and every member does hereby renounce all and every right of ownership of his present and future, movable and immovable, property, and leaves the same to the free disposition of the directors of the Society, elected by themselves.

(2) The Society elects out of its own members its directors and managers, who shall conduct the general business transactions, and exercise the general duties of the Society. They, therefore, take possession of all the active and passive property of all the members, and at the same time assume the obligation of the support of the latter; and said directors are further bound to give an account to the Society of all their business transactions.

(3) All the members of the Society do hereby promise to render due and faithful obedience to the orders and regulations of their directors, and to support them as much as possible in all the common business transactions of the Society.

(4) Casual contentions or disputes shall be decided by the aforementioned directors by majority vote in case they themselves are not accused or implicated in the same. Should this be the case, the Society shall elect

one or more persons in the stead of those who may be partial, until the number of three, five, or seven is filled.

(5) Withdrawing members cannot demand any compensation or restitution, either for property brought in or for their labors in the Society, unless a majority of the Society shall be willing to allow such withdrawing members a reasonable compensation.

(6) The Society may increase or reduce the number of its members according to its own best. judgment, but each action must always be based on the unity and the maintenance of the Society.

(7) Elections shall be held annually and according to the laws of the State of Ohio.

Attested by the Directors,
Zoar, State of Ohio,
April 15, 1819.
Johannes Breymaier
Joseph Georg Ackermann
August Huber[53]

CHAPTER 3

"What Is Good for One Is Beneficial to All"

The Separatists Create a Communal Society

What is good for one is beneficial to all—the advantage of an individual is the advantage of the community. There are no rich to despise the poor, no poor to envy the rich; so all are happy and contented, for there may be happiness even in a hovel when there is no palace in view to vex the eye with envy.
—*(Columbus) Ohio Statesman,* September 18, 1859

It is hard for us to imagine the sheer desperation in which the Separatists found themselves in 1819. How would they keep their community, and, above all, their church, together? It must have been a hard decision for some to make, to give up everything they might earn individually, even inheritances,[1] in order to survive in this new land. The decision to combine together communally—to pool their labor, their wealth, their very lives—showed a great commitment to their religious faith and to each other. There was no going back.

Sociologists have studied communal groups and their organizations,[2] comparing them with mainstream society. How are they different? The main difference seems to be in their wholehearted commitment to the success of the group. In this system, the reward is what is best for the whole, not the individual. Roles are assigned and people follow them because they know that if they deviate from them, they risk the failure of the entire enterprise. Peer pressure helps to keep all members in line. Those who can't follow the norms laid down by the group will leave on

Working together allowed the Zoar Society to survive as a group and keep their religious beliefs intact. (Courtesy of the Ohio History Connection, Louis Baus Collection, P223AV.)

their own accord or be driven out by the members who wish to maintain the status quo.[3] Thus by organizing communally during the early years of their religious movement for the security and survival it promised, the Separatists of Zoar accepted the disciplines communal living demanded, demonstrating what historians now call developmental communalism—a vital process of adjusting to changing realities that sustained their society for nearly a century.[4]

Zoar was not a pure democracy, however. The group decided to elect people to lead them and make decisions. The earliest Articles of Association provided for three trustees (called "Directors" in that document). This office never changed during the Zoar Society's history. One trustee, who, after Bimeler's death assumed the leadership of the three, was in charge of Zoar's agricultural pursuits. The second supervised the industries, which included milling, weaving and, later, the iron furnaces and foundry. The third had charge of the livestock, horses, cattle, sheep, but no hogs—the Separatists thought pork was unclean, as described in the Bible. Hogs were not raised until the advent of hired laborers employed by the Society.

Later, this third trustee had charge of the Zoar Hotel, opened in 1833 to cater to overnight visitors. The trustees, in return for their authority, were responsible for furnishing each member with the necessities of life. The member, in return, had to pledge to abide by the decisions of the trustees.

In November 1820, Joseph Bimeler wrote to Frederick Rapp of the Harmony Society describing the state of the nascent Zoar Society: "Our condition . . . is for the greater part good. Providence has blessed our business that now except for salt and iron we can save all expenditures for essentials." He complains that "in our area, trade is completely down, also the so-called barter affords many difficulties."[5]

Life was indeed hard in Zoar during those early years, despite the decision to become communal. Children were being born and mothers had to take time from other tasks to bear and rear them.[6] Something needed to be done so as not to deprive the Society of the work of these indispensable hands.

The religious ideal of celibacy was enshrined in Article 9 of the Separatists Principles: "All intercourse of the sexes, except that which is necessary for the perpetuation of the race, we hold to be sinful and contrary to the command of God; entire abstinence, or complete chastity, is, however, still better." Some Separatists had already embraced the more extreme belief of total chastity, and were either unmarried or lived apart from their spouses. Others had left their spouses in Germany when those spouses could not adhere to the Separatists' creed. Women, many of them widowed or unmarried, made up almost two-thirds of the community, and, as Edgar Nixon put it, they *were* the community.[7]

Around 1822, the Society adopted total celibacy and forbade men and women to live together. Each sex lived separately, with children living with the women, and a female served as housekeeper to the male households. Other communal groups, most notably the aforementioned Harmonists, were celibate, and they perhaps served as a model, but there is no extant record mentioning it, despite the extensive correspondence between the two groups in these early years.

It is hard to know whether this impulse was more religious in nature or economic, since their Pietist beliefs did exalt celibacy. The economic factor seems strongest, as the practice ceased in 1829 with the opening of the canal and the debt for their land paid. Two marriages took place in that year. In 1830 Bimeler married Dorothea Huber, daughter of Separatist preacher Stephan.[8] Undoubtedly, having all persons available to work, especially the arduous labor on the canal, contributed mightily to Zoar's success during the difficult period of 1822-29. Another way Zoar increased its wealth during this time was to send member Caspar Vetter back to Württemberg to liquidate inheritances of Separatists whose relatives had died. He made two trips, the first in 1819-20 and the second in 1823. He took with him powers of attorney from various members in order to amass the funds. His collections amounted to over seven thousand dollars, a welcome addition to the Society's coffers.[9]

A second, more detailed, Articles of Association was drawn up in 1824 that clarified some issues. The earlier document did not give a role or office to Joseph Bimeler, even though practically all business had been done in his name alone. In 1824 he was elected to the newly created office of arbitrator. Actually, the Articles specified that this office be a committee "of one to three persons," but no one but Bimeler was ever elected to the post. The duties of the "board of arbitration" were thus: "[The board] shall be bound to observe all the different branches of economy of the Society, and, whenever they may find it necessary, to give orders and instructions to investigate accounts and plans which may have been made by the directors or their agents; in short, all transactions of importance and of the value of more than fifty dollars, shall have to obtain the consent of said board of arbitration before they shall be considered binding and valid."[10] These powers obviously put the brakes on any trustees' (still called "directors" in 1824) actions, and placed immense trust in Bimeler's judgment.

Another new office in 1824 was that of cashier, whose duties were "to manage [the Society's] receipts, moneys and expenditures, and, besides him, no one shall be entitled to keep any moneys without the order of the Cashier," but specified that these funds were "to the benefit of the Society."[11] It should not be surprising that this office was also held by Bimeler until his death in 1853.

This interim document also specified the age when one could become a member (twenty-one for males, eighteen for females), detailed how the Society might collect members' inheritances, spelled out that "backsliding members" (Article 11) excommunicated from the Society could not demand payment for anything they had contributed, be it labor or money, and defined the role of children (the directors could act *in loco parentis* if needed—recall this was written in the midst of the period of celibacy).[12]

A third document provided the final framework for the Society's operation. After receiving funds from the canal construction to pay off its land debt (see chapter 5) and its steadily improving business enterprises, the

Society needed a firm legal basis for the community. It formally incorporated under the laws of the state of Ohio as "The Society of Separatists of
Zoar" in 1832 and revised its Articles of Association into a formal constitution in 1833. The incorporation gave the Society the usual legal rights and
privileges of a company. A corporate seal, incorporating the design of the
central garden, was chosen.[13]

This new Constitution was adopted by the membership on May 14,
1833.[14] Included were almost all of the provisions of the 1824 document,
but it is much more detailed than either of the previous two agreements.
Included are the mutual responsibilities of both officers and members.
The introduction states the motives of the Society:

> In order furthermore to secure our consciences that satisfaction proceed-
> ing from the faithful execution of the duties which the Christian religion
> demands, and to plant and establish the spirit of love as the bond of peace
> and unity for a permanent foundation of social order for ourselves and
> our posterity forever, we therefore seek and desire in accordance with
> pure Christian principles to unite our various individual interests into
> one common stock; and, conformable with the example of the primitive
> Christians, all inequalities and distinctions of rank and fortune shall be
> abolished from among us and consequently to live as brothers and sisters
> of one common family.

A new office, agent general, replaced the former arbitrator. Bimeler was
elected to that position, which he held for the rest of his life. Trustees were
elected for three-year terms and could be reelected as many times as members of the Society desired. A right of recall was specified for officers but
was never used during the Society's existence. A new group, the Standing
Committee, was formed to arbitrate disputes. These five men were elected
for five-year terms and became a training ground for future trustees. Joseph Bimeler was elected to this office for the remainder of his life also,
and held the titles of agent general, cashier, and member of the Standing
Committee all at the same time. All officers throughout the existence of
the Society were exclusively men, despite the fact that women could vote
and were not legally barred from office.

Since the resumption of marriage in 1829, Zoar now had a number of
children to care for. An educational institution was called for in Article 8,
requiring "all members to bind themselves to deliver up and place their

The first buildings in Zoar were necessarily of log construction, using timber from their forested land. The log Zoar Meeting House, where Joseph Bimeler delivered his discourses each Sunday, served the community for thirty-five years. The upstairs housed the girls' dormitory. (Courtesy of the Ohio History Connection, Louis Baus Collection, P223AV.)

children, after having arrived at the third year of their age or sooner" to receive "appropriate education and tuition" for the "attainment of scientific branches of knowledge," but also "the diverse branches of manual labor." After "their age, abilities and bodily condition shall permit," the children would be placed in the hands of the trustees "who shall give them such employment as they may be able to perform."

These *Kinder Anstalten,* also called dormitories or nurseries, were a short-lived phenomenon, presumably to instruct the young in communal life and free their mothers to work. Girls stayed in the upper floor of the log Meeting House and boys in the building across Third Street. Life in the dormitories was hard, with strict matrons who, it was said, were not suited for their profession.[15] Despite the former practice of keeping their children away from the church-run schools in Württemberg, children were required to go to school and work. Boys herded cows and braided ryestraw for hats; girls spun flax into linen thread and peeled apples for drying into "snitz." After trustee Jacob Ackermann refused to send his daughter there around 1840, sending one's child to the dormitories became optional at that time, and the dorms became orphanages until they were discontinued in about 1860.[16]

The 1833 Constitution formalized the process of admitting new members, which had been done on an ad hoc basis since the early 1820s. A probationary "first-class membership" was created. After one year, probationary members could apply to the trustees to become full second-class members. After a thirty-day waiting period, so current members could possibly lodge protests, the Membership Book was formally signed.[17] Children of members were not automatically enrolled as members; they, too, had to serve a probationary year after reaching the age of majority.

Not everyone who joined fit into the close-knit group. As probationers had to be cleared by the trustees before becoming full members, some, like T. Friederich Heim, were put off for years until they left on their own accord. Here is an excerpt from his letter of complaint, dated May 1, 1837:

> I undertook my long journey, in full trust and faith, to unite myself with you. This done, you required me to enter upon a contract with you, according to which you promised to receive me into the second class of the Society, one year after I should announce my intention. This first year passed and I gave notice, and you did nothing, but put me off to wait one year longer. This I did, and waited until it was three and a quarter years, and again gave notice. I was told I had not done so at the proper time. It was not this that excluded me, but rather your politics. You wished to punish me for certain wrong-doings; see that you punish these wrong-doings in the proper quarters. You put me at various tasks; these I did with all faithfulness and with all my strength. I brought to you a very healthy body; now, it is injured. . . . Where do you find in Scripture that honorable, faithful people should be sent away without wages or compensation, and where do the laws of men say this? Both say that the laborer is worthy of his hire. Therefore, I demand that you square your account with me by next Wednesday, and compensate me. If this is not done, I shall know enough to turn to the laws of our country. . . . Then we shall see who is in the right.[18]

It was not until a year and a half later he received any compensation from the Society, just twenty-five dollars.[19] He, like all members, full or probationary, who left the community, had to sign a quit-claim to declare null and void their previous contract with the Society.

Provision was made in the constitution that withdrawing members could present claims to the Standing Committee. Often small sums were given, as were personal effects and furniture. An existing inventory of items given to departing member Juliana Thiriet on March 13, 1852, has been preserved:

1 small Bedstead	$3.00
1 small Chest	2.50
1 ditto smaller	1.00
1 small Trunk	.50
1 Bed	25.00
Calico from the Zoar Store	1.50
2 Dresses from the Zoar Store at 1.50	3.00
2 Dresses at 1.00	2.00
2 Woolen dresses at 4.50	8.00
1 Woolen Dress at	3.25
1 Woolen Dress at	2.50
2 Woolen Shirts at 2.25	4.50
2 Linen Shirts	3.12½
4 Aprons	2.00
2 Aprons of Linen cloth at .75	1.50
2 Aprons of common cloth at .25	.50
1 Bonnet	.50
1 carpet	3.00
2 pairs Stockings	3.00
1 pair new Shoes	1.50
2 pairs old Shoes	2.00
l pair knitted Winter Shoes trimmed with leather	1.00
1 pair Boots—old	.50
1 Umbrella	.62½
	$77.00[20]

After this laborious tabulation, there is appended a short note: "She returned March 15, three days after she had left." Apparently not everyone was cut out for life outside the confines of the Zoar Society.

Elections were held each year the second Tuesday in May, as specified in the new constitution, with both men and women voting. Since there was a majority of women in the early community, many of whom worked as hard as the men, it was necessary for them to have an equal voice. A notice was posted twenty days before each election, indicating whose terms were expiring. Here is a typical announcement:

Notice

The members of the second class of the Separatists Society of Zoar, Tuscarawas County, Ohio, are hereby informed, that in accordance with the acts of incorporation, they are to assemble in the Meeting House on the second Tuesday of next month, that is, on the thirteenth of May, at seven o'clock in the evening, to elect the following directors of the Society for the ensuing year, namely: One trustee, in the place of Jacob Ackermann, whose term expires this year, and one member of the Standing Committee, in the place of J. P [Johann Peter, Joseph's son] Bimeler, whose term of office ends this year.
Zoar, O., April 10, 1856   J. G. Grötzinger

                                              Jacob Sylvan   Trustees

                                              Jacob Ackermann[21]

There were no nominations from the floor; ballots marked with members' preferences were placed in a small wooden chest. Presumably, likely candidates for the open positions had been discussed by all in the days beforehand. Terms were arranged so that only one trustee and Standing Committee member vacancy was open each year. Officers, once elected, usually served until death. When a death occurred, an election was immediately held to elect a successor.

The only punishment for violating Society rules was expulsion, quite a drastic outcome. A call upon one's better nature and peer pressure often worked, especially in the early years. When William Hinds visited in 1876, he was told: "We appeal to the conscience. What else can we do? We can't punish anybody. Formerly, if a member disobeyed the regulations of the Society, he was not allowed to attend the meetings, and that was punishment enough."[22]

By the time of the above interview, religious fervor in Zoar had declined so much that exile from the Meeting House was not the punishment it once was. During the time Bimeler was their spiritual leader, however, the offense of a member was sometimes remarked upon during the Sunday evening meeting and the congregation asked to help bring the guilty one to grace.

Trustees from time to time sent letters to an offending member or outside laborer. One Christian Bauer, a hired hand, was called to task by trustee

Ludwig (Lewis) Birk in 1848 for "certain habits or conduct which are somewhat offensive or annoying to various people," including bathing unclothed (some did bathe in undergarments at that period), being "negligently dressed" around others, and refusing to "eat what we eat." Birk concluded, "I hope you will correct these matters as quickly as possible."[23]

Exactly what offenses were the basis for expulsion were not enumerated in the constitution. Cases of actual expulsion are few, with most ending in court cases (see chapter 8 for a discussion of these cases).

The 1833 Constitution could be amended by a two-thirds vote of its members, but it never was; it remained in effect until the Society was disbanded in 1898.

CHAPTER 4

"He Loves Influence"

Joseph Bimeler

He loves influence, and has consummate skill in the exercise of it, and we could see oppression nowhere, abundance everywhere, but with the most rigid discipline connected with it.
— [Sophia Dana Ripley], *The New Yorker,* July 17, 1841

Joseph Michael Bimeler (born Bäumler) is an enigmatic figure for someone so important to the history of Zoar. He inspired reverence and revulsion, admiration and animosity. Loved by his followers and derisively called a "king" by his detractors. It is hard for a historian at this remove to put a finger on just what made him such a pivotal figure. Nothing in his background gives a hint as to what he would become. He was not formally trained in theology or business yet became a revered preacher and an astute businessman. His powerful personality kept the community together in the direst of circumstances and inspired the greatest trust—so much so that their property was kept and most community activities were transacted in his name alone.

Born in Merklingen in the Schwabische Alb in 1778, he was first trained as a weaver like his father, Peter. From 1797 through 1799 Bimeler had worked as a teacher at Grimmelfingen, a suburb of the city of Ulm. He married Barbara Danzer (1771-1804) from Merklingen in 1802, had two children, Barbara (b. 1803) and Johann Peter (b. 1804), and worked as a tobacco pipe maker. Seeking a better life, he received permission to become a citizen of Ulm, about twenty-five miles from Merklingen. Once an imperial free city, it was at this time a pawn in the tug-of-war between Napoleon Bonaparte, his German allies, and his Austrian enemies; Ulm became part of Bavaria in 1802 and then part of Württemberg in 1810. Bimeler's 1804 application contained a reference from the weavers' guild that had accepted him as a master weaver. (He had to become a citizen in order to join the guild.) In his letter, he testified he had recently purchased a home containing the "necessary things to run this business" and the funds (130 gulden) to do so. The rights of a citizen of Ulm were granted on May 2, 1804.[1]

Later that year, Barbara Danzer Bimeler died, leaving Michael (as he was known at the time) a widower with two young children. He became acquainted with Stephan Huber, the itinerant minister from Rottenacker, whose influence persuaded him to separate from the church. In Ulm, he was converted to Separatism around 1804 by Konrad Schacher and Georg Striebel of Rottenacker.[2] He drew together a few like-minded followers, including weaver Johan Georg Schaude, who would later emigrate with Bimeler to Zoar. But their illegal assemblies drew the attention of the authorities so, after being questioned, Bimeler promised not to spread his convictions or wear the star symbol of the Separatists. He attempted to preach separatism in his hometown of Merklingen with no success, and he got into trouble back in Ulm for his proselyting.[3]

It is not known just how Bimeler became part of the emigrant group. We know he participated in the ill-fated attempt to move to Brandenburg in 1816, as his name appears on a list of contributors to a fund to rebuild the estate's brewery,[4] the first mention of his interaction with the larger group of Separatists. He emerged as their leader on the ship, where he traveled with his young son, Johann Peter, age thirteen (daughter Barbara, fourteen, remained in Germany). One of Barbara Grubermann's prophecies had foretold that "In München sei ein Schulmeister" ("In Munich there is a schoolmaster"),[5] but Munich is 156 kilometers from Ulm, and Bimeler had only taught school for a short time, so this foretelling may be a bit farfetched. After the Separatists landed in Philadelphia, he was indeed their primary spokesman, much to the dismay of the benevolent and egalitarian-minded Society of Friends who greeted them upon landing.

As noted in chapter 2, Bimeler did not wish to be beholden to the Quakers and, from the first, pushed back against their advice, however benevolently it was intended.[6] He was not above using their assistance for his own aims, however. This "artful man," as Quaker Thomas Cope called him,[7] was willing to risk the ire of the Quakers to get what he wanted for his followers.

Once reaching Ohio, Bimeler showed his skills in management, business and, above all, spiritual leadership.[8] We will consider all of these qualities, beginning with the latter, which laid the foundation for the other two.

SPIRITUAL LEADERSHIP

By all indications, Bimeler was self-taught in matters of religion. His library of religious books, now part of the collection of Zoar Village State Memorial, included works by German theologians Jakob Boehme, Philipp Jakob Spener, Friedrich Christoph Oetinger, Johann Georg Gichtel, and Johann Heinrich Jung-Stilling. All of these authors explored mystical religious ideas. Presumably Bimeler obtained these books—most written and printed in the seventeenth and eighteenth centuries—in Germany and brought them to America. His knowledge of the Scriptures was profound.[9]

We know he had a horror of the professional clergy, so it is unlikely that he learned theology under the supervision of the established Lutheran church of Württemberg. One nineteenth-century reader of his *Discourses* says Bimeler believed that "all [the] strife of Christianity originated from a difference in ceremonies and this has turned it into priestcraft. Therefore the gentle, mild and peaceful Baeumler, whenever he thinks of a greedy priest, who has purchased his education in some school, gets into a real rage." Bimeler himself states: "[Priests] are neither selected by God nor are they authorized for the things they do. They have not received their wisdom from God, but they have learned it in the higher schools and preach to us for money. They teach well the word of God, but they do not understand it, and neither they nor their listeners obey it. . . . The true sense, however—the spirit and the power—they suppress. They presume the right to forgive sins and do not hesitate to forgive all without distinction." Jacob Sylvan in his introduction to the *Discourses* claims that separation from the "godless and unspiritual clergy" of the Lutheran church was a "necessary consequence" of those who wished to live a holy life.[10]

In one of his sermons printed after his death, Bimeler describes his own religious conversion:

> The more I searched and examined, the more distrustful I became toward my faith, and finally I discovered that I had no faith at all; this disturbed me greatly, and I struggled to obtain a better one. However, I turned onto the

Joseph Bimeler is said to have designed this new Meeting House, built in 1853, but he died before it was completed. Today it is the home of the Zoar United Church of Christ, which holds services there and the church is open for occasional special events. (Courtesy of the Ohio History Connection, Properties Collection, P365AV.)

broad road of destruction and remained there until God himself stopped me. . . . I saw myself obliged to take another way, for I now recognized that the road on which I had turned was the broad road, which would without a doubt lead me to ruin. I began to seek God but he kept himself aloof from me. He acted as if he did not want to hear my anxious sigh and my urgent cry. . . . It is no wonder that he did not want to hear me, for I had very much offended him.[11]

This is called a *Busskampf*, described by one scholar as "a struggle to attain forgiveness for a deep sense of sin and guilt." It is this struggle to become purer, more like Christ, which is the basis of Bimeler's teachings. He went on to describe his own delivery in these words: "nevertheless he [God] sent me his grace . . . and afforded me his protection: gladly I submitted to his guidance. Inestimable are the benefits, favors and blessings which I enjoyed from that time on."[12]

As he never was imprisoned like many other Separatists, Bimeler undoubtedly carried out whatever preaching he did before the emigration
in underground conventicles. As there are few documents on his life in
Württemberg, much of this is speculation. To have been so accepted as
the leader once in America shows that he and his religious teachings must
have been known to many before emigration. The four months on the ship,
difficult as they were, seem only to have strengthened his leadership.

Even before reaching Ohio, he had assumed the position of preacher,
although, with his horror of priests and ministers, he was careful never to
call himself such. Even his weekly discourses or meditations (*Reden*) were
never called "sermons," lest they remind their audience of the established
church they left behind.

Here he is described by Jacob Sylvan, fellow émigré and his successor
as religious and secular leader, in his preface to the *Discourses:* "He offered
a worthy example to his little flock, and himself practiced and personally
experienced everything he preached to others. . . . No one ever saw him
despondent, discouraged, or baffled in the midst of the myriad blows of
fate that worked against him and the Society."[13]

His preaching style was extemporaneous and conversational, not stri-
dent: "When I come here, I usually come empty, and do not yet know what
I ought to talk about. What I am supposed to talk about is only given to
my spirit here, and as soon as I begin to speak, there opens up before me
a broad, vast field of thoughts [*Vorstellungen*] from which to take whatever
seems to me most necessary."[14]

It is telling that the first volume of Bimeler's *Discourses* includes the
phrase *Die Wiedergeburt,* which means "rebirth," or born again. Religious
historian Elizabeth White says, "Bimeler sometimes likened this [struggle]
to the process of giving birth, which was never painless but which promised
relief in a safe delivery." Another reader of the *Discourses* agrees: "In these
speeches, Baeumler shows how man, after he leaves the state of innocence,
starts on the road of nature, which leads him to eternal damnation, but if
like the lost [prodigal] son he turns at the right time and cleanses his heart
by penitence he is again taken into the community of man."[15]

The *Wiedergeburt* demanded a "new, holy and pure way of life," which
theologians call "sanctification," or becoming more saintlike. The Lutheran
church emphasized "justification" over sanctification—man was saved by
faith in Christ alone, and sanctification could never be attained in this
life. As we saw in chapter 1, a swing away from justification was one of

the hallmarks of the first Pietist movement in the seventeenth century. Bimeler, the Radical Pietist, warned that "an inner transformation does not happen otherwise than through the *Wiedergeburt,* and you know, friends, what that demands of time and effort." The soul in travail needed to be reborn, to deny the "natural man," and to be guided by a "divine voice": Bimeler warns, "If he does not obey this inner voice, then grace will finally be withdrawn from him."[16] As Elizabeth White observed, "In short, man could attain salvation by both an effort of will and by some assistance from God, according to Bimeler." He thought man had the "capacity for improvement, ennoblement and perfection."[17]

To the Separatists, as to the original Pietists, true Christianity "has to be an earnest thing of the heart." All appeals to God should come from within. Nothing should come from the hated clergy, not even congregational prayer. "All prayers must come from the heart, free and unforced. Therefore, all prayer books are not only [dispensable] but injurious to the true Christian, because they promote babbling with the mouth."[18]

The Separatists viewed the Bible as "the touchstone of true and false." The "inner voice," mentioned above, was often called an "inner light" and was necessary to properly interpret Scripture. As Bimeler points out in one of his discourses: "The Spirit which operates in them teaches them perfectly what they need to know, without their needing to rely on books and various languages as the learned of the world do. . . . The true word of God is truly something different, something spiritual, which in an unseen way works powerfully in these souls which the Holy Spirit has illuminated."[19]

This light can be symbolized by "the bright signal star" that the Separatists adopted as their symbol. Seeking one's "inner light" is part of the beliefs of the Society of Friends as well and is one way the two groups may have considered themselves similar.[20]

To Bimeler, the Bible was allegory. He criticized narrow literal interpretations of the Bible, comparing them with the hated teachings of the Württemberg clergy. Not only did the Star of Bethlehem symbolize the formation of the Separatists, but the story of turning water into wine at the wedding in Cana became the transformation of the natural man into the spiritual one. Christ's birth became symbolic of the *Wiedergeburt.* Like Boehme, he saw earthly phenomena as mirrors of the unseen, with God the Father as fire, the Son as light, and the Holy Spirit as the divine light in us all.

Sin was consciously living without God. The Separatists did not believe in predestination, which Bimeler called "the most damaging absurdity," as

The Zoar Artist (probably Thomas Maier, 1778–1851?) painted this *fraktur,* which illustrates the story of the Separatists' emigration to Zoar. The upper left panel uses the suffering of Job to stand for the Separatists' travails in Germany. The upper right shows two angels looking over the New Jerusalem (which also inspired the plan of the garden in Zoar), with God promising a new life. The lower left panel shows the voyage to America with a Bible verse about faith and hope. In the last panel, an angel holds a scale with all-seeing eyes and a verse indicating God's approval. (Courtesy of the Ohio History Connection, H52086.)

it undermined man's role in becoming more Christlike. Original sin, like that of Adam and Eve, was part of an evil tendency in man, but could be overcome in the process of sanctification. Children were not born in sin but had the seed of evil, which did not sprout until the age of reason, and parents should guard against such self-will. In contrast to Luther, Bimeler denied that Christ died for man's sins to grant humanity so-called imputed righteousness: "I do not consider this faith. . . . The sinner will find that his sins all still remain and that he cannot be free of them except through contrition—namely through a penitent and holy life, thus can he be reconciled to his offended God."[21]

A journey to sanctification must include an encounter with the issue of sexual relations.[22] The Separatist Principles exalted celibacy as a religious ideal, with some Separatists living as celibates their entire lives, with the whole community practicing abstinence between 1822 and 1829. But unlike the celibate Harmonists, the Zoarites did not see marriage and child-rearing as impediments on the road to sanctification.

A denial of the sacraments (baptism, communion) put the Separatists at odds with the established Lutheran church. Bimeler stated that the sacraments were "merely the outward signs and [they] deny and destroy the power and the substance of the inner thing. True baptism is spiritual and occurs within, but the ceremonies of baptism and communion are worthless because they leave our souls unimproved." Marriages were considered by the Separatists to be civil ceremonies, performed before a justice of the peace. Several Zoar members held that local public office through the years.[23]

Funerals were simple, with the body buried quickly in the town cemetery and the grave unmarked, as all were considered equal in death. Tombstones, first wooden, then limestone markers, did not appear until later in the Society. One 1893 visitor saw two evergreens marking the graves of Bimeler and his wife Dorothea.[24] Today, in an open part of the cemetery, a simple granite stone, erected during the 1930s, indicates his grave, surrounded by the other dead of the early Zoar community, their graves unmarked. Often Bimeler would allude to the life and piety of the recently departed in his next Sunday discourse. After Bimeler's death, these funeral biographies were given by others and have been preserved.[25] In Württemberg these so-called "parentations" were read by the schoolmaster at the funerals.[26]

If one felt a fellow Society member had erred in either a religious or secular sense, Bimeler suggested the following: "One may say, 'Brother or sister, you should do this or not do that' or 'I wish you could view the matter from my point of view,' and so on. Such an expectation is not only not a sin but is even an imperative. Universal brotherly love demands that this be done." This admonishment was first done in private, but Bimeler was not above aiming a sermon at a particular offense or personally asking the offender to sit in the front row of the Meeting House when his or her faults would be revealed. To be singled out like this must have been embarrassing, but effective. In Württemberg, this was called *Kirchenzucht* (church discipline).[27]

The afterlife, according to Bimeler, was a more spiritualized view of the Second Coming, although in Germany the Separatists did believe in a physical return of Christ. According to a late nineteenth century observer, "They came to the conclusion that the kingdom of God would not come outwardly, but inwardly, and then slowly and by degrees. A state of grace would only be gradually attained by sincere repentance, just as a person could not exchange his sick body for a sound body by legerdemain. A new heaven and a new earth can be created only . . . as we ourselves become new." Again, this is the *Wiedergeburt*—a "taste of heaven"—and the "true resurrection" not of the body, but of the spirit, which would "arise from the sleep of sin" and "change into a new life with Christ."[28]

Most people, those with a mix of good and evil, would first go to *Reinigungsort* or a place of purification, sometimes called the spirit world. Here they would be assisted by teachers sent "from the highest regions to instruct the novices in the right way . . . and we find it not so very unreasonable when we describe it as purgatory." Souls here suffered spiritual, not bodily, punishments and could earn merit by which they advanced toward heaven. Lutherans did not make distinction for the degree of sanctification, which Bimeler called "most absurd and unjust."[29]

Hell was a series of seven abysses, with the first for those who committed abominations (of what kind he did not specify) to the lowest, the blasphemers, those who cursed against God. This resembles the description given by Barbara Grubermann, who claimed to have visited hell in one of her transports.[30]

Bimeler's description of heaven was highly social, much like communal life. He said there were no hermits in heaven, and one would seek the company of those who were spiritually compatible. The movement toward perfection and union with God would then culminate in the *Wiederbringung*, the restitution of all things, the ultimate salvation of everyone, including Satan (apocatastasis). "Since all had gone out [been created] from

God, and could not rest outside him, then one day all must return to him." This Platonic ideal Bimeler frequently referred to as "the indestructible spark in man" that "goes with the soul into the deepest recesses of hell" and would not allow the soul to rest until it had been fully purified.[31]

After Bimeler's death in 1853, the *Discourses* were printed (1855-60) in two octavo-sized volumes, *Die Wahre Separation* (*The True Separation*) and *Etwas Fürs Herz!* (*Something for the Heart!*) with copies given to each family. Bimeler's *Reden* originally had been taken down in shorthand by Johannes Neef for his father who was deaf. After Neef's 1832 death, another member continued recording Bimeler's words. Although the type to print the *Discourses* had been purchased as early as October 1853, just after Bimeler's death, serious work did not begin until a professional printer, Heinrich Hiserich, was hired in 1858.[32] Young men, including Eugene Wright,[33] were employed in the Print Shop, located in one of the original log cabins (and still standing today).

With the loss of Bimeler, several members, including Jacob Sylvan and gardener Simon Beuter, attempted to preach, but no one could fill Bimeler's shoes; no one could convey the force and spirit of the beliefs that made so many risk jail in Germany and emigrate to an unknown land. Even before the sermons were printed, Jacob Sylvan lamented the "waning zeal" of members and hoped the publishing of Bimeler's sermons could help.[34] But the slow process of drawing away from their unique religion was inexorable; church services became rote and consisted mainly of rereading favorite selections from the *Discourses*. There was no replacing Joseph Michael Bimeler.

MANAGEMENT AND BUSINESS

From the first, Bimeler assumed the mantle of supervising all aspects of Zoar life, the patriarchal "head of a great family," as historian E. O. Randall put it.[35] As we have seen, the deed for the land was in his name only, and business was transacted in his name. His name, not the Society's, is on a branding iron for barrels (now on display at Zoar Village State Memorial). Countless invoices in the Zoar Papers are in his name alone.

It's intriguing to speculate if Zoar would have survived as a community without his management. Would someone else, perhaps someone who had earlier left the group, someone who resented Bimeler, have stepped up? Did Bimeler's powerful, controlling personality prevent others from developing necessary leadership skills? Of course, we will never know, but it seems doubtful the Society would have endured without his guidance.

Even before the establishment of the communal society in 1819 and his assumption of the office of arbitrator in 1824, all business was conducted in Bimeler's name. He "had earned their trust and confidence by his intelligent and unselfish conduct already in the German fatherland, as well as later on the lengthy ocean journey,"[36] and that seemed to be enough for the others. His conduct inspired the conviction that he would act on behalf of everyone, not just himself. It seems the morality preached in his discourses carried over to business.

He was not above being possessive of community assets, declaring himself "the master" of Zoar's canal boat and listing in his receipt book a payment on "my note."[37] An argument was made both at the time and long after his death that Bimeler held himself above the other members. After all, didn't he live in a mansion (Number One House) when others still lived in one-room log cabins, and didn't he ride in a carriage while others walked? Yes, on both counts, but he lived in Number One with two other families,[38] and he rode in a carriage because he had a lame leg. But despite the utterances of his detractors, nothing can be proven that he did not act entirely for the welfare of the Zoar Society. US Supreme Court Justice John McLean (1785-1861) said of him: "Bimeler has a difficult part to act. As the head and leader of the society, his conduct is narrowly watched, and often misconstrued. Narrow minds in such an association, will be influenced by petty jealousies and unjust surmises. To insure success these must be overcome or disregarded. The most exemplary conduct and conscientious discharge of duty may not protect an individual from censure."[39]

Bimeler unsuccessfully fought to get the remaining funds from the Quakers in order to build a much needed gristmill (see chapter 2), since the closest one was in Sandyville, three miles away. He knew a mill would not only serve the Zoar community but bring in needed revenue. After building its first mill, without the money from the Friends, Zoar was selling excess unground wheat to mills in Canton in 1822.[40]

It is not known just how the Separatists obtained the contract to build their section of the Ohio & Erie Canal in 1826, but Zoar's portion undoubtedly had Bimeler's fingerprints on it. Canal contracts were let by the mile and were advertised in the newspaper. Whether he had any influence in picking the path along the Tuscarawas is unknown (there were several competing routes, including one that would have used the Sandusky River to reach Lake Erie). To have landed such a contract less than ten years after their arrival was a coup, but one that meant several years of exhausting work.

Bimeler himself probably did not participate in the physical labor of canal building, as he was reportedly "lame and walked with difficulty." It's unknown how he became disabled, whether it was before or after coming to America. "An element of mystery" surrounded his appearance. One eye was larger and more prominent than the other. Sadly, no photographs or portraits can confirm this description. In his discourses, Bimeler indicated he favored vegetarianism.[41]

Here is one description of Bimeler, given by Sophia Dana Ripley, one of the founders of the secular community Brook Farm, on a visit to Zoar in the summer of 1838:

> After breakfast . . . Mr. _____ went to pay his respects to B. whom he found rather advanced in years, dressed in a plain blue sailor's jacket and trows-ers, with a straw hat he doffs for no one. His address was polite, but very distant. No compliments were offered by him, and no interest expressed in what was going on abroad. His countenance is striking, decided but calm, with a full grey eye, very mild in its expression. He is evidently nothing of a philanthropist, and this lessens our interest in the community. His business talents are great, and he bears lightly the responsibility of all the pecuniary transactions of the society, which are extensive. He loves influence, and has consummate skill in the exercise of it, and we could see oppression nowhere, abundance everywhere, but with the most rigid discipline connected with it.[42]

His expertise as a homeopathic physician was tested on the voyage, where he tended to the sick onboard, which led to his assumption of leadership of the group in Philadelphia. Such medical knowledge was said to have been acquired "by his own efforts."[43] In Zoar, he continued as a doctor, most notably during the 1834 cholera epidemic where he ministered to the sick without regard to his own health.

Homeopathy, a medical concept developed by the German Samuel Hahnemann in 1796, theorized that "like cures like"—a patient takes a very dilute dose of a substance that causes the same symptoms as his ailment. It was quite different from the "heroic" medical procedures of purges and bloodletting then practiced, what Hahnemann derisively called "allopathic" medicine. Perhaps homeopathy appealed to Bimeler's mystical belief that there was a secret harmony in all things.

The Society hired local doctors as well, including Dr. Edward Caspari, who practiced in Zoar in 1843-44. Caspari, who would later testify in a court case against the Separatists, had nothing good to say about Bimeler ("Bimeler rules the members with an iron rod; they are more afraid of him than about any thing on earth"), but he never mentioned Bimeler's medical proficiency, or lack thereof, in his testimony.[44]

Bimeler became Zoar postmaster in 1826. One of the perks of office was free postage, of which he took full advantage. Not only were letters *from* the postmaster sent free of charge, but letters *to* him were free as well. Zoar was on the "state road" between Canton and New Philadelphia,[45] as well as parts of two other postal routes (Millersburg to Hanoverton and New Hagerstown to Leesville) and its post office also served the surrounding area.[46] As postmaster, he subscribed to both German and English newspapers and magazines, including the *Ohio* (now *Canton*) *Repository, Scientific American,* the farm journal *Ohio Cultivator,* and, perhaps surprisingly for the leader of a community supposedly closed off from the world, the *Phrenological Journal,* detailing the pseudoscience of comparing bumps on the head to personality traits, which was all the rage in the 1840s.[47]

In an inquiry from postmaster general William T. Barry in 1834, Bimeler proudly described the village: "The improvements in and near the village consist chiefly in: 1 flouring-mill, 2 saw-mills, 1 oil-mill, 1 woolen and linen manufacturing establishment; 1 warehouse; 1 new and commodious hotel; 1 store, and various other places of industry and mechanical business. There is also a blast furnace building at this time by the society of Zoar, situated about 2 miles north of the village on the Ohio canal."[48] Bimeler was involved in all aspects of these businesses. Members supervising each industry reported to him on production, and carried any cash received to him, where all transactions were carefully recorded by his hand in meticulously kept receipt books.[49] One gets the picture of someone with ink-stained fingers seated at a desk surrounded by the letters and ledgers needed to keep such a varied enterprise running. He was noted for his careful record keeping of even the most inconsequential documents.[50]

Although we will probably never know exactly how the system worked, as there are no extant notes of meetings, presumably Bimeler received daily updates from the three trustees charged with the different parts of the Society's work. The agriculture trustee reported on fields plowed and crops harvested. The livestock trustee gave updates on numbers of animals born or slaughtered and those animals needed to be traded or sold and also reported on the hotel, including the number of guests and the food and labor needed. The industry trustee would report on the production of all of the shops and factories, noting supplies or equipment needed. Bimeler recorded it all in his books, using different pages for different items.

He recorded shipments on the canal, the tonnage, and where they were bound. He kept day-to-day records of funds coming in and out of the Society. In the receipt book, any money was said to have been "delivered to" Bimeler. Journal pages indicated buying trips to New York or Philadelphia by Society members to purchase supplies—using either cash or "drafts," due bills for goods previously sold to others, like those from Cleveland commission merchant N. C. Winslow and Co.,[51] which were used like cash in these days before national banking. The Zoarites sent on these buying trips then presented a careful accounting of their expenses upon their return.[52] Printed blank contract forms from the 1840s show they were made between the contractor and Bimeler, not the Society.[53]

Bimeler used his own name to act on behalf of the Society in multiple ways. Stock, such as that purchased in the Farmer's Bank of Canton and the Sandy and Beaver Canal was in his name, with the canal stock going through probate at his death.[54] And, of course, the deed to the land was in his name alone. This usage is perhaps understandable before the Society incorporated in 1832, as, until then, the Society was not a business entity, just a collection of individuals. But it is harder to understand why Bimeler continued in this manner until just two weeks before his death.[55] Was it "old habits die hard" or ego? If he would have signed over the land earlier, he would have perhaps saved the Society a lot of anxiety and legal fees, as we will see in chapter 9.

Bimeler's will, signed on his deathbed on August 16, 1853, in a very shaky hand, reads as follows:

> I, Joseph Michael Bimeler, of Zoar, Tuscarawas County and State of Ohio, being weak in body but of sound and disposing mind, memory and understanding do make and publish this as my last will and testament. That is to say: I give and bequeath all my property, real, personal and mixed, of whatever kind, be the same in lands, tenements, trusts and otherwise, bonds, notes, claims, bank accounts or other evidences of debt of whatever nature, to the Society of Separatists of Zoar, and to its assigns forever, hereby

declaring all property I ever held, real or personal, within the County of Tuscarawas, has been the property of the Society, for which I now return it.

And I do herby appoint John M. Grossinger, Jacob Silvan, and Jacob Ackermann, trustees of said Society, as my executors, to carry out this, my will, into effect.

In testimony whereof, I have hereunto set my hand and affixed my seal, this sixteenth day of August A. D. one thousand and eight hundred and fifty three.

Joseph M. Bimeler [seal]

Signed, sealed and declared by the above named J. M. Bimeler, as his last will and testament, in the presence of us (the words "and its assigns forever" interlined [inserted?] before signing).[56]

Jacob Blickensderfer, Joseph C. Hance

Even over a span of over 150 years, one can imagine we can hear the deep sighs of relief from the trustees that the Zoar lands and wealth now *really* belonged to the community.

Bimeler's estate was probated as follows:

Amount collected on book account		$5192.55
Amount collected on notes & bills		$6386.46
Amount proceeds on RR stock		$1360.00
Amount proceeds State stock		$1350.00
Amount interest on State stock		$ 322.87
Amount bank certificate		$ 12.00
	Total	$14,683.88
Less cost of inventory, will		25.70
	Total	*$14,658.18*
Unable to collect: Agency German Society		$ 27.88
F. M. Weiss & Co		$237.28 [business failed?]
Sandy & Beaver Canal		$10,000.00[57]

Despite Bimeler's intransigence about signing over the property, there is no doubt he was beloved by his followers. Jacob Sylvan, in his introduction to *Die Wahre Separation* deserves the last word on Bimeler's character:

Our loyal departed friend and brother in faith was appointed as the only appropriate and capable person for this position, which he occupied with the greatest endurance and loyalty from 1817 until his blessed end in 1853. Not only in this office, but at all times, he offered a worthy example to his little flock, and himself practiced and personally experienced everything that he preached to others.

But just as for all true servants and beloved of God, so here too in full and even excessive measure, this man found himself despised, ridiculed, maligned and persecuted by Satan, the world, and the children of evil. Most of all, he was maligned by the unfaithful and lapsed members who were sometimes present. But he followed his Lord and King Jesus, patiently and courageously bearing this crown of thorns, and no-one ever saw him despondent, discouraged, or baffled in the midst of the myriad blows of fate that worked against him and the Society. Like a good shepherd and hero, he stood before his little flock and protected them when hell's wolf wished to creep up and break in. In truth one can say: he fulfilled, with as much fidelity as is possible for a human being, the office and calling laid upon him by God himself.[58]

CHAPTER 5

"Engaged in Agricultural Pursuits"

Agriculture in Zoar

Men and women alike engaged in agricultural pursuits. At harvest time all the
able-bodied inhabitants went into the fields to cut the grain with the sickle; all
were again employed in corn husking,
  —George B. Landis, "The Society of Separatists of Zoar, Ohio," Report
  of the American Historical Association, 1899

The Society of Separatists of Zoar obtained most of its wealth from agriculture, and, according to Edgar Nixon, "the bulk of the life of the community
centered around it."[1] Farming was the occupation of the majority of its
inhabitants. Whether they were directly involved or not, all Zoarites paid
close attention to the state of the crops, the weather, and the harvest. Although he is the only one to have left us his observations, gardener Simon
Beuter conveyed the thoughts of everyone in Zoar when he described in
his *Tag-Buch*[2] the date that the wheat was harvested, whether it was wet
or dry, and when the first furrow was turned.

As we have seen, one of the three trustees supervised the Society's
agricultural pursuits, and was considered the "lead" trustee, showing just
how important the growing of crops was to the community. Animal raising was supervised by a second trustee.[3]

By 1850, the Separatists' original 5,500 acres had grown though land
purchase to 8,826; by the 1898 dissolution, the extent of their holdings

was 7,300 acres.⁴ Most of the property southeast of town, too hilly to farm and known as the Zoar Woods, was timberland. Alexander Gunn gives us a picture in his *Hermitage-Zoar Note-Book:* "In the afternoon I persuade Christian Ruof, the landlord, to go with me through the great woods. I am afraid to go alone, for there are about three thousand acres, and so much broken that there is a chance of being lost. . . . The prospect is strikingly beautiful in all directions; range after range of rolling hills fading away into a faint purple haze, some covered with woods, others with the intense green of winter wheat. My companion seems to take a very practical view of everything, and knows how much wheat or corn may be expected from an acre."⁵ Gunn has left us indelible vignettes of Zoar agricultural life, despite his tendency to romanticize: "In the large field east of the village many teams are plowing the long furrows, stretch[ing] nearly half a mile without turning. I go up and see them pass, smelling the fresh-turned earth, than which there is no more delicate perfume."⁶

The Separatists were fortunate that the rich land ("the Plains") along the river had been used by the Delaware Indians and required little clearing in 1818 when their first crops were sown.⁷ Fields were given names to differentiate them and give directions to the laborers. Names included Bolivar Plains, Church Plains, both located along the road to Bolivar; Sulphur Spring Field, Kugel Berg (Cannonball Hill) on the Mineral City Road; Spring Field, Good Field, near the river bridge; Dover Hills, on the Dover-Zoar Road and Ghost Field on the road to Zoar Station (now Zoarville). The "ghost" name came from a mysterious reflection of moonlight that seemed to emanate from the field on clear nights.⁸

The Separatists often contracted to outsiders to clear land to be farmed, leaving members free for more important work. Here is a typical contract dated April 4, 1839. (Note that it is between the contractor and Bimeler, not the Society, and that his pay was two-thirds in trade at the Zoar Store.)

The said J. Wolfe is to grub the above described land in a workmanlike manner and pick off the brush clean, and rake the chips together and burn them; and cut all the timber off, excepting a few dead trees and several green trees—too large—in a word, make it ready and sufficiently clean tor the plough; and make a fence around said ground in the manner agreed upon. . . . That is to say, a fence 7 rails high, then stakes and riders, making it altogether 8 rails in height. . . . And the said J. M. Bimeler is to pay to James

Wolfe eight dollars per acre for as many acres as the above described lot
shall be found to contain; and cleared in the manner above described. And
the said J. M. Bimeler is to accept of Orders for flour, pork, etc. from the sd.
J. Wolfe as the work progresses along, and when said job of clearing shall
be finished, the sd. J. M. Bimeler is to pay one third of the whole amount
in cash, and the remainder that may be due him in trade.[9]

Some Zoar land was farmed by tenants, some for yearly rent, and others
on shares. Here is part of another contract: "To repair and put in good Order all the fences around said improvement, and Keep them in such repair
and Order, and to farm the said place well and in workmanlike manner,
and to deliver unto said J.M. Bimeler or his agents the One Third of all the
grain they may raise in said premises."[10] In 1879 the Society received 1,565
bushels, 55 pounds of wheat and 1,615 bushels of corn as their "shares"
from fifteen people leasing various parts of their land.[11]

The crops grown were those characteristic of a nineteenth-century Ohio
farm. In 1858, a typical year, the Society planted 355 acres of wheat, 70
acres of corn, 219 acres of oats, 62 acres of rye, 8 acres of buckwheat, and
21 acres of barley; it harvested 800 bushels of potatoes. Farm equipment
included fifteen plows and harrows ("with iron teeth"), three cultivators,
a threshing machine and a reaper (valued at a hundred dollars each), two
drills, and two windmills.[12]

The Separatists applied their German agricultural methods to the Ohio
landscape. Essayist P. F. D., a German himself, in 1832 boasts that "one
finds evidence of German diligence everywhere and, as far as the land has
been cleared at this time, one also observes a method of farming which is
typically German."[13]

The Separatists' expertise was admired by agricultural experts in the
pages of the *Ohio Cultivator:* "At Zoar, we were favorably struck with the fine
appearance of the crops on the very extensive grounds belonging to the
community. The corn was the best we had seen in this season and the wheat,
oats, and grass were equal to any not on better land."[14] A large farm equipment maker, the C. Russell Co. of Massillon, bragged in an 1875 advertisement
that the "Zoarites have continuously been using [our] rear cut machines
[reapers] for over 25 years."[15] In 1861 the Separatists subscribed to the German edition of *The American Agriculturalist* as well as the *Ohio Cultivator.*[16]

Not all Zoar harvesting was "modern," though. The use of the hand

As the labor of all is necessary for a communal society's survival, both men and women worked together in Zoar's fields and elsewhere, with some women performing traditionally male jobs. (Courtesy of the Ohio History Connection, Zoar Photograph Collection, AV9.)

cradle to harvest grain, with a line of cradlers followed by rows of rakers and shockers continued through the years and was seen in a circa 1890 photograph that has become an iconic Zoar image. The flail, a wooden pole with a shorter wooden piece attached by a leather thong, used to beat the chaff off the grain, was used to harvest rye as late as the 1890s, since the Society wanted the long rye straw to braid for hats.[17] An 1882 visitor observed, "We were attracted to the sound of flails. Really and truly, the rhythmic beating of the flails upon the barn floor! . . . Long, long ago it was a familiar noise—one that we had never expected to hear again."[18]

Flailing, and much other farm labor, was done by the "strong and industrious"[19] women of the community, a practice much remarked upon by visitors: "[The women of Zoar] delve into the gardens and toil in the fields, carry huge bundles on their heads and rake with their stout arms. At the time of our visit . . . the Zoarites were gathering in their grain . . . and the girls were following in the wake of the rakers over the field, picking up every straw and head of wheat, in order that nothing should be lost or wasted."[20]

After the 1834 cholera epidemic, the Society began to hire outsiders to assist with the farm work, as well as to labor in their ironworks (see next chapter). Most of these hands were Swabians,[21] who boarded in the Bauer Haus (farmers' dwelling). Some came with families and boarded in Society-owned homes, both inside and outside of Zoar. Bringing so many strangers into a closed community had ill effects. William A. Hinds was told, "They tempt our young people into bad habits."[22] These included drinking, swearing, eating pork, smoking, and singing secular songs. But most of all, the paid laborers, working for wages, brought a cash economy into a community where that concept was foreign. In 1873 the Society paid out $8,490 in wages, typical for the period. Workers were paid $10 to $15 per month, half in cash and half in trade at the Zoar Store.[23] Most, if not all, hired laborers never became members of the Zoar Society. Zoar instead became a safe place for newly arrived Swabian immigrants to get on their feet. Often their descendants visit Zoar today and declare their ancestor once was a Society member, but in most cases, they were hired workers who stayed only for a short time and are not included in the membership rolls.[24]

The first mill at Zoar, south of the village, was built in 1821, shortly after the Separatists' arrival. Society accounts relate that thirty farmers brought their grain to Zoar that year and the Society was buying wheat to sell to larger mills in nearby Canton.[25] A dam on the river provided the power for this mill, plus the sawmill, Planing Mill, and Woolen Mill, all located along this mill race.

> A mill, well designed in the English manner and supplied all year long with sufficient water from the Tuscarawas River, by means of a very special canal, is capable of not only filling the rather considerable needs of the whole community, but also in addition, of delivering every year two thousand barrels of flour for sale which is shipped by way of Cleveland to New York on the barge canal. This mill operates without strenuous work of human hands, since the machinery itself performs nearly all the labor. A large number of customers from all around Zoar call at the mill, so that a great part of the need for flour is already gained in the customers.[26]

The writer is referring to the "toll," or portion of a bushel of grain taken by the miller as payment for grinding, which, as he indicates, made up a large part of the Separatists' flour production. In 1845 this first mill was replaced by the larger and more modern Custom Mill, which stood until

This huge mill along the Ohio & Erie Canal was built in 1837. Never very successful as a mill, it later served as a warehouse for community-made goods. (Courtesy of the Ohio History Connection, Properties Collection, P365AV.)

the early 1930s, when the upper stories were moved to Zoarville to become Ehlers' General Store.[27]

In 1837 a second mill was built along the Ohio & Erie Canal. This mill spanned the canal, with a trap door over the waterway so boats could be loaded directly. "The old mill . . . spanned the beautiful stream. A great arch it was, that reached from one green bank to the other, while the mill itself, above, was unbroken and worked on with its rush, and buzz, and whirl of machinery within, just as though that was a common way of making mills to stand astride of noisy, onward-rushing rivers."[28] This huge frame structure, which took two years to build, was never as successful as the other mills; its turbine froze during the winter and its machinery was deemed obsolete even at the time of construction.[29] It eventually became a warehouse for all types of Society goods shipped on the canal. It stood until the 1920s, and its foundation can still be seen along the towpath.

The Society sometimes hired outsiders to run the mills. One early contract was made in 1837 with Henry Usher, "late of New York," to run the Canal Mill at a yearly salary of four hundred dollars. His flour was to be good enough "such as will pass inspection in the eastern cities," and he was to run the mill "day and night if it be required of him," with "a sober, industrious and moral behaviour."[30]

An additional mill was located at One Leg Creek, near Zoar Station, three miles south of the village. It, too, was run by an outside contractor.[31] This mill was traded for land in Guthrie County, Iowa, in the 1870s.[32]

By 1837 the Society was shipping two thousand to three thousand barrels of flour per year (each weighing 196 pounds) to New York by way of Cleveland, Lake Erie, and New York's Erie Canal.[33] Bimeler's Receipt Book shows many barrels of flour shipped via Zoar's canal boat *Friendship* from the 1840s through the 1850s. In later years, Zoar flour was shipped by rail.

To facilitate sales of their products to distant markets, the Society relied on commission merchants, who acted as agents between buyer and seller. One such merchant was N. C. Winslow of Cleveland who had a long relationship with the Zoarites.[34] Typically, the Separatists would send their products to him on the canal to be stored in his warehouse until he could find a buyer in a distant town like Buffalo or New York. On receipt, Winslow would send a "note" with a monetary value of the goods back to Zoar, which the Separatists could use in lieu of cash with other businesspeople. Often, a Society member would travel to Philadelphia or New York to purchase supplies, armed with notes ("drafts") of various values in order to buy essentials.[35] These IOUs are how business was transacted in the first half of the nineteenth century when there was little hard money and no national banking system.

After harvest, the grain was stored in two large barns on the eastern edge of the village. The oldest, the Granary, was built in 1821 and featured a steep roof and doors on either side that allowed a wagon and team to drive through. The second, known as "the barn built before breakfast," indicating the speed in which it was framed, included a full cellar underneath. Threshing was done in the nearby Thresh House, originally with flails, as mentioned, and later with more modern machinery.[36]

The Society bought and sold miscellaneous agricultural products through the Zoar Store. These included wool, hops, flaxseed (for oil making), and woad (a plant-based dye that, when fermented, made the distinctive "Zoar blue").[37]

The Society raised livestock—cows for milk, cheese, butter, meat, and hides, sheep for wool and meat, chickens for meat and eggs, and horses and oxen for transportation, plowing, and hauling. One of the three trustees supervised all of the livestock operations. For the 1850 census, the Society listed the following animals at a total value of $4,010:

53	horses
16	working oxen
105	milk cows
61	other cattle
1090	sheep
76	swine[38]

Although at this time, the Society refrained from eating pork, pigs were raised for meat to serve to the hired help and to visitors at the hotel. By the time the Society dissolved, most Zoar members had added pork to their diet.

The number of dairy cows remained fairly constant over the years, as one hundred cows were advertised in the 1898 auction poster.[39] They experimented with various cattle breeds, finally settling on Durham and Devonshire.[40]

P. F. D. describes Zoar animal husbandry in his 1832 essay "Harmony Builds the House":

> In general the Society of Zoar seems to bestow extraordinary attention to the raising of cattle and sheep. This is shown especially by the fact that in the very beginning, before they began building more comfortable and spacious houses for themselves, they erected next to the existing and still useful old barns or stables two very large structures, which were more comfortable and healthy for the animals. These buildings compared favorably to those which in former years could be seen in the Royal Estates in Stuttgart, Ludwigsburg and Monrepos. The cattle as well as the sheep . . . remain constantly under the supervision of herdsmen [while in the fields], and are not allowed to run freely without such supervision, as is usually the case on American farms. When the weather is favorable the oxen, cows and sheep are driven every morning after breakfast in three separate groups to the pasture, and then in the evening again back to the barns at the proper time. In this way the milk cows can still be milked before nightfall, for which purpose one female is assigned seven cows. The milk is then immediately transported to the Springhouse in a vat which is fixed on a small cart especially built

for this purpose and pulled by a horse. There it is stirred into thoroughly scalded clean pots by women especially entrusted to this job.[41]

Dairy products were not just for home consumption. Cheese and especially butter were sold on the open market via the canal. Butter was shipped in 100-pound kegs, with some Zoar butter sold by commission merchants to buyers as far away as New York City.[42] Butter was considered so valuable that it was not distributed unsupervised in the Springhouse, as was milk, but was given out each Friday afternoon under the watchful eye of the overseer of the Magazine.[43] An accounting of butter and cheese production was made in 1879:

Butter used in Zoar Society	5451 lb.
Cheese used in Zoar Society	1668 lb.
Butter used in Zoar Hotel	773 lb.
Cheese used in Zoar Hotel	842 lb.
Butter sold in Zoar Store	478 lb.
Cheese sold at Zoar Station	448 lb.
Cheese sold at Zoar Store	5768 lb.
Butter in all	6702 lb.
Cheese sold and used	7726 lb.
Cheese made this year	8729 lb.[44]

P. F. D. describes the dairy industry in 1832 (and disagrees with the size of the butter casks):

Besides the great quantities of milk which are consumed daily in the community, partly with coffee, partly in other ways, there still remains so much left over that they are able to prepare a kind of Swiss cheese from it, which likewise, for the most part, is consumed by the Society. Almost with every meal they enjoy cottage cheese prepared in three different ways, in addition to butter. . . . Notwithstanding the considerable quantity of butter which is used in the different boarding houses, in part for cooking, partly enjoyed on bread. . . . every year several thousand pounds are put aside and shipped in small casks (or vats) weighing approximately forty to fifty pounds on the canal to Cleveland, and from there by way of Lake Erie and Buffalo to New York. In this way the Society of Zoar is amply rewarded for the care which they take of their cattle, because they have plenty of butter and milk all through the year. . . . Their neighbors, who let their cows run freely day and night, summer and winter, without shelter, often must do without milk and butter.[45]

Descriptions of the dairy with its dairymaids, cows, and their vast barn are plentiful in the accounts left by travelers and journalists. Sophia Dana Ripley, in 1838, described the Springhouse (located under the store and adjacent to the Dairy) as "cool as an icehouse, with running water passing through it. Pots of milk, with the cream rising, were ranged around. Small new cheeses were piled on the shelves, and large tubs of butter in the centre." She describes the sound of cowbells marking the return of the cattle to the barn for evening milking and the dairymaids carrying tubs of milk on their heads.[46] Constance Fenimore Woolson gives a quite accurate description of straining the milk brought from the barn: "A venerable 'milk-mother' in white cap and clogs, stood down in the lower story, and ladled out the strained milk into innumerable pails, each with its hieroglyphic sign on the cover, denoting to which household it belonged."[47]

The huge cattle barn intrigued other visitors, with one calling it "a milker's palace."[48] Geoffrey Williston Christine, writing for *Peterson's Magazine* in 1889, described it thusly: "The stables in which these cattle are kept are models of their kind. Their drainage, ventilation, and facilities for light are perfect, and every device that ingenuity can suggest and an unlimited expenditure [can] carry out has been utilized to make their sanitary conditions as perfect as possible. The stalls extend in long rows on either side of broad aisles. The name of each animal is painted above her resting place, and the surprise of the visitor, upon reading such fanciful appellations as "Maud," "Lily," "Ethel," and "Rose," fades away when he learns that each young woman has the privilege of naming the cows she milks."[49]

The Dairy Barn, two and half stories (the upper story held hay and straw for the animals, accessible by a ramp in front) and over two hundred feet long, stood until about half was removed to accommodate the Zoar levee in the mid-1930s. The remaining barn stood until 1980, when its roof, weakened by lack of maintenance, caved in during a windstorm. The building was later demolished, but its foundation can still be seen.

The large flock of sheep was kept in barns near the Shepherd's House, just outside town on the Mineral City Road (today's Second Street). They were housed in barns overnight and taken out to the fields during the day.

"The sheep, though not of the finest wool, are bred with a view to the profits arising from them, and divided into small droves, each of which has a shepherdess assigned it, who takes some light work in her hands, and with the assistance of a dog trained for that purpose, moves her flocks slowly off to their hills in the morning, and gradually returns them to their fold again, by the time the sun is down and, the men are returned from their work."[50]

Men also tended the sheep, as Maximillian, Prince of Wied, traveling on the canal in 1834 observed: "Just as I was at this spot [the Canal Tavern], the shepherd drove a numerous flock of sheep over the bridge, and answered my questions in genuine Swabian German. His entire dress and equipments were quite in the German fashion: a shepherd's crook, a broad leather bandolier, ornamented with brass figures, a flat broad-brimmed hat, and a large grey coat; a costume very uncommon in America."[51] The sheep were taken to pens near the Granary to be shorn each May, a procedure done by women and a few boys. Afterward, a celebratory *brodesse* of fresh bread and butter was served.[52] The shorn wool was bundled and taken to the Woolen Mill to be processed (carded, spun, dyed and woven). Products of the Woolen Mill will be considered in the next chapter.

Most households had their own small flock of chickens, but the eggs and meat needed for patrons at the hotel were raised at the *Henneberg* (chicken keeper's hill), just south of town. Excess eggs were packed in straw in barrels and shipped north on the canal to be sold.[53]

Orchards dotted the landscape around the village. P. F. D. describes them in 1832: "All along the roads in the town of Zoar and on the cleared land belonging to it, the fruit trees put on quite a show with their luxuriant growth. Besides that they have several orchards, some of them laid out on a high knoll [now called Cherry Hill] so they can . . . look forward to a rich fruitful harvest in future years, even if the fruit should thrive only moderately well."[54]

Zoar earned the moniker "a little village in an apple orchard" due to its abundance of apple trees.[55] The fruit was dried into "apple snitz," pressed into cider, made into apple butter, and stored in barrels in cellars to be eaten out of hand. Some apples and dried apple snitz were sold.[56] The trees grew everywhere, not just in orchards, but along the fences and roads, along the mill race and the picnic grounds; "all kinds of apples, sweet and sour, early and late, even crab apples."[57] Apple picking was done mostly by children, supervised by an adult, and everything had to be picked, even

This view northeast from the hotel cupola shows Zoar's tannery (*left*), granary (*center, upper left*), barns, and other outbuildings, all now gone. Included in the foreground is a tiny fruit-drying kiln for producing dried apple *snitz*. (Courtesy of the Ohio History Connection, Properties Collection P365AV.)

the windfalls. The snitz were peeled and sliced in the evenings by groups of neighbors and dried in small houses equipped with slatted drawers on each side; one was located near the hotel. Apple butter stirring was a community activity each fall.

Gardener Simon Beuter specialized in fruit culture, developing the Zoar Sweeting apple and the Zoar Beauty pear.[58] Young trees from his nursery were often sold to outsiders.[59] The nurseries contained twenty-five varieties of cherries, thirty-seven kinds of apples, and many other fruits.[60] Orange and lemon trees were grown in the greenhouse and were much remarked upon by visitors: "This garden contains a hot house in about which were a variety of plants and small trees that require its protection during winter, among which were several lemon trees, one of which was loaded with lemons, of handsome size some being verry [*sic*] large."[61]

No discussion of Zoar agriculture would be complete without a mention of the Zoar Garden, the town's focal point. Although visitors' accounts mention that a few vegetables were grown there, it was its floral beauty, its symbolism, and its tranquility that were most noticed by visitors.

In the Centre of these lots they have their Gardens and on the out corners
and outside is their houses and shops. On the North side of this is [a] green
House Containing almost all kinds shrubs some orange and Lemon trees
with all kinds flowers. In the centre of the Garden is a circle of Rose Bushes.
Perhaps 20 ft in circumference in the middle is a bed of flowers of all kinds
planted in circles which makes it quite beautiful. There are twelve walks
four feet wide beautifully lined with flowers and s[h]rubs and all terminat-
ing in [the] centre. Besides these there are three walks running each parallel with the square at equal distances from the edges and each other. This
accordingly will make some of their beds (which contain common garden
vegetables such as beets carrots, etc.) in the form of a triangle, others of a
right angle and many other shapes equaly [sic] odd.[62]

This early description of the Zoar Garden gives a rough outline of its geo-
metric shape, which was symbolic of the New Jerusalem in Revelation 21.
The center tree is the tree of life, or Christ, and the circle (here described as
rose bushes and later as a hedge) is Heaven. The twelve slip junipers outside
the hedge are the Apostles. The twelve radiating walks, depicting the twelve
gates and the twelve tribes of Israel mentioned in Revelation, also represent
the paths taken in life. The path surrounding the entire garden is the world;
to be saved, one has to get on a path that leads to Christ, but one may go
astray on the inner path that runs between the flowerbeds. However, looking again toward Christ can put one on another path toward Him.

We know the central garden was not in the original town plan, as the
log home of Christina Petermann, the first child born in Zoar in 1819, was
located on this block.[63] George Washington Hayward's 1829 diary informs
us that the garden was thriving then, so we can probably date its establishment to at least 1827, if not earlier. Perhaps the Separatists, working so
hard on the canal at that time, needed this tangible symbol of their faith
to keep them true to it during their labors.

No one knows who designed the garden or from whence the idea sprang,
other than from their deep faith. The castle at Ludwigsburg, where some
of the Separatists were employed while imprisoned, has beautiful formal
gardens even today, so seeing and perhaps working in those gardens may
have been the impetus for the one in Zoar. In addition to the flowers and
vegetables, more apple trees lined the perimeter fence.

Cider, fresh and "hard" (fermented), pressed from the many apples,
was a staple drink for the Separatists, especially the men. It was served to

workers in the fields, and barrels of it were kept in the cool cellars under each home. The pressing was done in the Cider Mill, built in 1854 with the assistance of the communal Harmonists (see page 98). This newer building replaced an earlier, smaller press. Simon Beuter wondered if such an extravagant structure was needed for just a single purpose, and if it might encourage a population already, in his opinion, inclined to drink too much.[64] After completion, the cabinet shop moved to the upper story to share the mill's steam engine. The Society did custom pressing for nearby farmers, another source of income.[65]

Beer, made from homegrown grain, barley and hops, was produced at the Brewery, west of the village. Beer was also brought to workers in the fields on hot days, and female laundresses were allowed a glass of beer on Monday washdays.[66] It was served at the hotel bar; it's unclear how much was sold outside of the community. From January through May 1870, eighty-seven barrels were produced, according to records (today's barrel of beer is thirty-one gallons).[67]

The Separatists' experiments with viticulture, with both imported and native grapes, were unsuccessful, but great quantities of currants were grown to make wine, which was produced mainly by each household. Children, with their small fingers, picked the tiny currants.[68]

Maple sugar was produced from the surrounding woodlands, as P. F. D. describes: "This sugar is also produced and prepared on their own land from the sap of their sugar maples which starts running in the very early spring. There is an extraordinary large number of these trees growing in various locations on their lands. Their yearly yield of sugar amounts on the average to several thousand pounds each year produced in five different sugar camps." The 1850 census shows the Separatists produced 2,000 pounds of maple sugar that year.[69]

Other agricultural products—clay, hides, and flax in particular—were transformed by manufacturing and will be considered in the next chapter.

CHAPTER 6

"The Wealth They Have Accumulated Is Enormous"

Doing Business in Zoar

The wealth they have accumulated in the half century that has since elapsed is enormous.

—"A Day with the Zoarites," *Elmira (NY) Telegram,* June 3, 1888

TRANSPORTATION

The key to Zoar's success in trade was its location on the Ohio & Erie Canal. The canal provided an easy way to get its goods, both agricultural and manufactured, to market. Digging seven miles of it, building one lock and supplying the outside contractors who constructed the other locks and connecting sections,[1] brought the Separatists out of debt, allowing them to build larger homes, barns, and mills and develop an iron industry that would have been unprofitable if the pig iron produced by these furnaces had been shipped overland.[2] Zoar might have been just another short-lived communal experiment, a footnote perhaps, if it had not been for the canal. Essayist P. F. D. put Zoar's canal-related success in biblical terms: "For the Society, therefore the words of Solomon the wise, Proverbs, Chapter Ten, Verse Four, have been fulfilled literally: 'He becomes poor that dealeth with a slack hand, but the hand of the diligent maketh rich.'"[3]

The presence of the canal greatly increased the value of their land. By 1830, a mere twelve years after their arrival, the Separatists began to develop new industries, shipping products in earnest, and, again in the words of P. F. D., "had become the trading center of the whole region."[4]

The influence of the canal was not unalloyed—it brought the world to Zoar, as passengers on packet boats and rowdy "canawlers" (canallers) disturbed the community's isolation, but unlike the railroad would prove later in the century, the influx was as slow moving as the waterway itself. Besides, the Separatists could see a profit in serving these outsiders, building first the Canal Tavern in 1829, which mainly served the canal workers, and, in 1833, the Zoar Hotel.

The route of the canal parallels the Tuscarawas River, crossing Zoar land at a diagonal, northwest to southeast. Exactly how the contract was made with the state of Ohio is unknown.[5] What is known, is that after more than two years of backbreaking labor digging the ditch, the Separatists received twenty-one thousand dollars for their efforts,[6] more than enough to pay off the debt for their land to the heirs of Gottfried Haga, who had since died.

Everyone worked, including women, who carried the dirt away in baskets on their heads. The celibacy then practiced in Zoar proved fortuitous, as Nixon says, for "without the aid of the women it is doubtful if the work could [have been] undertaken."[7] Moreover, by doing the labor themselves, they were spared the excessive destruction of the landscape that might have occurred with a more careless outside contractor.

In addition to the canal bed, the Separatists constructed a feeder canal that came right into the village, allowing boats to dock adjacent to the Woolen Mill, and Planing Mill. A guard lock (which can still be seen today) was constructed "at joint expense of the state and the Zoar Community."[8] This lock and a feeder dam were kept in good repair by the Separatists, who were paid one hundred dollars per year by the state.[9]

The Society operated its own canal boats—the *Industry,* used in the 1830s until at least 1841,[10] and the *Friendship,* used throughout the 1840s—until at least 1854.[11] A flatboat, the *Economy,* was used to haul bulky items. The *Friendship* was replaced with another boat, probably with the same name, in 1849, built by Jacob Barnhardt of Peninsula, Ohio, a center of boat manufacturing located on the canal north of Akron. Bimeler provided the specifications:

> Said Boat shall be built of such size, as to Carry at least Sixty Tons, it shall not be of the largest kind of Boats, but shall be large Enough to fill up the Locks so far, as not to leave a greater apace in length than from twelve to

Eighteen inches; To have One Bow Cabin of the full length of One Locker, with a Cabin next, thereto attached, Calculated for State-rooms; Also One Stern-Cabin, large enough to have one Kitchen struck off from same, Commodious for Cooking, and have room for the Necessary Cupboards or Closets for Kitchen-furniture, and a Space under the Stern, Sufficiently large enough for the Boat-hands to Sleep in. . . . Said Barnhardt shall also have the Midships so arranged, that a Commodious Stable for two horses shall be placed about the middle of the Boat, and the Boat shall be furnished with Six Hatches, One on Each side for Each Midship, and one on Each side for the horse stable; Said Barnhardt further agrees to furnish the sacking frames, the windows, and to paint said Boat well and thoroughly, and fit it out Complete in Every respect, ready for Navigating the Ohio Canal.[12]

This completed boat was, before received by Bimeler, to be "accepted by two impartial witnesses as to soundness of construction." Cost for the new boat was $1,100, with $300 down and $100 paid monthly. To measure how quickly the canals were supplanted by the railroad, it, or perhaps another Society boat (a name is not specified), was sold for just $500 in 1855, only six years later. A spur of the Cleveland & Pittsburgh Railroad had just been built at Zoar Station, two miles distant.[13]

The Society had at least two members who captained its boats: John Petermann and John Brunny.[14] Petermann's wife, Christina, traveled with him on trips to Cleveland, leaving their two young daughters behind in the Girls' Dormitory.[15] Though presumably his lameness kept him from actively being on board, Bimeler was calling himself "the master" of the Zoar boats in 1834-35.[16] Outsiders were also employed as captains, most notably James Rutter, "late of Pennsylvania," who helmed the *Friendship* from 1839 to 1843. He was paid $218 per month, and promised to "Keep such orderly and well behaving hands, against whose behaviour & deportment no reasonable objections can be raised." Bimeler could discharge any crew in violation of this rule, as the contract was made with Bimeler, not the Society.[17] Rutter further agreed: "Not to keep any spirituous liquors on board of said Boat, nor shall he suffer any of his hands to keep any, but on the contrary use his best diligence to keep them sober and not to allow any blasphemous Cursing or swearing on the same, as that kind of deportment can have no other but an evil tendency and lead to no other but bad and destructive results. But on the other hand he is to treat his hands kindly and with a due tendency to preserve peace and good order,

Having the Ohio & Erie Canal traverse their property contributed mightily to the success of the Zoar Society. Not only did building it help them pay off their land debt, but it also allowed their products to be more easily marketed. Here a boat approaches Lock 10, the one closest to Zoar. (Courtesy of the Ohio History Connection, Zoar Photograph Collection AV9.)

and especially to conduct himself honorably and kindly towards his Employer [i.e., Bimeler] in all matters and things between them."[18]

The Zoar boats carried all kinds of products, from green apples to "old rags," but mostly butter, flour, and, above all, pig iron from the Society's two furnaces, all of which were transported to consignees in Massillon, Akron, Cleveland, Toledo, Buffalo, and New York City.[19]

Travel on the canal was a seasonal affair. The typical season lasted from April through November. At the close of navigation in the fall of 1843, the Zoar boat *Friendship* was "stopped at Bethlehem [now Navarre in southwest Stark County] by the Ice, and could not come home, arrangements were then made to send a Team to Bethlehem for the Furniture of the boat and some few articles of loading."[20] Presumably, the *Friendship* remained at Bethlehem until spring or at least until warmer weather.

Boats came unsolicited to offer their services to the Separatists. A surviving notice reads: "Dear Friends: The Propellor "Whale" is on her way for

Akron and on her way back wants all the butter you can make from this time and will take it at the market price. Have the butter put up in firkins or stone Jars in good shipping order, also wish you would buy in all the eggs you can for me, have them put up in good packages. Measure the oats you use in packing the eggs so I will know how much to pay for. I will also take all the green apples you can get for me, want them in good shipping condition. Do the best you can for the Whale in Butter, Eggs and apples."[21]

There were four locks in the three miles between Bolivar and Zoar (Locks 7-10), so traversing this short distance gave captains, crew, and passengers ample time to spend in the vicinity while "locking through." Since traffic moved at the pace of a horse or mule, and two-way traffic had to yield to whomever came to the lock first; passengers could get out and walk from lock to lock on the towpath, exploring the area. Passengers on the "packet boats," those designed for people, not freight, spent the night in the adjacent canal towns, not on the cramped boats, hence the need for hostelries like the Canal Tavern and the Zoar Hotel.

The tavern catered to the rough canal trade. A blacksmith shop was located next door to service the mules and horses pulling the boats along the towpath. The accounts of the tavern show that money for both lodging and freight was collected here, along with room and board for the boat crews. In 1842 the high water mark for canal traffic, $1,115.41 was collected at the Canal Tavern in lodging, meals and freight.[22]

The proprietor of the tavern had to hew a fine line between the needs of his customers, the canal captains, and their crews, and the strict rules of the Separatists not to drink, swear, or gamble. As you will see in chapter 9, the tavern's proprietor, Johannes Goesele, went over that line repeatedly and was expelled from the Society in 1844, resulting in a landmark US Supreme Court case in 1852.

Records show that by 1846, the tavern was costing the Society more than it was taking in,[23] which, in addition to the mismanagement by Goesele, may be another reason for closing it. A few months thereafter, the tavern was closed for good, and became the home of the overseer of the Canal Mill.

The Society, or rather, Bimeler, invested in the Sandy & Beaver Canal, a feeder which ran from the Ohio River in Columbiana County west to the Ohio & Erie Canal at Bolivar.[24] It joined the Ohio & Erie at Bolivar via a wooden aqueduct over the Tuscarawas River. Begun in 1834, plagued by construction delays (two tunnels had to be cut through solid rock), the financial Panic of 1837, and changes in management, the completed canal ran for only two years, from 1849-1851, until the bank of a reservoir at the summit gave way in April 1852, destroying the midsection of the canal.[25]

During the final phase of its construction, Zoar provided "good gray mettle [*sic*]" to Joshua Malin of Minerva in Stark County to cast parts for the locks of the Sandy & Beaver Canal there.[26] The decision for Zoar to operate a general store from about 1841 to 1854 in Waynesburg, twelve miles east of Zoar, may have been due to its location on the Sandy & Beaver Canal.[27] Bimeler contracted with a Joseph Doll in 1841 at three hundred dollars per year to keep the Waynesburg store. Bimeler would furnish the goods and coal for heating and keep all receipts. Noted on the 1842 renewal of the contract were the stipulations that Doll was not to sell on credit "except to men of property and good standing (& only for 6 months or less)" and not to purchase goods in Bimeler's name without his consent.[28]

Bimeler bought a hundred shares of Sandy & Beaver stock valued at a hundred dollars per share on a 5 percent margin in 1835.[29] These shares were still in his name at his death in 1853, and listed in the record of probate

By the late 1850s, the Cleveland & Pittsburgh Railroad had fairly supplanted most traffic on the canal, but the waterway was still used for heavy freight until the disastrous flood of 1913. (Courtesy of the Ohio History Connection, Louis Baus Collection, P223AV.)

filed by the Society trustees, with their ten-thousand-dollar value marked as "unable to collect."[30]

Although the Ohio & Erie Canal continued to be used to transport bulky and heavy freight until it was destroyed by the flood of 1913,[31] the "canal era" was essentially over by the time a spur of the Cleveland & Pittsburgh Railroad (between Hudson in Summit County and Millersburg in Holmes County) was constructed nearby in 1855. As the road was contemplated, the Separatists purchased $1,350 worth of C&P stock in 1852.[32] In 1857, in the wake of that year's financial crisis, Cashier Christian Wiebel inquired of Zoar's commission merchant, N. C. Winslow of Cleveland, "an experienced business-man," whether the Society should be worried that the C&P was now paying its dividends in "scrips" and a "coupon bond" payable in distant 1867 and 1870. He asked if all stockholders were getting paid that way, and if the company would start paying dividends in cash in the future.[33] Wiebel must have also written to the railroad itself as well, and received a reply from E. Rockwell, its secretary, on October 29, 1857: "The prospects of our road are still encouraging,—but the present financial circumstances of the country have somewhat effected the profits . . . & we cannot tell now when we shall be able to declare another dividend."[34] The economy recovered, and in May 1863, in the midst of the Civil War, the Society purchased another $1,260 of C&P stock.[35] Eventually, this line became part of the Pennsylvania Railroad.

The C&P tracks did not come into town—that did not happen until 1882 when the Wheeling & Lake Erie opened a station in the southern part of the village—but instead ran near the Society's property at One Leg Creek and the now-shuttered Fairfield Furnace two miles south. The Separatists took advantage of "Zoar Station" (now Zoarville) to open a general store there. The "Station Store" was operated by generations of the Ehlers family, who received it in the dissolution, and Ehlers General Store remained a community fixture there through the 1980s.

The impact of this new mode of transport so far from town seemingly was minimal—hotel guests now often arrived by rail instead of canal boat, and shipping and the occasional out-of-town travel by the Separatists was easier—but the two-mile distance between the town and rail line was beneficial in keeping the villagers isolated. Often visitors to the hotel would be picked up at Zoar Station by the village omnibus (the "Black Wagon"), a multi-passenger, horse-drawn vehicle that also transported Zoarites to Bolivar for voting or Zoar band members to concerts.[36]

A visiting journalist in 1882 saw presciently what the building of the Wheeling & Lake Erie line right in town might do to a cloistered Zoar:

> A railroad is in progress of building that will unite them to the world. Ere long its throbbing pulses will be felt at Zoar. The glitter of the engine will cast its shine upon the great windows of the church on the hill, and the rushing trains will jar the peaceful graves of the dead, and people will walk the wide street in the little village and curl their lips "half in pity, half in scorn," over the cumbrous tiled roofs and old fashions and sacred customs of this united colony which was once a poor handful of strange seed sown in peril and with misgivings and sorrow in the New World across the vast Atlantic.
>
> The Community gave generously to secure the location of the railroad near them. The changes that follow its advent will be marked in more ways than one.[37]

It was not just the railroad itself: by the 1880s Americans had more leisure time to take day trips. Day-trippers, especially German Americans, took the Wheeling & Lake Erie from its station in Cleveland to Zoar on weekends to sample the good Zoar beer, the hearty food at the hotel, to stroll through the garden and gawk at the strange folk who lived there. As we will see, the Separatists, never ones to pass up an opportunity to make money, catered to these tourists. Although it seemed like good business at the time, tourism was one factor leading to the Society's demise.

BUSINESS PRACTICES

Judging by his meticulously kept account books, not a penny was spent by the Society that was not accounted for by cashier Bimeler, who held that office as well as that of agent general. He even recorded a donation of twenty-five cents given to a "blind black man" in 1846.[38] After Bimeler's death in 1853, the books were kept first by trustee Jacob Sylvan until he died in 1862, then by three different cashiers: Christian Wiebel until his death in 1872 (although Wiebel was cashier from the time of Bimeler's death, Sylvan kept the ledgers), Jacob Ackermann until his death in 1889, and, lastly, by Christian Zimmermann until the corporation was officially dissolved in 1900. Ackermann served as both trustee and cashier from 1872 to 1889, although he had been a trustee since 1832.

Anyone who had business with the Zoar Society stopped at the Zoar Store, which sold both Zoar-made items as well as those purchased from outside suppliers. Nonmember workers were paid partially in cash and partially in trade at the Store. Society members could obtain goods from the store, but only with permission of the trustees. (Courtesy of the Ohio History Connection, Properties Collection, P365AV.)

The Zoar Store, a large frame building with a long stone-flagged porch, served as the Society's business hub; it also housed the post office. Goods sold there ranged from items manufactured outside the community and purchased by the Society on business trips to the East, to surplus items made in the village shops and factories. Those persons having any business with the Society—be they creditors or debtors—called first at the store, which served the surrounding countryside as well as the village. The cashier or his delegate managed the store and acted as the Society's purchasing agent.[39] Hired workers got their pay half in cash and half in trade at the store. Around 1860 laborers were given slips of paper stating the amount of work done signed by their supervisor to redeem at the store.[40] Later, account books were used to record the balances. As mentioned, the Society had a store in Waynesburg as well as ones at the two iron furnaces, the one at Fairfield Furnace was supplanted by the Station Store after 1855.

Society members could obtain merchandise from the store only with permission of the trustees. Especially in the early years, members had no cash to pay for goods anyway. It does not seem from the extant manuscripts that any records were kept of items from the store doled out to individual members. We do know that members could request specific items to be purchased on buying trips: in a small memorandum book of "Goods Wanted" dated 1857 are listed a "Homeopathic Box and Book [for] Mr. [Mathias] Ubele" and a "Tenor Horn for C. [probably Johannes C.] Breymaier."[41]

Trusted Society members traveled to Philadelphia, Pittsburgh, and New York to buy supplies for the store, carrying "drafts" from commission merchants to use as cash.[42] These IOUs, indicating the writer of the draft owed the Society a certain amount of money for Zoar goods previously received, would be traded, often at a discount off the face amount, for merchandise. Specie, gold or silver, was scarce and dangerous to carry long distances. Here is a letter of introduction given by Bimeler to his surrogates in 1851:

> To all whom it may concern, Be it known that the bearers of this are Georg Stoerl and Christian Zimmermann are hereby authorized and in my Name to purchase goods for me in the City of New York or in some other Eastern Market to the amount not over five thousand Dollars ($5,000) and on Such conditions and prices as the parties may agree and also to give their Notes when required for said purpose in my name.
>
> Zoar, O. April 28, 1851   J. M. Bimeler[43]

These drafts were the norm in the days before national banking. It must have been difficult to keep track who owed what to whom, and who to trust to pay their debts. One example from the Zoar Papers shows that Bimeler was not above bringing a lawyer into the mix to collect:

> W. B. Curtis, Atty.
> Mt. Vernon
>
> Zoar, Tuscarawas Co., Ohio
> December 7, 1840
>
> I beg to inform you that the note of Munson, Case & Co. $550 d. & 4/100 from August 20 was received by me from J. D. Dare & Co. of Zanesville in payment for 20 tons Pig Iron in good faith, that it would be paid at maturity and that in accordance with commercial usage I have a right to return the note to Dare & Co. and claim the payment for what I sold them from themselves.

If you cannot collect the note by the usual process of law I would request
you to return the same to me by next mail and oblige.

Yours respectfully,

J. M. Bimeler[44]

After the Civil War, the banking system started to resemble that of today. By 1868 Zoar commission merchants and customers were depositing
their drafts to pay for goods purchased from Zoar in the Second National
Bank of Cleveland.[45] By 1872 the Separatists were using checks from that
bank (as well as other banks, including the First National Bank in nearby
Massillon) to pay for goods received.[46]

After Bimeler's 1853 death, the Society continued to make money. In 1864,
at the height of the Civil War, it declared a profit of $16,161.00, on which it
paid $819.10 in federal income taxes that had been levied during wartime.[47]

A goodly portion of the Society's postwar income was taken up in pay
for outsiders. In February 1875, $778.25 was expended in labor, with $319.23
of that for work on the farm and $261.46 for work with livestock. Some
of the names on the list of farm workers were the sons and daughters of
current members; these folks decided not to become members and instead
to work for wages. Certainly having people working for wages laboring
alongside Society members, no matter if they were related to one another
or not, made for an interesting dynamic. Just who worked the hardest?
And at what cost?

The leadership of the Society became surprisingly well-versed in American business practices from the beginning. There are very few surviving
business documents from the 1820s, so we must imagine what it must have
been like to have been dropped into the wilderness of a foreign country
and not be familiar with its language and customs, much less the ways of
doing business. It is obvious that Bimeler and his associates were quick
learners, participating in the agricultural market by 1822, selling wheat in
Canton and by 1825 contracting to build their section of the canal.[48]

Even before Bimeler's death, the Society began to enter the financial
markets, buying stock and securities, reflecting the sophistication of the
Society's, as well as American, business.[49] Bimeler was the seventh-largest
stockholder in the Farmer's Bank of Canton, with two hundred shares,
valued at five thousand dollars, purchased in January 1839. The stockhold-
ers included many early Canton leaders, including *Repository* newspaper
publisher John Saxton.[50]

Inside the back cover of the account book started by Bimeler in 1841 and continued by his successors through 1873 are statements of net worth from 1853 (after Bimeler's death) to 1861. In just eight years, the value of the Society's assets (not counting its real estate) went from $35,887 to $67,656, almost doubling. This dramatic increase occurred during the financial panic of 1857 and without the hand of Bimeler to guide the community. The trustees during this period, taught by Bimeler, were good stewards.

In an effort to improve the efficiency of the huge 1837 Canal Mill, in 1864-66 the trustees spent $22,300 in repairs to its machinery ($1,733 of that amount was "Society labor"). This considerable expense was largely in vain, as the mill still did not operate properly, and reverted to again being used as a warehouse.[51]

As its wealth accumulated, the Zoar Society started to act as a bank. In 1859 and again in 1860 Zoar lent the cash-strapped county commissioners of Tuscarawas County two thousand dollars for one month at 8 percent interest. During the Civil War, the county borrowed funds to grant to needy families of soldiers (see chapter 10). A journal shows multiple pages of deposits in the 1860s by individuals, ranging from one hundred to fifteen hundred dollars, for which the Society paid 5 to 6 percent interest, after a six months' deposit. It was a safe place to keep your money when you had no local bank, and the Society had use of the funds for the length of the deposit.[52] The Society's reputation for honesty, a fair rate of interest, and good recordkeeping made trusting your money with them a much better bet than hiding your funds under your mattress. At the end of 1873, these deposits (called "liabilities" in the ledger) totaled $20,995.41 "foreign" (outsiders) and $2,918.98 "domestic" (Society members). At the Society's end in 1898, $10,340.00 in "foreign" deposits were still on the books. Presumably these amounts were eventually returned to depositors, although their disposition was not indicated in the ledger.[53]

Continuing its role as local banker, the Society's ledger shows outstanding loans totaling over $15,000, with $2,548.25 of that sum listed as "domestic," and $13,070 "foreign" at the end of 1872. Most loans were $1,000 or less, with some rolled over from year to year, after interest was paid. The Society earned 4 percent to 6 percent interest on these loans,[54] but still, a lot of their capital was tied up in possibly risky loans, which then was not available to reinvest in their own businesses. All of these loans are shown to have been paid off by the 1898 dissolution.

MANUFACTURING

The Ohio Gazetteer, an 1841 state travel guide, described Zoar's manufacturing facilities:

> Every agricultural and other implement, and every machine used in Zoar, is manufactured by the Zoarites themselves. The clothing that covers them is made by their own tailors, of cloth woven in their own mill, from wool sheared from their own sheep. The stoves that warm them and cook their food are cast in their own foundry, from iron smelted in their own furnaces, from ore found upon their lands. Their shoes are made by their own shoemakers, from leather prepared by their own tanners, from hides obtained from their own cattle. In every department of trade, they have their own mechanics, who serve not only the Zoarite Community, but also the surrounding country, doing all work entrusted to them in a most honest and faithful manner. Their carpenters, masons, hatters, blacksmiths, tailors, cabinetmakers, wheelwrights and other artisans are all thoroughly skilled workmen.[55]

With a bit of exaggeration (they purchased a lot of their machines and equipment from the outside), this statement fairly sums up manufacturing in Zoar. This author of the above quotation called Zoar "an active manufacturing village."[56]

How did it get that way? Many of the Separatists arriving in 1817 were artisans—Bimeler was a weaver, Johann Georg Nädele was a carpenter, Johann Gottfried Banzhof was a cart maker, Georg Friedrich Holzhoy was a tailor, David Raiser was a shoemaker, Johann Friedrich Bachofer was a baker.[57] Expertise in many trades was available; it was up to the Separatists to develop it.

Nixon likened Zoar to a medieval manor: production was primarily for use and not for profit. Any excess was sold, but only if the needs of the community had first been met.[58] Manufactured items—furniture, tin ware, shoes, and the like—were sold individually, not in bulk. As Zoar's reputation for quality grew, special orders were taken and filled when the skilled workers had time. Other workers repaired items for locals.[59]

The Separatists utilized others' manufacturing expertise as well as their own, purchasing rights to use various inventors' US patents, which included everything from churns to cultivators, shingle cutters to stave makers for barrels.[60] Such use of patents shows the Zoarites were not so isolated from mainstream America as once thought.

Early on, the Separatists exploited their location on the Tuscarawas River by building a dam and diverting water to a mill race that powered many of its manufacturing facilities as well as its flour mill and sawmill. "All manufacturing in Zoar is done by water power," noted a women's magazine of the day. "The Tuscarawas River, by means of a dam, is made to flow with sufficient volume and swiftness to supply from thirty to forty horsepower to the various mills and factories, all of which are provided with machinery made by the Zoarites themselves in the large millwright [machine] shop which they have always maintained."[61]

Outside visitors often remarked upon the Separatists' entrepreneurial skills. Charles Nordoff, in his 1874 survey of communal groups, didn't expect much of the Zoarites with their "dull and lethargic appearance" but said, "I was struck with surprise that they have been able to manage successfully complicated machinery, and to carry on several branches of manufacture profitably. Their machine shop makes and repairs all their own machinery; their grist-mills have to compete with those of the surrounding country. . . . They have found among themselves ability enough to conduct successfully all these and several other callings, all of which require both working skill and business acuteness."[62]

IRON INDUSTRY

Geologically, Zoar sat atop land layered with abundant coal, iron ore, lime-stone, and sandstone, all of which made it a likely place to develop an iron industry. The sandstone ("ganister") was used to line the furnace stack, the limestone for "flux" to help separate the iron metal from the ore, and coal for fuel. Charcoal, an additional fuel, came from its forested land. The Ohio & Erie Canal provided easy transportation for ore and fuel as well as the finished product, which was measured in tons.

The Separatists weren't the first to see the potential: the partnership of William Christmas, James Hazlett, and William Hogg of Canton opened the "Tuscarawas Steam Furnace," an establishment about two miles south of Zoar on One Leg Creek, sometime around 1831, just after the opening of the canal, which was about a quarter mile away.[63] The success of this venture gave Bimeler and the Separatists the idea to develop a similar furnace on their own land. A story in the May 5, 1835, *Tuscarawas Advocate* boasted: "Another vast help to the trade and business of our county is the new furnace lately being erected and put into operation in the vicinity of this beautiful village [Zoar]. We now have 2 furnaces in the county."

Zoar Furnace was built in 1834 just off the canal a mile or so north of the village. A short spur from the canal aided delivery of raw materials and shipment of "pig iron," the small iron bars cast in sand from the melted iron, so-called because the resulting branching structure of the cast iron resembled piglets feeding on the mother sow. Their small size made handling and shipping easier. Attendant buildings at Zoar Furnace housed an office, pattern shop, a horse barn, and a blacksmith shop. A foundry to cast the iron into useful ware like stoves and frying pans was built closer to town, near the other industrial buildings along the millstream. All this investment, costing over twenty thousand dollars according to the records, came to Zoar the same year as did the cholera.[64]

Just the next year, the Canton partners offered to sell their Tuscarawas Steam Furnace to the Separatists at a similar price of $20,000, which included 1,716 acres of land. An immediate sum of $4,000 and yearly payments of $4,000 plus interest were the terms.[65] Renamed Fairfield Furnace, for the adjacent township in which it was located, this facility produced a finer quality of iron, using the Upper Freeport ore nearby, rather than the Lower Mercer ore available at Zoar.[66] A story in the July 29, 1835, edition of the *Tuscarawas Advocate* describes the purchase:

> Extensive sale of real estate—The property known as the Steam Furnace, bought by Mssrs. Christmas, Hazlett & Co. in 1831, for $15,000, was a few days since sold to the Zoar Community for the sum of $20,000. This last purchase is considered a very cheap one. . . . Its situation is peculiarly romantic, within a few rods of the Tuscarawas River and a little south of the junction of a principal branch [One Leg Creek] of the Conotton with that stream. The hills in the vicinity contain inexhaustible beds of iron ore and stone coal, and are covered with the finest timber. Several veins of ore have been opened within less than ½ mile of the furnace, from 3 to 5 feet and upwards in thickness, from which the furnace has been principally supplied. Much of this ore is of the best quality, and the iron made here will compete with any made in this western country. The amount of castings and other metal will average about 4 tons every 24 hours when the furnace is in blast, and employment is given to 75 or 80 hands daily. We are glad

that the property has fallen into the hands of the Zoarites—whose active exertions spoil nature's rugged works as it were with ease, and turn them into places to be desired—as the beautiful spot where they live in unity and peace will clearly illustrate.

Bimeler placed an announcement in the October 13, 1835, and several subsequent editions of the *Tuscarawas Advocate,* advertising goods made at the two furnaces, as well as other items. Note that he speaks as if he himself owns all of the establishments mentioned:

NOTICE TO THE PUBLIC—The subscriber wishes to inform merchants and the public in general that as his TWO FURNACES (the Zoar Furnace on the Ohio Canal, and the Tuscarawas [Fairfield] Furnace on the Tuscarawas River) have been for some time in successful operation, and have now on hand a considerable variety of castings, such as Franklin and cooking stoves, 10 plates and 7 plates; Box and coal stoves and grates, fancy and common; kettles of most all sizes; teakettles, pots, spiders, etc.; wagon boxes, ploughs, and plough shears. . . . Application can be made either to Francis Simpson, manager at the [Tuscarawas] Steam Furnace or Matthew Macy, manager of the Zoar Furnace; and as I continue to buy wheat, rye, corn, flaxseed, beef, pork, bacon, lard, butter, linen, wool, etc. Merchants, traders and farmers will find it advantageous to themselves to call and trade, either of my mills, stores or warehouses. A supply of fish & salt is generally kept on hand for sale.

Zoar, Tusc. Co. Ohio, October 13, 1835   J. M. Bimeler

A foundry for making castings like those mentioned above, was included with the buildings at the newly acquired Fairfield Furnace, and the advertisement seems to indicate it was still being used in 1835, but eventually all casting was done at the foundry in Zoar.

It's unclear how Zoar-made ironware was otherwise marketed. "Zoar Stoves" were advertised in the Wooster (Ohio) *Republican Advocate* in 1837, so the name must have meant something to buyers. It's worth noting that Wooster, about thirty-five miles northwest of Zoar, is not on the canal, so the heavy stoves must have been shipped by wagon.[67] Ten-plate stoves, so called because they were assembled from ten separate pieces, with "Zoar Furnace" molded into the design of the side panels, can still be seen in several of the Zoar museum buildings.

Managers and workers at the furnaces were primarily outsiders. One Separatist, Michael Miller, managed the Fairfield Furnace for a number of years during the 1840s. Contracts to make charcoal and mine iron ore and coal were made with nearby farmers. Pay for workers and the contractors who supplied the raw materials helped the Society's profitability, as they only received half, or sometimes a third, of their pay in cash; the remainder was in trade at the stores established at the furnaces or at the Zoar Store in town.[68]

Structural details of the two furnaces are sketchy, but a contract to build a new stack at Fairfield Furnace in 1842 specified that it should stand 27 feet high, 29 feet square at the base, and 19 feet square at the top. The pig iron made at Zoar was described by Christian Wiebel as being "a soft grey texture, a quality much sought for in the market."[69]

Michael Miller submitted a statement of daily operating expenses for 1846:

A Statement of the Expences of Fairfield Furnace per Day supposing She makes 3 Tons of Iron. This is running her 36 charges –

1. It will take 10 tons of Ore, cost $1.50 per ton	$15.00
2. It will take 650 bus[hels] charcoal, cost @ 5¢ per bus.	31.50
3. It will take 80 bus. Stone Coal @ 4¢	3.20
4. It will take 2 Engineers	1.50
5. It will take 2 Fillers	1.33
6. It will take 2 Keepers	1.36
7. It will take 1 Gutterman	.57
8. It will take 2 Bankmen	1.47
9. It will take 1 Founderer	2.00

Other Expences for Lard & Oil etc.   1.50
Boarding of Hands Included   Total $59.25
Suppose 3 Tons of Iron worth $22.50 pr Ton which will make $67.50
Take 59.25
Which will leave a bal. of $ 8.27
June 20/46   M. Miller[70]

It is not clear if the estimated worth per ton (the $22.50) includes shipping on the canal. If not, the profit margin by 1846 is quite slim.

In the year 1844, a total of 982 tons of pig iron was produced, 498 at Zoar Furnace, 484 at Fairfield Furnace. Shipped on Zoar's canal boat *Friendship* was 874.25 tons of it, mostly Fairfield Furnace production, which stands to reason, since this iron was deemed better quality. Also, the foundry for casting stoves and other items was located closer to the Zoar Furnace, and, presumably, the remaining production was used in the foundry. In 1844 shipments were made to consignees in Buffalo (Jewett and Root); Monroe, Michigan; Toledo; Detroit; Niles; Akron; New Castle, Pennsylvania; and New York City (S. Sage & Co.). Most shipments that year went first to Zoar's commission merchant N. C. Winslow and Co. in Cleveland, who forwarded the cargo on to its final destination, but direct shipping was made to buyers in nearby Canal Fulton, Massillon, and Niles, Ohio.[71]

Also in 1844, an inventory worth a total value $6,543.36 was made of the items, including the equipment, at Zoar Furnace. Listed were "Stove Castings" 10, 7, and 6 plate; cooking stoves (including the number in stock, their weight, and costs), coal stoves, kettles, pots, and the names of patterns, including those for plowshares, mold boards, and cultivators.[72]

In 1835, shortly after it was built, a fire broke out in the Zoar Furnace coal house, the storage shed for charcoal, the principle fuel then used. An advertisement appeared in the February 3 edition of the *Tuscarawas Advocate* [New Philadelphia]:

Whereas it seems most certain to the subscriber that a certain individual calling himself Mathias Smith (a German) has,[73] in the night from the 22nd to the 23rd inst., absolutely laid fire to one of the Coal-houses, stocked and filled with charcoal on the premises commonly called the Zoar Furnace (the property of the Separatist Soc.) which fire destroyed the said building entire, and whereas the said Matthias Smith came afterwards in the same night to the house and residence of Joseph M. Bimeler at Zoar, with the intention to break in and rob the property of the said Separatist Society, under the care of said J. M Bimeler.—Therefore, I offer the following reward of One Hundred Dollars to any person or persons who may bring him up and deliver the said Smith to B. S. Belknap, Justice of the peace at Bolivar, or to the subscriber; or Fifty Dollars for securing said Mathias Smith in any county jail or other safe custody, by giving due notice to the subscriber. Otherwise, I offer a reasonable compensation to any person who will give proper information which may lead to his detection, in order to have the said Mr. Smith brought to justice, and to be further dealt with according to law. Said Mathias Smith is supposed to be about 35 years of age, slender built, 5 feet 10 inches high, red face, no whiskers, black hair, walks straight, is very fond of spirituous liquors, and is always praising Hungary his native country. Had on, when last seen, a straw hat and probably wears either blue or gray coat and pantaloons.

Zoar, Ohio, January 31, 1835   J. M. Bimeler

Three weeks later, on March 24, the following appeared in the *Tuscarawas Advocate:* "ARREST: Mathias Smith, the person who is charged with having set the fire to the coal-house adjacent to the Zoar Furnace, was arrested in the town of Beaver, Pa., and safely lodged in the jail of this county [Tuscarawas] on Tuesday last. He was 3 or 4 years a member of the Zoar community in which he might have lived in peace and comfort, had his conduct been such as to entitle him to their protection." A Matthias Schmidt did join the Society on July 2, 1831, as a full member. Probationary, or first-class, membership did not begin until the Constitution of 1833. His name in the membership record is crossed out with the date 10 February 1834.

And on April 14 in the same newspaper: "Mathias Smith, who was committed a few weeks since on a charge of burning the coal-house at Zoar, was convicted by a chain of circumstances, irresistibly establishing his guilt; sentence, 7 years in the penitentiary. After his conviction, on being remanded to prison, he pretended to confess himself guilty of having murdered a man on the canal not far from Zoar, a year or two since. This confession has not, we understand, seemed worthy of attention." Other Zoar historians as well as Zoar descendants have claimed that no Separatist had ever been convicted of a crime during the Society's existence.[74] Apparently no one remembered a fire in the Zoar Furnace coal house and one Mathias Smith [Schmidt].

In 1845 Zoarite Michael Miller, manager of Fairfield Furnace, warned Bimeler that the furnace there was operating at a loss.[75] With the midcentury discovery of better ores around Lake Superior and the financial Panic of 1850, Zoar's iron industry began to wane. Bimeler asked the outsider manager of Fairfield Furnace if, during this "difficult time in Every Branch of Business," he could take a cut in pay:

We have found it Necessary to bring about a Certain Reform with our laboring hands throughout, in reducing their wages. . . . whereas you must be aware yourself, that the furnace Business itself has for some time past been Carried on rather to my disadvantage. . . . For how much less of a

Salary would you be willing to save me in the same Capacity you now do, for the future, in case I should continue it yet longer, to continue the Business, at the Furnace & Store. . . . You will probably see, that under Existing Circumstances a reform throughout is pressing itself upon me, and if you can convince yourself, that this is the Case, you will be kind enough, after Considering on the subject, to give me your Candid reply.[76]

Unfortunately, we don't know his "candid reply."

Although the Fairfield Furnace was still operating in 1854, the Separatists attempted to sell it that year to their commission merchant, N. C. Winslow, to no avail. Sixty acres of the land already had been sold to James Moffit of New Philadelphia in 1853. In 1858 Fairfield Furnace was sold to the nearby Dover Iron Co., which paid the $10,000 price (with interest) in yearly installments through 1862. It's not clear how much land or equipment this included, as the Society let a contract to take the Fairfield Furnace stack down in 1863, and the blast cylinder of this furnace was sold for scrap in 1864.[77]

It is also unclear to what happened to Zoar Furnace; perhaps nothing. Letters were exchanged with a J. B. Salisbury of Chicago in 1855 to buy the Zoar Furnace land, emphasizing the fire clay nearby. Samples of ore were sent, Salisbury was not satisfied, and no deal was made.[78] (This fire clay deposit was not exploited until the advent of the Zoar Firebrick Co. after the 1898 dissolution.) We do know that a dormitory at Zoar Furnace for iron workers was moved around 1857 into town and became the Bauer Haus, or farmers' dormitory, replacing an earlier building.[79]

The Society continued to sell ore to others, especially the Massillon Iron Co., which purchased ore from 1855 through 1862. Nixon cites ore sales as late as 1881 and castings in the foundry in 1875.[80]

Although the iron industry was comparatively short-lived and unprofitable at the end, it did give the Society expertise in the business world and gave employment to many outsiders in the area—be they furnace workers, charcoal burners, or surface miners. These men and their families were paid partially in trade at the Society's stores, boosting the local economy, as well as that of the Society. As Nixon points out, "It is highly probable that the gain to the [Zoar] community was greater than that derived from the actual sale of iron and castings."[81]

WEAVING INDUSTRY

The weaving of linen, wool, and, to a much lesser extent, silk were important Zoar industries. Here is P. F. D.'s fulsome description:

> The spinning of home-grown flax is an important activity in Zoar. In the wintertime all females age six years and up (and often even still younger in years) are occupied with the spinning of flax by hand, from early morning until late at night, unless they are busy with other jobs. Some of them have developed great skills, either as far as general dexterity is concerned or in the spinning of fine materials. In the store of Zoar one can certainly find a quality of linen spun by local females and also bleached locally, which in the delicacy of material and beauty is probably not surpassed by the linen of Silesia. Only tow [the coarse part of the flax] is being spun into linen on spinning wheels . . .
>
> The wool, obtained yearly from the one hundred head of sheep, amounting from three thousand to four thousand pounds, likewise is spun by them, and indeed, depending upon the quality of the wool, into a material of a considerable fineness of delicacy. Out of this wool-yarn three other females, well-skilled in this procedure, manufacture on three especially-equipped looms woolen materials, cloth cassinets [wool weft and cotton warp] and rugs, as well as cloth for garments for the community, or for sale, and also for a few customers. Of these would be many more if they could be served. One female no longer capable of performing any other work, manufactures the spools for those weavers.
>
> In a dye and print house, only recently set up by a trained German master dyer, wool is dyed, as well as yarn, as are the already finished products. They do a beautiful job of printing pieces of clothing for the feminine sex. This dye house also has quite a few customers from the neighborhood. The Separatists of Zoar have good reason to say to themselves: "Because we sing our songs, because we drink our drinks, and wear our own garments, things flourish on our land."[82]

Both the Weaving House, where linen was woven, and the Woolen Mill were built, and flax and wool were being raised by the time Bimeler sent his detailed description of village industries to postmaster William T. Barry in 1834 (see page 90).[83]

As P. F. D. describes, linen was made from flax fibers spun by hand on slender drop spindles (some of which are in the Zoar museum collections), a task performed mainly, but not exclusively, by the young women of the community. As previously noted, this was done in Zoar's early days by the residents of the Girls' Dormitory.

Another description of the making of linen is by an English visitor in 1837: "The spinning of the linen yarn furnishes employment during the winter for the aged women and young children: being very fine, it is in much repute, and sells in the shops for one dollar (nearly 5s.) a pound." Although both he and P. F. D. mention linen was for sale at the Zoar Store, the author has yet to find mention of it specifically, but flaxseed was sold in 1862. Linen towels (bleached twenty-five cents, unbleached eighteen cents) were sold to a Cleveland concern, also in 1862.[84]

Flax was grown in a meadow behind the Weaving House (still standing at the corner of Main and Fourth Streets). After the seeds were removed to press into linseed oil, the arduous processes of preparing the flax for spinning began. They consisted of retting (soaking the flax plants to rid them of the bark and leaves), drying, scutching and braking (beating the fibers to loosen the outer plant layers), and hackling (running the fibers through an upright block of iron teeth until the fibers are free of bark, separated, and ready to spin). These processes were performed at the Hackle (also Heckle) House, on the banks of Goose Run off East Second Street, where the tall bundles of flax were soaked. The Separatists had a mechanical flax brake to make the process a bit easier.[85]

After spinning, the linen yarn was taken to the looms in the walk-out cellar of the Weaving House. Linen thread must be kept damp, both when spun (spinners dipped their fingers in water) and woven, so the dampness of the cellar helped the process, but not the health of the workers. Three grades of linen were woven: fine, for handkerchiefs and sheets; medium, for shirts and other clothing; and coarse, for bags and bed ticking. This last utilized the "tow" or the shorter pieces of flax left after hackling. Linen did not take well to the dyes then available, so colors were limited to blue and, more rarely, pink, which were woven into checks with the white.

After weaving, the linen was bleached by the sun on a field west of the Weaving House and Bakery. It was kept damp and the lengths of fabric turned frequently.[86] Examples of all types of linen can be seen in the Zoar museum collection.

Wool from Society sheep was processed in the Woolen Mill, built in 1830 on the mill race south of town. A receipt for a "double carding machine," a "jack with g. b. spindles," and a "power loom" is dated July 27, 1838. Taxable valuations of equipment vary from $1,003.00 in May 1847 to $842.00 (presumably allowing for depreciation of the equipment) in 1853 for the following: "1 Set Carding Machines, 1 Spindle-jack, one pr. Satinet Looms, one pr. Broad Looms, one pr. Hand Looms, one pair Napping Machines, one Picker, 1 Shearing-& Brushing Machines, 1 Fulling Mill, 1 Cloth Press, 2 double Carding Machines."[87] One of these broad looms must have included a Jacquard mechanism, one that attached to the loom and used a series of wooden punch cards on a continuous loop that raised and lowered different warp threads to create the intricate patterns of the Zoar coverlets, some of which are dated 1845. A similar, but undated, list of weaving machinery specified that it took seven to eight horsepower to run.[88]

The Woolen Mill did custom work for outsiders and carded their wool.[89] An adjacent dye house processed colored wool, spun and unspun. One natural dye, woad, after fermentation, made the distinctive Zoar blue. The Separatists sold sixty-five pounds of woad to the Harmonists in 1857.[90]

The following price list appears in the papers. Dated June 4, 1868, it seems to be an attempt to drum up Woolen Mill business after the hiatus of the Civil War, as well as give information about fabric production:

6-shafted doeskin cassimere weighing 10-12 oz. per yard	75-80 cents/yd
Fine worsted cassimeres	75-80 cents/yd
Sattinets	55 cents/yd.
Crossbared [checked?] flannels 1 yd. wide	50 cents/yd.
Indigo blue and madder red	
Blankets 1 yard wide finished fine	45 cents/yd.
5 yards for blanket	$2.25
1 yd. fine twisted cassimere requires 1½ lb. good wool	
1 yd. heavy doeskin requires 1¾ lb. good wool	
1 yd. lighter doeskin requires 1½ lb. good wool	
1 yd. sattinet requires 1 lb. good wool	"　　　"
if not clean requires 1¼ lb. good wool	
1 yd. flannel requires 1 lb. good wool	
Carding, spinning and reeling clean wool	18 cents [per pound]
Ditto　　　　　　　unwashed wool	20 cents　　"

Carding rolls [cleaned, combed wool to spin yourself]   6 cents per pound

Grease additional [to make it easier to spin][91]

From this list, it seems the mill accepted and processed raw wool from outsiders and additionally made some fabrics on order. That same year, 1868, the Society produced fabrics (labeled "flannels, cassinets, 'cloth,' jean, woolens and yarn") worth $3,021, some of which was listed for sale.[92]

In 1890 the Woolen Mill was directly soliciting business from the public. The following advertisement appeared in Dover's *Iron Valley Reporter* on November 27 of that year: "Having refitted our Mill for manufacturing woolen goods, such as yarns, flannels, cassimeres, satinets, and a special line for farmers and mechanics wear, we respectfully invite the attention of the public to the same. All our goods are manufactured from pure Ohio wool, and are therefor [sic] free from shoddy and cotton. The Zoar Society."[93]

During the 1840s, the Zoar Society attempted to start a silk industry. Mulberry trees were planted as food for the silkworms, and a house, still known today as the Silk House, was given over to the challenging production of raising and feeding the worms, "reeling" and spinning their cocoons, and weaving and dyeing the fabric. Advice was sought from the Harmonists, who had much more experience in this field (see chapter 7). Zoar silk manufacturing lasted only about ten years, and it's not known how many of the silk items in the Zoar textile collections, consisting of bonnets, ribbons, and scarves, were actually made here.

OTHER INDUSTRIES

Most other shops in Zoar made items primarily for domestic use by Society members, but some things were sold—whether the buyer made contact through the craftsman directly or if the Zoar Store made these arrangements is not clear. The receipt book for 1841 to 1873 is peppered with transactions for "custom work" at the saddle shop, cabinet shop, cobbler shop, and tannery.[94]

Trees and plants were sold from the garden at the rate of about two hundred dollars per year in the mid-1840s. Some of these transactions are marked as going through the store, some as cash given directly to agent general Joseph Bimeler by gardener Simon Beuter.[95]

Tubs of butter were sold to individuals, including in 1853 to attorney Henry Stanberry, who purchased a keg of butter the same year he argued the Society's landmark case before the US Supreme Court. Goods like butter were traded as well. A keg of "fresh butter for winter use" was traded for a subscription to the *Cleveland Herald* newspaper in 1866.[96] In the accompanying letter Wiebel writes, "We don't like to send money by mail, if we can avoid it."

Services such as those at the hotel, the Canal Tavern, its nearby blacksmith shop, and the stores at the iron furnaces were made available to outsiders as sources of income, illustrating Zoar's good business practices. The Separatists were not afraid of the outside world but wanted to shape it to their will, to get from it what they wanted, not what the world necessarily wanted from them.

CHAPTER 7

"We All Greet All Those Who Heartily Wish It"

Zoar and Other Communal Groups

These and such questions I should very much like to see answered, in order . . .
to have a correct view of your regulations. . . . I and those with me surely can
depend on your friendly attitude. . . . We all greet all those who heartily wish it.
—Joseph Bimeler, Zoar, to Frederick Rapp, New Harmony,
November 27, 1820

The Separatists who settled the village of Zoar were not isolated in their
communalism. Throughout their history, they corresponded with two
other German communal societies, the Harmonists of New Harmony,
Indiana, and Economy, Pennsylvania; and the Inspirationists of Ebenezer,
New York, and Amana, Iowa. A fledgling communal group, Ora Labora,
petitioned the Zoarites for advice. The Zoar Society also had contact with
the Society of Believers in Christ's Second Appearing, or more commonly
known as the Shakers.

The Harmonists were from the same area of Germany. Led by the char-
ismatic George Rapp, they were also a part of the Radical Pietist Separatist
movement in the late eighteenth and early nineteenth centuries. Rapp led
his followers to America in 1803, where they established their first home
in Harmony, Pennsylvania. In 1814, perhaps because Harmony was too
far from good transportation, they moved to Indiana and founded New
Harmony. After eleven years in Indiana, they returned to Pennsylvania and

settled on the Ohio River, twenty miles northwest of Pittsburgh,[1] ninety miles from Zoar.

The Community of True Inspiration was likewise formed of Separatists from Germany. Their name comes from the fact that their leaders, or "instruments," were endowed with the gift of revelation, or "Inspiration." One instrument, Christian Metz, migrated to America with his followers in 1842, and founded the town of Ebenezer (also spelled Eben-Ezer), near Buffalo, New York. Between the years 1855 and 1865, the Society removed to Iowa, where it became known as the Amana Society.[2]

The history of the three German groups is parallel in some respects. They all had their roots in the German Radical Pietistic movement, and the writings of the mystics are evident in their beliefs. All endured persecution in Germany and therefore emigrated to the United States to escape such treatment. Their religions were similar in that all eschewed formal religious ceremonies and had an ascetic attitude toward life. Their chief differences were in the application of this attitude and their views on revelation.[3]

Secularly, the organization of the three communities was similar. Trustees were elected by the members to manage the affairs of the society.

As can be seen by these similarities, the societies shared much in common and might be expected to correspond. Their German language and the relative isolation of these communities may have prompted them to seek others who shared the same experiences.

The Zoarites and the Harmonists corresponded from the Zoar Society's very beginnings. Many of the Separatists had relatives and friends in the Harmony Society. Johann Henger, a Zoarite, had a brother Wilhelm, a shoemaker in the Harmony Society. Visits were made and letters sent to New Harmony, Indiana, through Henger.[4]

Upon their arrival in Philadelphia in summer 1817, two members of the Separatists wrote to their godmother "in the Harmony" to join them: "Ah, dear godmother how much we would like to have you with us, especially because we have heard Rapp is so strict over his fellow brethren."[5]

Frederick Rapp, George Rapp's adopted son and the business leader of the Harmony Society, was in Philadelphia in August 1817, the same time as the Separatists' arrival there from Germany. He spoke there with Joseph Michael Bimeler, who had assumed leadership of the immigrants on the voyage.[6] Frederick Rapp asked his agents in Philadelphia to keep tabs on the Separatists and to give them a letter of recommendation to the Harmonists' Pittsburgh agents.[7]

There is some question as to whether the proposal had ever been made to settle the Separatists with the Harmonists. A letter dated September 30, 1817, from George to Frederick Rapp, gives question: "No one need be surprised if the Quakers give them [the Zoarites] that land; they will have their own advantage from it. I regret the trick. I would prefer them on our land."[8] Which land Rapp refers to is not known.

The Rapps were kept well informed by their agents, Boller and Solms of Philadelphia, of the progress of the Zoar settlement and the differences the Separatists had with the Quakers.[9]

Godfrey Haga, the Philadelphia merchant who Harmonist historian Karl J. R. Arndt calls the Harmonists' "true and valuable friend,"[10] sold the Zoar Separatists their Ohio land. This same land in Ohio had been inspected and rejected by George Rapp on his arrival in America in 1803.[11] Perhaps Haga was introduced to the Separatists by Frederick Rapp or his agents, Boller and Solms. Haga, too, kept the Harmony Society informed of the doings of the Zoarites: "The Rothenackers [the town in Württemberg from which many Zoar Separatists emigrated] who bought my land are well satisfied, but I do not believe that they will make as much progress as you have made. They do not have a Father Rapp and son. They still have everything in common and seem to be united in this."[12]

Bimeler, as leader of the Separatists, corresponded with Frederick Rapp during these early years of the Zoar Society, and eagerly sought information from Rapp. "I also wish to see a letter from you, to give me news about several things which would be useful to me in my situation and climate. I greet you and all those who are interested in me. I hope I can call you my friend, just as I hope to be yours. [signed] Jos. Mich. Bäumler."[13]

Less than three months later, in September 1818, Bimeler was granted his wish, and in addition, received one hundred dollars from the Harmonists, a "pleasant surprise" that received his "heartfelt thanks" for "the large present received from you." The letter from the Harmonists, now lost, apparently asked for information about the Society's land purchase, details of which were given willingly by Bimeler. In an addendum, he states, "If I have not reported as fully as you wish, then ask me again. I will very gladly do your wish, as much as time and conditions allow."[14]

It seems as though letters were not as forthcoming to Zoar from New Harmony as Bimeler would like, and in a letter dated November 27, 1820, he complains that his last two letters had not been answered, and reminds Rapp of "your services of friendship which you promised to provide."

Bimeler especially needed advice, since the Zoarites had joined together communally in April 1819, and he no doubt had many questions that the Harmonists could answer. Bimeler states that "our association must daily suffer much persecution since its establishment both from acquaintances and strangers."[15]

Religion usually did not enter into the correspondence between the two societies. Customarily, it was referred to at the close of a letter, as in Bimeler's letter of September 11, 1818: "We are and remain according to the work of union in Christ Jesus our King, your friends."[16]

Sometimes, especially in hard times such as the disastrous harvest of 1859 referred to in this letter from Jacob Sylvan of Zoar to R. L. Baker of Economy, a short "sermonette" was given:

> The presumption, the disregard, the misuse of God's blessings, and the ingratitude of mankind in these times, has been raised to the highest pitch, and the wrath of God so aroused, that it is inevitable that such judgment be passed, in order to restore the balance. Of course, we have to suffer with the others, for in these matters we also are not guiltless. At all events, everything comes back to this: God is righteous, and His judgments are also righteous; and when He permits chastisements to be visited on His people, it is with the intention of making them better, and of drawing them more closely to Him, and in this way we will make such punishments profitable.[17]

Perhaps the worst intrusion religion made in the relationship and correspondence of the two societies was the notorious "pork incident" in late 1859. The Separatists refrained from eating pork due to the biblical injunction. During a visit to Economy by the Separatists, pork was served at dinner. The Zoarites declined the dish without comment, but Harmony trustee Jacob Henrici remarked: "You will not touch pork, but you are not so careful about other flesh!"

This celibate Harmonist was referring to the Zoarites' condoning of the marital state. The Separatists left the table in indignation. A letter from Harmony trustee R. L. Baker following this visit attempted to heal the breach: "Worthy Friend: Thou revealest too much self love and weakness through the mentioned grievance; for it is not a sin, but a duty toward a friend, to give him a hint as to an error when such is against God's Word. We find in your Book of Sermons [Bimeler's *Discourses*], many points, which according to our understanding of the Word, are not in harmony with the Bible.

However, it is not our business to enter into a religious disputation. These two Societies are two kinds of flowers and will remain thus. Let each one be sure of his ground and loyal to his conviction."[18] The relationship was soon mended, but very little reference to religion can be found in letters after 1859.

Since the societies were organized so similarly, it stands to reason that many letters would refer to that theme. Joseph Bimeler asks questions in the letter dated November 27, 1820, about the communal organization of the Harmony Society, especially about dissension among members.[19]

It was a question well taken, as both societies had problems dealing with lawsuits of disaffected members. In particular were the cases of *Goesele v. Bimeler* (1852) for the Separatists and *Nachtreib v. Baker* (1857) for the Harmonists. Both cases involved former members or their relatives who wished to receive a portion of the assets of their respective society.

In the Goesele case, the German relatives of a deceased member, Johannes Goesele, one of the original Separatists, who died in 1827, wanted to receive a share of what he had contributed to the Society before his death. This case was melded with another case, previously dismissed by the state courts, that of Johann Georg Goesele, a cousin, who had been dismissed for cause by the membership of the Zoar Society in March 1845.[20] This younger Goesele was the manager of the Canal Tavern and had allowed drunkenness and "had operated the Tavern in a manner contrary to the rules of the Society."[21] The German Goeseles instituted a suit in the US Circuit Court in 1851. All was for naught, as the Society's case was upheld in the Circuit Court and again on appeal in the US Supreme Court, where the majority opinion was written by Justice John McLean in 1852 (see chapter 9 for more details about *Goesele v. Bimeler*).

Jacob Sylvan, a trustee of the Zoar Society, did his best to keep the Harmonists informed of the case's progress: "The judge, still young but very understanding, has gotten such a clear insight into our case that we were surprised. We are very glad to have gained victory over our enemies once again with God's help, and we feel obliged to thank our Father."[22]

The Harmony trustees congratulated the Zoarites on the outcome of the case.[23]

The Nachtreib case was similar to the Goesele case, but Joshua Nachtreib willingly withdrew from the Harmony Society in 1846, after signing a release and receiving a two-hundred-dollar cash gift given ordinarily to departing members. In spite of these precautions, the Harmony Society was sued in November 1849, for an equal share in its property. The trustees were asked to render an account of the Society's business dealings for the twenty-seven years Nachtreib was a member, and after protracted investigation, the lower court awarded Nachtreib $1/321$ of the Society's estate, or $3,890, in 1855. Two years later this finding was appealed to the US Supreme Court, which reversed the lower court's decision, using the Zoar case as precedent, and barred Nachtreib from all claims.[24]

Trustee R. L. Baker, in a letter to Jacob Sylvan, rejoices in the verdict: "It means that here (in this country) the communal spirit has the freedom to stay alive, although in many regards this is offensive to the prevailing Zeitgeist. Therefore, be of good cheer thou faithful Zoarist and also thou faithful Harmonist, suffer, endure, and bear patiently whatever may be in store for you, so that the communal rose under [illegible] affliction will fully develop and be fit to be incorporated and entwined eternally into the flowery wreath of the Great Higher Community."[25] This letter was appended to a copy of the Supreme Court decision on the Nachtreib case.

These court cases were mentioned again as late as 1896 when John Duss, the last Harmony Society member, wrote the Zoar Society requesting copies of the *Goesele* case for use in his dismantling of the Harmony Society.[26]

Most letters between the Harmony and Zoar Societies concerned business. On the whole, Zoar provided the Harmonists with raw materials, including flax, clover seed, rye, wool, woad (a dyestuff), and Russian duck, probably a stiff cloth. Zoar also ordered raw materials from the Harmonists, as in an 1883 order for "wood to make barrels."[27] Economy bought cattle, and Zoar bought "cotton yarn" and "rabbitt fur hats."[28]

The Harmony Society, for its part, was called on for assistance in technical matters. The Zoarites purchased looms from the Harmonists in 1846.[29] The Zoar weaver, Gottfried Kappel, discussed with them his problems with his loom.[30] The Separatists purchased a fulling mill from Economy in 1867 but had to return it because the wood was too rotten to use.[31]

Both societies cooperated in an effort to build a cider mill in Zoar. Jacob Sylvan admired Economy's cider mill and asked many questions about it in a letter dated October 30, 1854. Later, Jonathan Lenz of the Harmony Society was sent to Zoar to supervise its construction. Two years later, Sylvan reported, "We are producing 40 barrels a day of good clear cider. We are able to make cider to sell to outsiders who pay 50 cents a barrel."[32]

Relying on the Harmonists for their expertise in machinery, the Zoarites

Also German Radical Pietists, the Harmony Society had previously immigrated
to America in 1803. Despite the Harmonists' celibate lifestyle, the two communal
groups had much in common, and traded goods and sought advice from each other.
(Engraving from *Communistic Societies of the United States* by Charles Nordhoff, 1874.)

fired off inquiries about steam boilers, steam dryers, beet cutters, and corn
shellers.[33]

Using the Harmonists' example, the Zoarites attempted to start a silk
industry in Zoar in the 1840s. Zoar sent representatives, one the community
weaver, Gottfried Kappel, to examine their "silk-manufacture," as stated
by their letter of introduction. Later, trustee Sylvan asked that "Katherina,
most capable in this line, be sent again to Zoar." On one occasion, Bimeler
sent silkworm eggs as a present to George Rapp.[34]

The Separatists also purchased silk fabric from the Harmonists, including "handkerchiefs, ribb[on], white silk for undershirts and satin vesting
with modest flowers interwoven."[35]

The two societies were alike in their love of music, and in 1863 trustee
Henrici helped select a Steinway piano for the Zoarites. The Separatists

purchased three unspecified musical instruments from the Harmony Society in 1855.[36]

The Harmonists did business errands for the Separatists in Pittsburgh and both recommended suppliers to each other.[37]

Many of the letters concern visits to and fro. Some of these visits terminated Separatist business trips east. Christian Zimmerman, on buying trips for the Zoar Society, visited Economy in April, 1855, and again in April 1858.[38] Employees from the Zoar Store visited Economy on their way back from a Philadelphia buying trip.[39]

Another reason for visiting Economy was to inspect machinery, as mentioned above, in connection with the cider mill and silk industry.[40]

At the conclusion of these trips, the Zoarites often took home gifts, necessitating the need for thank-you notes upon the return home.[41] Jacob Sylvan reported that the eggs they got from the Harmony Society hatched chickens that were "exceedingly well and beautiful."[42]

Unfortunately, no letters survive recording details about the Harmonists' visits to Zoar, but a quote from the diary of Alexander Gunn, a wealthy outsider who lived in Zoar during the last years of the Society, may capture a sense of the atmosphere: "January 5: The Economites will go home to Harmony today. There has been no lack of hospitality shown them; valiant tipplers both, it has been their own fault if they have drawn a sober breath during their stay."[43]

The last visit of the Harmonists to Zoar was in 1897 for a *Swabenfest,* a picnic held in Zoar for Swabians, natives like themselves of southwest Germany. John Duss's Harmony Band performed at the event.[44] This was billed as a *Sängerfest,* a "singing festival," that included Swabian groups from Cleveland, Canton, Toledo, and Economy.

Many of the letters contain personal references. During 1823-24, a series of letters passed between George Schillinger of Columbiana County, Ohio, to Henry Haug of New Harmony, concerning the disposition of Haug's property (mainly cows) in Zoar. In September 1823, Bimeler wrote to George Rapp in regard to this transaction and added a personal postscript: "To date, except for a few members who left here or were driven off, we are well and cheerful, with the exception that we have become somewhat sickly, but this summer no one has died yet."[45]

Health and sickness were frequently mentioned in the letters. The death of leader Joseph Bimeler was reported in a letter of Jacob Sylvan, dated

December 2, 1853: "His death has hit us hard, the more since there is no one who can take his place."[46]

In a subsequent letter, Sylvan, a Zoar trustee who had stepped somewhat uncertainly into Bimeler's role in the community, lamented further about the hole that the death of this dynamic business and spiritual leader had left in their lives: "I can't describe how difficult it was right after the very big loss which we have suffered by the death of our loyal friend and brother J. M. Bäumeler, under whose loyal care we lived as carefree children. Right after that we were attacked and one subpoena followed the other [referring to the above-mentioned court cases], because we didn't have anybody who was able to handle these things."[47]

Letters contained personal references. Writing to inform the Harmony trustees of the death of his wife, Pauline, David Sylvan asks that his friends "Gertrud Baker, the motherly friend Elizabeth Baumgartner, and Boehm," be informed of her death. Bimeler frequently ended his letters with the phrase, "We greet all those who heartily wish it."[48]

Members of the Zoar Society wrote letters of recommendation for former and potential members of the Harmony Society. Simon Beuter, the Zoar gardener, wrote on behalf of John Mayer, a former Harmonist who wished to be reinstated: "His most ardent wish is to return to Economy, which would be best for him in any event. . . . However, I shall advise him to reunite himself with you in all loyalty, and not to go away again, for he does not belong in the world."[49]

Beuter wrote reluctantly to Economy on behalf of an outsider who desired to become a Harmonist. He "claimed to be a communist, but on what principals his communism is based, I don't know." The outsider wanted his son to learn music. "I don't know if this man is honest, but I don't like him. . . . Now I have fulfilled my promise [to this man by writing this letter]. Please answer."[50]

Gardener Beuter wrote yet again to the Harmonists, this time on behalf of his own son, Jacob Albert:

Dear Friend: With tears in my eyes, I inform you that my son Jacob, 18 years of age, will apply to you for employment. Kindly give him an opportunity in this direction. If you can make a good Harmonite out of him, I shall bless you forever; bitter would it be for me if he should fall among the world. He has had experience with garden, greenhouse and nursery work, binding of books, and has substituted for me, at times, in teaching school. He is talented particularly in music. Since his thirteenth year, he has played first violin in church and the first alto in the band. He has spent his evenings during three years at the piano, and thus becoming the butt of ridicule on the part of the boys and girls, so that already last winter, he complained about this, and has asked me to permit him to go to Economy, where he would be free from such like, and where there would be greater opportunity. . . . And so far as I know, he has always conducted himself in a proper and moral manner. He has no vices, and as to love affairs with the other sex, which is a troublesome cancer, his piano has been his all.[51]

Albert Beuter as he called himself later, did find opportunity in Economy and in the world. After his music study at Economy, he held music professorships in Pennsylvania and Illinois and was a noted composer and arranger until his death in 1892.[52]

Other Zoarites also wrote for personal favors. Michael Miller asked the Harmonists to take in his son and give him work. Simon Beuter recommended a former Zoar hired laborer to Economy.[53]

Current events seemed not to be a topic of discussion in the letters—with the lone exception of the Civil War. Sylvan mentions "the impending war" to Baker in a letter dated January 3, 1861. Later, he laments that fact to Baker that thirteen young men left the Society to join the Civil War, forsaking the Zoar Society's principle of pacifism.

Correspondence and visits slowed during the waning years of both societies. The Harmony Society, due to its celibate nature, dwindled in number until just one person, John Duss, was alive at its eventual dissolution in 1905. The Separatists did not have that problem, but still were losing members in other ways. Simon Beuter shared his feelings with Duss in an 1892 letter: "What is going to become of us? The young ones are running away on a massive scale, leaving the old, the crippled and the lame behind."[54]

Zoar's relationship with the Inspirationists of Ebenezer and Amana was not as close or as lengthy as the one with the Harmonists. Distance may have been a factor, but religious differences may have been a greater reason.

The Inspirationists tended to admonish the Separatists about religion. In reply to some religious disagreement, Charles L. Mayer concludes that the Separatists were "totally inaccessible to admonition." He goes on to say, "The testimonials of our brother C. M. [Christian Metz] are the words of the Lord," and "are in perfect harmony with God's work, revealed in the Holy Scriptures, being identical in spirit and emanating from true witnesses." In closing he bade the Separatists "to look after your own eternal salvation and not yield to the spirit of slander. God does not suffer himself to be mocked."[55]

When the Inspirationists' *werkzeug* (instrument) Christian Metz visited Zoar in 1843, he experienced an "inspiration." It so impressed the Separatists that they talked about it thirty years later to William A. Hinds: "The Separatists at Zoar gave me a most sensational account of the contortions and tremblings of Christian Metz while on a visit to their Society. They were not favorably impressed by the scene."[56] The inspiration in question compared Zoar's perceived errors in spirit to a faithless bride who has forsaken her bridegroom. The helpful Metz made a copy of the testimony and left it with the Separatists.[57]

It should be noted that the Separatists themselves had an "instrument," Barbara Grubermann, while in Germany, but by 1843 had discounted such mystical revelations.

If the Zoarites were not impressed by Metz, the Inspirationist leader himself was not impressed by the religious services he experienced in Zoar, which contained "little spiritual life."[58] A quote from Metz's diary reads: "On Sunday we went to their Meeting, but found no inner life, and heard merely the outward sound of the music which accompanies their singing, and a verbose and spirit-poor sermon from their leading official, Bäumler." Also in his diary, Metz noted that Bimeler had "lost and forsaken the true purpose and way of God."[59]

However they disagreed on religion, it did not prevent the Separatists from purchasing copies of the Inspirationists' *Psalter-Spiel* (psalm book) as early as 1846.[60] Copies were ordered on a regular basis until 1872.[61]

The Ebenezer newcomers were also curious to know how the Zoar Society was organized, much as the Separatists had asked the Harmonists in 1820. Charles Keilman wrote to Jacob Sylvan in 1853, asking about the Society's membership qualifications.[62]

An 1858 letter praises the Zoar Society's "simplicity": "What pleased me especially concerning you was that you had kept your simplicity, and are not so proud and ambitious as many here are who would be addressed only as Sie [the formal form of "you"]; Brother Mayer agrees with me, that in Zoar there is generally more humility than here. But that is just the reason why we have to leave this place by God's command and go west, and with but little inclination, because the intimacy of our young people with the world becomes greater and greater."[63] The move west to Iowa was discussed in other letters but in a business context.[64]

Trade between the two societies was mainly one way. Zoar bought yarn and cloth (sheeting, shirting, etc.) from the Inspirationists,[65] plus the aforementioned *Psalter-Spiels*. No letters could be found for a reverse trade, although a journal entry in the 1850 Commercial Ledger indicates that the Ebenezer Society purchased a cookstove from Zoar.[66] Trade stopped after the move to Iowa; perhaps the freight was too costly to continue.

The last letter from Amana is a request for information on Zoar's brewery. Did the Separatists have to pay taxes on the beer brewed and consumed within their community as the Amanaists did?[67]

An interesting, but unanswered question rests with the land the Zoarites bought in Guthrie County, Iowa, near Des Moines, in the 1870s.[68] Did the Inspirationists have anything to do with the purchase? It is thought that the land was bought on speculation for a proposed railroad route. Did they learn of the route through the Inspirationists? No letters have been found to confirm or deny this theory.

Visits between the Zoarites and Ebenezer were not as frequent as those to the Harmonists. One perhaps unwelcome visitor to Ebenezer from Zoar was a Dr. Caspari, a representative of disaffected former Zoarites, who tried to get aid from the Inspirationists in a rebellion against Bimeler (see chapter 9). To his credit, Christian Metz turned him away, recording this in his diary: "We urged his members to obedience and to greater earnestness and prayer, since they had completely forsaken these, and like Bäumler, had lost and forsaken the true purpose and way of God."[69]

No letter indicates other visits from Zoar, although a "Ph. Zimmer" (possibly Philip Zimmer) extended an invitation to one "Grotzinger" (perhaps Georg, the hotelkeeper) to visit him in Ebenezer: "Herewith let me inform Grotzinger, that if he wishes to visit me, that will please me greatly; table and bed are prepared, he need only come and make use of them."[70]

The Metz visit in the spring of 1843 was notable for a reason not yet mentioned. While at Zoar, he met Charles L. Mayer, business agent of the Zoar Society.[71] Mayer was a native of Württemberg, thirty-seven years old and unmarried. He was a first-class member of the Zoar Society, a probationary membership class.[72] Metz described him as one "who had a good command of the English language and who knew the laws of the country." While in Zoar, Mayer and Metz dined together. "On Sunday afternoon he invited us to visit him in his room, which we did. Here we talked about Zoar from a spiritual point of view. He [Mayer] then told us how he had gone to Zoar for the sake of his faith, but that he had not been able to accept Bäumler's beliefs, for which reason he did not attend their meetings. At the same time, he told us how he had been awakened by God, but how he had again lost the path of grace. During the days when he had been eating with us, he had experienced an inner emotion which had drawn him to us."[73]

Mayer subsequently received some correspondence from Metz. "[This letter] stirred up a certain joy inside me, that assured me that it was the Lord's will that I should go to your community." He soon gave Bimeler his resignation. Bimeler was skeptical: "He [Bimeler] thinks I am taken in by you."[74] Mayer soon left Zoar and joined the Ebenezer Society in late August 1843, and later became their business agent. Metz writes in his diary: "It was the hand of God which led this man to the Society at a time when such support was indispensable. . . . He soon became one of the strongest supporters of the community."[75] As with many converts, Mayer became overzealous and is the author of the letter admonishing the Zoarites quoted earlier.

Another visitor to Zoar was Zimmer, a mason from Ebenezer who wrote to the Separatists to thank them for the "large box of presents" that he had received on his visit to Zoar and that he had distributed to the sick and children.[76]

There are few personal messages in the Inspirationist-Zoar letters. The Zimmer letter, above, is the most personal of all, showing a real friendship between individuals. Perhaps because of the distance between the communities or the differences in religious doctrine, no friendships developed.

A fledgling German communal group, Ora Labora (Pray and Work), established in Huron County, Michigan, on Saginaw Bay, wrote to Zoar in 1864, asking for advice on everything from communal organization to how to make straw hats and how to keep its women employed. The community's founder, Emil Baur, had been a German Methodist preacher in nearby Dover, Ohio, and had become acquainted with the Separatists and the Harmonists in his travels as a minister and made plans for his Michigan society while preaching in Dover.[77]

To start his community, he received twenty thousand dollars from the Harmonists for a mortgage on a Michigan land grant.[78] In the lone letter in the Zoar files from Baur to Zoar, the idealistic Baur does not ask for money, but enthusiastically describes the log houses and sawmill built for the 160 members. He also complained of the opposition and attacks by local clergy to his community.[79] These attacks, a lack of capital, and the conflict of private and communal interests by members caused the demise of his society in 1868. After all was adjudicated in the Michigan courts, the Harmonists received just $4,500 of their $20,000 outlay.[80] Perhaps the Separatists were lucky—they made no investment, and no answer to Baur's many questions is indicated on the back of the 1864 letter.[81]

With four Shaker communities in Ohio, one just sixty miles north in North Union, one would suppose the Shakers would have had a close relationship to their fellow communal society members in Zoar, but a search of the extant correspondence of both societies finds no letters or invoices for goods exchanged.[82]

That is not to say there was no contact at all. There were visits and two very disparate demonstrations of both societies' innate kindness and humanity.[83]

The Shakers at Union Village (present-day Lebanon, Ohio) took in three refugee women from Zoar "to escape the wicked hands of their persecuting husbands." These women "who speak english but poorly" stayed with the Shakers from the fall of 1823 until at least June 1824. The Shakers praised them for "faithfully living up to the light they have already received" and were tolerant of their differing beliefs, despite the fact that the two groups may not have seen eye-to-eye on religious matters.[84]

Even though the communal Shakers had four Ohio settlements, there was little contact between the two groups. (Engraving from *Communistic Societies of the United States* by Charles Nordhoff, 1874.)

This husband/wife dispute was alluded to by historian William A. Hinds in an interview of a Zoar Society trustee, who, when asked about seceding members, said: "The first party left soon after the Society was established and consisted of six men, all of whom, save one, were married, but their wives remained with us."[85] It may be supposed that the couples may have quarreled over Zoar's decision to become celibate in 1822, a choice both religious and economic in nature.

The second instance of contact between the two groups involves the reverse situation. In March 1824, Elder Issachar Bates (1758-1837), a Shaker preacher and musician and author of the group's songbook, *Millennial Praises,* was traveling alone from Union Village (where the Zoar wives had taken refuge) northwest to North Union Village (now Shaker Heights) and "wished to go by the way of Zoar, & visit that society of Dutch people." On the third day of this more than two-hundred-mile trip, in a late-season snowstorm, his skittish horse threw him and then kicked him in the leg. He continued his trip, in great pain, with his leg "as big as two legs and black as bacon" until reaching Zoar. He was carried into a home in the village, was "seized with a violent fever" and remained, mostly incoherent, in bed there for forty-seven days.[86]

Some of his Shaker brethren, wondering what had become of him, found him at Zoar, and arranged to take him home in a straw-lined carriage. He tried to pay the Separatists for "their care & trouble with me," but they would take no money only his "kind thanks."[87]

The only other Shaker connection to Zoar is a farm laborer named Amasa Blodget (1787-1877), who was recognized as a former Shaker from the Enfield community.[88] His birthplace in the 1850 census is listed as New Hampshire. How he came to Zoar is not known. He became a probationary member of the Zoar Society in 1846 at age fifty-nine.[89] Perhaps Blodget's communal Shaker roots made him more acceptable to this insular society.

Commonalities in religion, social order, and business interests allowed these communal societies to correspond and visit one another. Their visits, writings, purchases, and inquiries allow us a fascinating glimpse into the inner workings of these otherwise cloistered societies.

CHAPTER 8

"A Life Free from Care"

Everyday Life in Zoar

To them it was a life free from care, worry and excessive work. They literally took no thought for the morrow. They lay down in comfortable homes at night, in certain and satisfactory knowledge that they would be equally well provided for on the succeeding day. What boon in life greater or more desirable than that?

—E. O. Randall, *The Society of Separatists of Zoar,* 1899

It helps to remember that the Zoar community, albeit organized into households, was really one big family. Sylvan, in his introduction to Bimeler's sermons, repeated the latter's belief that all lived together as one family, and it was important to maintain "a good order, and bring about an equalization in all things among the members."[1] By midcentury, family relationships were intermingled, as the marriages of members had to be with other Society residents, not outsiders. Those who married outsiders had to leave the Society.[2] Everyone knew one another—their habits, quirks, foibles, and style of work—very well. As with all successful communal societies, potential conflicts were tamped down with peer pressure, as things worked much more smoothly when everyone worked together.

We have seen in chapter 5 how the trustee system functioned to handle business affairs. The elected trustees worked with the agent general Joseph Bimeler and later cashiers Christian Wiebel, Jacob Ackermann, and Louis Zimmermann to get Zoar products to market and purchase materials for

Society use and sale. But to produce the goods and services needed, the Society's members (and later hired help) had to work as one, despite the all-too-human tendency of wanting to do things in one's own way. The trustees had to understand how to assign work to the best persons to get the best results and how to work around those who might not give their full cooperation.

Each day began just before daybreak with the blowing of the Assembly Horn, or later, with the Assembly House bell.[3] Those without job assignments met here, at the corner of Main and East Third Streets, to receive their daily assignments from the trustees. They met again at noon before lunch to get further updates from the trustees. Those with skilled occupations, like the tinsmith, went directly to their workplaces, unless it was planting or harvest time or if other jobs needed a fuller complement of workers.

It might be assumed that occupations were assigned arbitrarily by the trustees—one job one day, another, the next. E. O. Randall in 1898 observed that the trustees "consulted the inclination and peculiar abilities of the member, endeavoring to fit each man into the place for which he was best

The first image we have of Zoar was drawn by historian Henry Howe for his 1847 book, *Historical Collections of Ohio.* Shown are the Zoar Store and Number One House on the left and the hotel cupola and the Wagon Shop on the right. Interestingly, two of the female figures are depicted with a hoe and a wheelbarrow, indicating Zoar did not shy away from using females as farm labor. (Engraving from *Historical Collections of Ohio* by Henry Howe, 1847.)

adapted."[4] Trustees were not exempt from labor; they worked alongside their fellow members. A newspaper story from 1837 states, "Such persons [who] have no stated employment assemble upon a given signal upon the house of Bäumler and each of the directors chooses the person whom he considers best qualified for his particular business. The directors are, however, obliged to take a personal share in the most difficult part of their labors, and to excite their workmen by their example."[5]

In a study of the four censuses that list occupations (1850–1880) done by the author, arbitrary assignment does not seem to be the case. Most occupations listed by the census taker were for males; only a few females had job titles (e.g., "female institute [girls' dormitory]" and "head of Dairy"). Of the sixty-four men (and one woman) who had occupations listed in consecutive censuses, forty-three stayed in the same job. Only nine went from job to job. Nine others started with one job and went to another and stayed. The most common jobs were "farmer" or "farm laborer" or just "laborer" and presumably it was these folks who met daily with the trustees.[6]

The 1834 cholera epidemic forced the Society to begin to hire outsiders to work. Some lived on outlying Zoar properties to help clear them ("The said J. Wolfe is to grub the above described land in a workmanlike manner")[7] or raise their own crops as tenant farmers and pay the Society "a third of all the grain they may raise."[8] Bringing strangers, even German ones, into such a closed community was problematic. William A. Hinds was told, "They tempt our young people into bad habits."[9] Habits like using tobacco, eating pork, swearing, singing secular songs, and above all, using money. Hinds, who visited around 1876 was told that there were 171 persons, including their families, who worked for wages paid by the community at that time. Single men boarded in the Bauer Haus, a large residence at the end of East Third Street. Worker families lived in empty Zoar houses, either in town or outside, with their rent deducted from their pay, which was given both in cash and trade at the store, so the Society could make a little profit on goods purchased. Many hired workers came directly from Swabia; working in Zoar gave them a head start on life in America, where they could speak German and be somewhat shielded from the shock of a new culture, at least for a while.

The Separatists also made use of childhood indentures. Parents outside of the Society who could not care for their children themselves or wished them to learn a trade—or both—legally entered into agreement with the Society to care for the child, provide him or her with the necessities of life, and impart a trade or skill. There are at least a dozen indentures of children in the Zoar documents. Mary Ann Short, "a poor girl . . . aged four years," was indentured on May 31, 1830, and ultimately stayed with the Society.[10] She became one of only two known non-German Society members (the other was the former Shaker Amasa Blodget), and married wagon maker Bernhardt Beiter.

The Society acted as legal guardians for other children. Ludwig Birk, a Zoar trustee, became the guardian of Stephen Bührer (1825-1907) on October 30, 1832, after his father died.[11] Bührer grew up in the Society, learned to be a cooper and, at age seventeen, left for Cleveland to ply his trade. Later he specialized in the contents of those barrels, distilled spirits, and a tonic called "Gentian Bitters." In 1867 Bührer was elected Democratic mayor of Cleveland, serving for two terms.[12] The Separatists purchased barrels and spirits from Bührer through his long life.[13] One of his products was "Bührer's Wolf Mountain Spring Water," bottled from Zoar's *Wolfberg Brunnen* on the south side of the Tuscarawas River.[14]

Zoar households, many consisting of more than one family, extended family, or unrelated single members, were numbered to identify them, as it was far more convenient than using family names, as there might be numerous last names involved. The earliest mention of numbered houses is an 1833 document stating that school elections would be held in House Number 19.[15] Common articles—such as the cloths used to wrap bread (*brot-duchlie*), pails for obtaining flour at the Bakery and milk from the Dairy, and bed linens and clothing (in the days before each family had its own laundry)—were marked with the house number.[16] Nixon states, "Once a member was assigned a house, he usually lived in it until he died. When his children married they usually lived with him or within a few minutes' walk. A house continued to be occupied by the same family for years and in many instances for generations. The physical attributes of the family were grounded more firmly in Zoar than in the world outside."[17] When, on occasion, a family moved, either into a newly built home or an existing one, they took their house number and all the numbered paraphernalia with them.

It is hard to pin down an exact number of residents or, for that matter, the number of actual *members,* in Zoar through the years. The census gives totals, but that includes nonmembers and sometimes those who lived in surrounding Lawrence Township. Bimeler states that Zoar had "about 300 inhabitants" in 1834, right before the cholera took away fifty-six of them.[18]

Cholera, an acute intestinal infection caused by the bacteria *vibric cholera,* seemed to follow the path of the Ohio & Erie Canal. In August 1834 a traveler named Allen Wallace died soon after his arrival at the Zoar Canal Tavern and was buried in the Zoar Cemetery.[19] Soon his wife and two children appeared, asked that Wallace be disinterred so she could obtain the valuables that had been buried with him.[20] That night cholera broke out in Zoar.

The disease, known today to be caused by contaminated water or food, rapidly dehydrates its victims. Sufferers, including many young children, died so quickly that coffins could not be made fast enough. Bimeler ministered tirelessly to the sick. Hilda Morhart tells the story of one elderly woman who, contrary to prevailing medical practice, demanded water and then became well, so thereafter water was given to patients and many recovered.[21]

Despite the contagious nature of cholera, Sunday services were held. One victim of the disease was Johannes Breymaier, he who had called Napoleon an angel of the underground while in German prison and had advocated that Zoar become communal in 1819. In his August 17 discourse, Bimeler reflected on the events of the past week, in which twelve Society members, including Breymaier, had died: "You, my friends, may well be excused from asking what our text for today should be, since the frequent deaths of the past week remind us daily, that the object or our considerations during the last two discourses was this: that we should examine the state of our souls. And this may well be the most important and the most necessary today also . . . since no man is sure what day or hour he may be called from this earthly life."[22]

In all, fifty-six persons, nineteen of them under the age of two, died in the cholera epidemic. Such a rapid decrease in population might have driven another group to disband or despair, but not the Society of Separatists of Zoar. Now, however, this shortage of labor required the Society to hire outsiders to do jobs that they once might have done themselves.

Such outsiders lived in Zoar, and their presence makes it hard to separate them from Society members. An 1859 list gives the names of eighty men over the age of twenty-one residing in Zoar, but some of them, perhaps thirty, according to a cryptic notation, were hired workers. A handwritten list, probably made for the 1850 census, lists 249 persons in Zoar.[23] The 1850 census agrees with that number, also reporting thirty-seven households. The remaining census figures are as follows: 1860, 275 persons in 41 households; 1870, 325 persons in 45 households; and 1880, 277 persons in 47 households. (The 1890 census, destroyed in a fire in Washington, DC, is not available to consult.) Again, these figures include outside hired workers. How many of these are actual members, either full or probationary, is for another researcher to discover.

From the Zoar Society's beginnings, women had an outsize role in the community's everyday life. Because there were so many of them and so few men, when the decision was made to become communal in 1819, women were given equal voting rights to elect officers and were permitted to hold office, although none ever did. (This was the nineteenth century, after all.) In answering William A. Hinds's question about women's role in the community, a trustee (probably Jacob Ackermann) replied: "Our Constitution says nothing against their holding office, and in my opinion they could, should they be elected to an official position. They generally exercise their right to vote."[24]

Zoar women with their "stout arms" worked alongside men in harvesting,[25] did the heavy work of threshing grain with flails, milked the cows, and supervised the Dairy: "The women does [*sic*] all the spinning, weaving & besides almost all of the work on the farm such as mowing, raking and drawing hay, reaping, raking and binding, cutting hemp, pulling flax, dressing flax, etc. The men are nearly all mechanics. The number of women exceeds that of the men."[26] As time went on and the Society hired more and more outside labor, the work of Zoar women became less arduous. "After the Society reached its prosperous stage, the lot of the women was an easier one. Their household cares were lighter than is usually the case with housewives."[27] But the Zoar work ethic persisted, even after the disbanding of the Society in 1898.

Each household had a cook. An 1832 observer noted: "Not every household or family takes care of their own meals, but certain women known for their know-how and cleanliness and who are able to prepare a rather tasty and healthful diet, are designated as cooks. Each of these women cooks for ten, fifteen, twenty, up to twenty-five persons, who are assigned to them and depending upon the number of these customers or boarders, one or more helpers are appointed to do minor chores, like fetching water, washing cooking utensils and dishes, and to carry bread, meat, butter, and milk from especially designated houses."[28] Later, kitchens were added to each home, some in detached buildings, like that which can still be seen adjacent to Number One House. In homes with multiple families, the cook was the woman who lived in the house the longest, a custom set to cut down on argument, one presumes.

Meals were cooked in *kestle-ofens* (kettle ovens), a firebox with an iron top with removable "eyes" into which kettles with flanged rims were sunk. Since women often worked away from home, main meals were based on one-dish (*eintopf*) soups and stews that could be simmered over the fire for long periods of time.

Zoar Separatists ate five meals a day, as opposed to the typical American "three squares." Meals were centered around work: a light breakfast, perhaps just bread and butter, an hour after sunrise and a midmorning breakfast of cold meat, rye bread, and cider. Lunch, or "dinner," was the most substantial meal of the day: a hot dish, often cooked in one pot, consisting of meat, grains, vegetables, and fruit, accompanied by *kuchen* (cake) and coffee. A midafternoon snack, similar to today's coffee break, consisted of bread and butter, a soft pretzel, *kuchen,* or a cookie with cider or beer for men and coffee for women. Called *brodesse* ("bread meal"), it was often brought into the fields to the workers. "Supper" was eaten around 6 P.M. and consisted of cold meats, cheese, radishes, and pickles. Dinner variations might include a bowl of soup, perhaps left over from noontime, and a dessert of fruit.[29]

The Zoarites continued the German peasant tradition of eating small quantities of meat. They refrained from eating pork until late in their history but served it to hired help and hotel guests. Beef, veal, chicken, and lamb were raised and butchered. Venison and rabbit were also available. Meat was obtained at the Butcher Shop on Tuesdays and Fridays.[30] Sausage was made from parts not eaten whole, and variety meats, such as liver, tongue, lung, and brains, were prized by the frugal Separatists.[31] "The butcher shop is located next to the bake-house. Whenever a fatted calf, which is not suitable for breeding, is slaughtered, each cook, having been informed in advance, has the meat necessary for her boarders delivered to her, and always receives a commensurate (or proportionate) quantity of meat, since the number of boarders is known to the butcher,"[32] according to essayist P. F. D.

Due to the prohibition of pork, frying was done in old butter, rendered beef tallow, or chicken, duck, or goose fat. Oil may have been obtained from crushing or boiling nuts. Lard, according to Edgar Nixon, was only used for shining shoes.[33]

Supplies for food preparation were obtained from the Magazine, or storehouse. Located on the corner of Main and West Third Streets, near the garden and diagonally across from the Assembly House, the Magazine provided staples like sugar, rice, salt, spices, tea, and coffee. Butter was distributed here, rather than the Dairy, so the Number One House cook, who oversaw the Magazine, could keep an eye on how much was taken, as butter was also sold in bulk for Society income. A long numbered shelf, still seen in the restored Magazine, held the articles meted out to each household every Friday, or *Ins Fassa*. At one o'clock, housekeepers assembled to collect the items in their *fass-korb*, or gathering basket. Spices, matches, and toilet soap were distributed from the nearby kitchen, where an even closer eye was kept. According to local historian and descendant Hilda Dischinger Morhart, "searching questions" were often asked about how such precious commodities were to be used.[34]

However, no records were kept on how much food each household consumed and extra rations were even given when members had out-of-town guests.[35] But each member kept a vigilant eye on his neighbor to see that not a crumb was wasted. Peer pressure at work.

Potatoes and onions were grown communally in large fields and distributed to store in sawdust or straw in special root cellars under each Zoar home.[36] Each home had an adjacent kitchen garden where vegetables and fresh herbs were grown. Food preservation for use in the winter months was done through drying (apples and other fruits), pickling (cabbage, cucumbers), salting (meats), and sugaring (jams, jellies, preserves). In the days before Mason canning jars, sauerkraut and pickles were kept in the cellar in covered barrels, and preserved fruit in crocks sealed with wax. Meats were cured in a smokehouse near the Butcher Shop, which was first located in the southwest corner of the village and later near the Brewery northwest of town. Cut apple "snitz" was dehydrated in a tiny fruit-drying house near the Cobbler Shop and then distributed to each household. Honey from a "bee house" and hives near the Garden was distributed at the Magazine.[37]

Later in the Society, hand-built iceboxes on back porches kept perishable foods cold during the warmer months. Ice was cut each winter from the canal, river and bottomlands especially flooded for this purpose, taken to the nearby icehouse, and packed in sawdust.[38] Ice was also used when necessary in the Dairy Springhouse to cool the milk and raise the cream.

A communal bakery stood on the corner of West Fourth and Main. P. F. D. observed in 1832, "To be sure, there exists in Zoar also a special bake house, where several women turn out a very good tasty and wholesome bread, similar to the Stuttgart *Kronenbrot* [king's bread], but only for the Society as a whole but also for sale. The canal boats that pass through usually purchase their necessary bread supplies for several days here, certain proof of its quality and pleasant taste." This same writer declared that the bread was often enjoyed "with a refreshing glass of beer."[39] His observation that the bread was purchased by outsiders is borne out in Bimeler's Receipt Book, where cash received and "orders" (perhaps this was put on account to someone; it is unclear from the ledger) totaled about two dollars per week from 1847 to 1853.[40]

Bread was mixed the evening before, allowed to rise overnight, formed into loaves and baked in the morning, and distributed in the afternoon, when it was often picked up by schoolchildren returning home. Hilda Morhart relates the story of hungry children pulling out and eating the soft bread in the interior of the loaves, leaving the crusts for their families.[41] The fresh bread was wrapped to take home in the numbered bread cloths mentioned above.

Early bakers were women, Anna Maria Link and Maria Platz,[42] followed by the men Jacob Ackermann, John Kuecherer, Frank Sylvan, Benjamin Rieker and, lastly, Frank Ackermann, who received the Bakery in the 1898 dissolution and continued to operate it for a few years afterward.[43]

Everyday bread was brown: whole wheat or rye. A mixture of mashed potatoes, flour, salt, sugar, and a tea made of hops steeped in water served as yeast. Sometimes the bread just wouldn't rise and this was jokingly called "bumpernickle" bread. Elderly residents received a weekly *Mittwoch-leib* (Wednesday loaf) of bread made with white flour along with a bottle of currant wine as a special treat.[44]

Thick gingerbread, wrapped in grape leaves to impart a special flavor, and other bakery treats were also made here, many for the hotel. Ginger cookies made an appearance at Christmas time, cut into hearts, stars, and bells with cookie cutters from the Zoar Tin Shop.[45]

Beer, cider, and wine were all consumed at Zoar. Drinking to excess was frowned upon. Beer, considered "liquid bread," was brewed from malt, barley, and hops grown in Zoar. The Brewery, constructed on the northwest edge of the village in 1831, had a large cellar where the beer was stored. Beer was sold to visitors at the hotel, and a limited amount to nearby residents. Without pasteurization, it could not be shipped. Beer was taken out to the fields for the afternoon *brodesse* during the summer, and a glass was given to laundresses on washday.[46]

Cider, made from the many apples grown from this "village hidden in an apple orchard,"[47] was processed in the Cider Mill. A new structure to replace a smaller older one was built in 1854 with the help of the Harmonists and featured a steam-engine press and an elaborate apple washer. Built on two levels into a bank, the apples were unloaded on the top level and dropped down into the press.[48] The Cabinet Shop was moved from a separate building to the first floor and shared the steam engine. The Cider Mill also did custom pressing for neighboring farmers. Cider was mainly served at meals and taken out to the fields in a special wagon.

Traditional wine grapes like those grown in Germany did not do well in the northeastern Ohio climate, so the Society made wine from currants grown on the *Weinberg,* north of the village. Such wine was dispensed from the cellar at Number One House. However, each family also made its own wine from table grapes, currants, and berries.[49]

Women normally drank coffee, and lots of it, all day long. Regular coffee was reserved for Sundays; a coffee substitute made of rye roasted in the Bakery ovens was the everyday drink. Children drank skim milk, as the cream was reserved for making butter.[50]

The Dairy, on Second Street, between the Zoar Store and the Cow Barn, processed the milk from the Society's large herd of dairy cattle, which numbered 105 in 1850.[51] The Dairy, unlike other Zoar industrial or agricultural enterprises, was supervised by women for most of Zoar's history.[52] Dairy maids, mostly young, unmarried girls, were assigned to care for and milk a number of cows daily. They then carried the milk the short block between barn and Dairy on their heads. According to a newspaper of the time, "The heads of the females seem to be made of sterner stuff than those of our worldly women. We have seen one of them carrying in each hand a basket and on their heads a bucket full of water or milk nicely balanced, from which not a drop was spilled."[53] A small, round cushion made of wool and stuffed with rye chaff helped balance the full tubs of milk.[54]

The milk was strained and cooled in the adjacent Springhouse, a cellar under the store. Cool water, sometimes supplemented with ice, surrounded flat pans of milk, allowing the cream to rise and be skimmed to make butter. Water from the seven springs located on the hill near the present Meeting House were piped in a gravity-fed system to storage cisterns at many households, including the Dairy. The butter was churned using horse power. P. F. D., the anonymous author of the 1832 piece "Harmony Builds the House," described the Dairy: "The author of this essay has seen the springhouse with his own eyes and can vouch for the fact that it is perfectly clean. In general the greatest cleanliness possible is found in their dwelling places as well as in their linen clothing; [it is clean] even in the cattle barns."[55]

Others also observed how clean the village appeared. Comments such as "spotlessly and scrupulously clean," and "their chief object seems to be the attainment of the highest possible degree of cleanliness," were common in the accounts of those who wrote about the community. Saturday was the day reserved for cleaning.[56] In 1859 a reporter for *Ohio Statesman* described the scene:

> The women seem as if to be perpetually scrubbing, and in every house we passed, we heard the mop in motion. Floors, porches, benches, pavements, trees, stables, children, and animals, all things in short, undergo the same daily manipulation, as if the least speck of dirt was the enemy of every house-wife in the village and must needs be simultaneously wiped out by combined effort. Cleanliness and order was everywhere manifest, and the most important business as well as the simplest household duties are performed with the regularity of the old fashioned clock which ticks with dignified stolidity in the barroom of the village tavern.[57]

Hilda Morhart argues that the use of mops was "a lazy man's way of working," and describes how floors were scrubbed on hands and knees and scoured with sand. Cellars were whitewashed on a yearly basis with a mixture of lime and water by a Society member called the *weissner* (whitewasher).[58] Morhart also describes how pots and pans were thoroughly cleaned with a special brush made of bulrushes, with iron skillets and kettles cleaned with brick dust.

Soap, so necessary for cleaning, was made from rendered beef tallow mixed with lye made from wood ashes and water strained several times in a barrel filled with straw until the liquid was strong enough to float an egg. The lye and tallow were boiled and stirred to the proper consistency to pour into molds, then cut into cakes after it hardened. "Soft soap," that which did not harden, was used in the laundry. "Toilet soap," less harsh and used for face washing and bathing, was purchased outside and distributed at the Magazine. In the early years, candles were made for the community both from tallow and beeswax by the same woman who made the soap.[59] Later soapmaking was done in each household, and kerosene lamps supplemented candles. "The linen for the whole community is washed clean and with great care always on the first two days of the week, in two separate wash houses and by a specially delegated woman. The coarser wash or material is [placed in] steam kettles (or washing machines using steam). In this way no dirty laundry piles up in the home, which usually creates an evil smell and attracts vermin."[60] Originally, laundry was done communally, as P. F. D. describes above. There was a "Wash-House" located on either side of the village. Washing machines were indeed used, as an 1832 letter attests: "Please furnish the Bearer Geo. Hrezuiger with a large Pot, which he can best describe to you as wanted. The pot we need for a patent Washing Machine, which we wish to fit out on a larger scale."[61] Later, separate laundries were added to the maze of outbuildings at the rear of each household that often included a privy, henhouse, woodshed, and detached kitchen. Wet clothing was then taken to the *washplatz,* on high ground west of the garden where linen was laid on the grass or strung on lines to dry. Zoar women also did washing for outsiders, with payment coming back to the Society's treasury.[62]

Women's clothing, men's shirts, and bedding were made in the Sewing House. The Tailor Shop made men's outerwear. P. F. D. explains:

> About twelve women have been assigned to a so-called sewing house, erected for the specific purpose of manufacturing new shirts and new pieces of clothing for members of the female sex, as well as mending old shirts. They do this work for the whole Society. Several persons whose job it is to knit and mend stockings, are employed at all times; they also take care of other work. In a separate shop a number of skilled tailors take care of manufacturing and mending pieces of clothing for the men, and in a shoemakers shop, right next door, shoes and boots are manufactured and repaired for the whole community and in addition to some customers living in the neighborhood.[63]

Zoar women's clothing, simple and unadorned, did not conform to fashion. In an 1862 article about Zoar in the *Summit Beacon* (Akron), one J. B. L. opines, "The women wear no hoops, and, in my eye, at least, are not so beautiful to behold as the charming lasses out in the world."[64] Early clothing resembled that of their German homeland. An 1845 woodcut by Henry Howe, the first image we have of Zoar, shows three women seen from the back: one with a long, double-sided pinafore-type apron (called a "tire"), one with a triangular neck scarf, and a third with a neck scarf and apron.[65] (It's worth noting that one of the women is carrying a hoe, and the other is wheeling a wheelbarrow, thus illustrating Zoar women's role in the community's labor hierarchy.) Other commentators remark on the dresses' high waists ("waists under the arm-pits") and the "enormous hats" that can also be seen in the

Howe woodcut.[66] Dresses in the present-day Zoar museum collection are of later vintage, as presumably worn-out clothing in early days was made into rag rugs and not saved. These dresses are simple shirtwaists with a full skirt and a tight-fitting bodice with a row of buttons down its center. Aprons and neck scarves, dark for everyday and white for Sunday, completed the costume. Photographs taken in the last decades show women's hair pulled back tightly from the face in a low bun. Morhart says Zoar women were not allowed to part their hair, as it was "a way to Satan," and refrained from braiding it as the Bible prescribed.[67] Caps were worn over the hair, both indoors and out, with bonnets, quilted in winter, worn when outside. Shawls and capes provided winter warmth.

According to memories of Zoar descendant Helen Burkhart, a typical Zoar girl had three dresses: one for every day, one for Sunday, and one "picnic dress" for special occasions. Old, patched dresses with the sleeves cut off and worn over a lightweight undershirt were worn in hot weather or for messy jobs and were nicknamed *so lauf rock* (casual dress). One of these "pinafores" can be seen at the museum in Zoar.[68]

When a new dress was needed, a Zoar woman went to the *Näh Haus* (Sewing House). In the early days of the Society, permission had to be granted ("Requests concerning the need for new articles of clothing are usually directed to the spouse [Dorothea] of the leader Baeumler, who is in charge of this area," reported P. F. D. in 1832),[69] but it is unclear if this was still true in later years. Fabric was chosen from the limited kinds of material available. Woolens and linens were manufactured in Zoar, but cottons had to be purchased. "One fitting was all a Zoar woman ever received; the clothes were made big enough the first time," former Zoar member Salome Beiter told Edgar Nixon in 1932.[70] Dresses were all made alike, as Society members were uncomfortable in clothing that differed from the norm. The author interviewed Mrs. Helena Beuter Class, a descendant, who told the story about receiving a dress made from a different bolt of fabric than all of her young friends. Seventy-five years later, she still had hard feelings about being "singled out."[71]

Men's outerwear was made in the Tailor Shop, located on Main Street next to the Zoar Store. In Howe's woodcut, the lone male figure wears a tallish hat, trousers, and a jacket ("roundabout") cut short in the front and long in the back. Maximillian, Prince of Wied, passing by Zoar on the canal in 1834, encountered a shepherd near the Canal Tavern. "His entire dress and equipments were quite in the German fashion: a shepherd's crook, a broad, leather bandolier, ornamented with brass figures, a flat broad-brimmed hat and a large grey coat; a costume very uncommon in America."[72] Three decades later, Constance Fenimore Woolson reported, "All the males in the village were dressed exactly alike, in tight, short, blue pantaloons, long-flapped calico vests, scanty, short-waisted, blue dress-coats, with two brass buttons behind; scow-like shoes, and broad-brimmed white fur hats—which being a sign of masculine superiority, were never removed on any occasion." As we have learned, no Separatist removed his hat to anyone, as no man, not even Napoleon Bonaparte, was thought superior to another.

The few pieces of men's clothing in the Zoar collection include a linen shirt, with the tail cut long to serve as underwear.[73] Other shirts are made of heavy wool. An unassembled pair of trousers is made of felted wool, the fabric presumably of Zoar manufacture. The collection of the Western Reserve Historical Society includes clothing said to belong to Joseph Bimeler, which is very different. It includes a regular 1840s' style coat made of blue broadcloth, not the short-waisted version described by Woolson. A black top hat, a pair of yellow-striped suspenders and a brown-figured silk vest, all very fashionable, complete the costume.[74] Perhaps, as the public face of the Society, Bimeler thought he needed to dress the part.

One of the tailors acted as community barber. Separatist men had clean-shaven faces, with a fringe of hair around their face and chin, similar to today's Amish. Moustaches were not worn until late in the Society's history, as they were thought to look too much like the military.[75]

An account book, the "Clothing Register," in the Zoar Papers shows the amount and variety of clothing supplied not just to members but to the indentured children, apprentices, outsiders, and even the needy for the years 1833 to 1860. Men's clothing—shirts, "roundabouts," pantaloons, suspenders—and women's clothing—dresses, shifts, aprons, bonnets, capes, and "raiments" (perhaps cloaks?)—and shoes for all are listed under the name of the person, or under the husband's name if married. Interestingly, the various pieces are all given prices, even for members. In some cases, personal funds of members and nonmembers alike or those funds supplied by others are listed on the credit side of the ledger page, to offset the cost of the clothing.[76] Personal items like combs, penknives, spectacles, and Bibles, along with their costs, are listed here too. Presumably these items were acquired from the Zoar Store.

CHILDHOOD, ADOLESCENCE, AND MARRIAGE

After placement of children in the dormitories became optional in 1840, family life in Zoar became a bit closer to mainstream America. Life as a child in Zoar, especially in the early years, was not carefree, however. Each child was expected to work hard, just like their elders. Jobs for boys included herding sheep and cows and working in the central garden; girls spun linen and wool and milked cows. Hands, even small ones, were never idle. Other jobs included boys helping steer the plow in the fields and driving the cows to and from the fields to graze. Girls worked in the fields, raking after the cradlers, stowing hay in the mows, herding the sheep, carrying food to men in the fields, and working in the Dairy.

Nixon says the attitude of the older Separatists toward their children was "puritanical in its severity." Even small demonstrations of affection, like hugs and kisses, were carnal impulses (*fleischglotz*). P. F. D. declared that "ill-mannered children are not tolerated in the community."[77]

Schooling through the eighth grade took place in a Zoar building leased to the local Lawrence Township.[78] The original School House was a frame building on East Third Street, which still stands. In 1868 a brick building, also still standing, was constructed on a rise northeast of the village. Teachers were often Society members, who turned their salaries over to the trustees,[79] or were hired outsiders. One Thomas White was employed by the Society's school directors in 1837. His contract specified the teaching of "reading, writing and arithmetic," and keeping the school open six hours a day and two hours in the evening at eighteen dollars per month for three months. By 1850 the school year had lengthened to five months.[80] In later years, teachers in the Zoar school participated in periodic "teachers institutes" for county educators.[81]

Essayist P. F. D., who may have been a hired school teacher, lists the following subjects taught in the school in 1832:

1. Reading, according to the phonetic method, invented by Dr. Stephan in Bavaria and now widely initiated in France and England. This method makes it possible to teach the more gifted children reading and correct pronunciation in a very short time (usually four weeks) and is applicable to English as well as to the German language.
2. Writing—with German and English letters.
3. General grammar, to prepare pupils to express their own thoughts.

4. Arithmetic, according to new methods, little known in America, to speed up and streamline computation processes.
5. Theoretical and practical geometry.
6. Geography and description of the earth.
7. Music, singing, piano forte and violin[82]

Subjects were taught in both English and German until 1884, with German taught on Tuesdays and Thursdays. Some in the surrounding area sent their children to Zoar to learn German.[83] Music was part of the curriculum, and the school furnishings included a piano. Religious instruction was not neglected, as an order for schoolbooks included "½ dozen testaments."[84] English schoolbooks included *McGuffey's Readers* and *Ray's Arithmetic,* books used in many country schoolhouses. A German textbook was F. P. Wilmsen's 1854 *Deutscher Kinderfreund für Schule und Haus.*[85] A book supplier was asked "to supply this place with Books of an Excellent moral tendency."[86]

Hilda Morhart relates that in the latter years of the Society the school played a large part in Zoar life, with plays and holiday celebrations performed by the children for their parents. Each spring, students went on a *Spazierengehen* (spring walk) in the Zoar Woods to a memorable place, a cave (named, for some reason, *Die Hölle* [Hell]) where ferns grew, wildflowers bloomed, and water trickled down from high rocks.[87]

At about age fifteen, Zoar adolescents took up occupations assigned to them by the trustees. Boys, especially, had the opportunity to try out different jobs as helpers when school was not in session. Were job placements arbitrary or did the trustees use skill in assigning them, finding just the right person for the right job? Or were Zoarites so accustomed to obedience that they just accepted what was offered them? We have two reactions, one female and one male. The first is from Sarah Ott, writing in 1866 to her twin sister Rebecca Feucht, who had left Zoar and, amid scandal, married Benjamin Feucht, a former member of the celibate Harmony Society. "If I am forced to teach school this winter I will leave. The maid from not around here who worked at the inn has left. Now Lois is supposed to work at the inn and I should help Christiana. But she won't let Lois go. And I don't want to be her servant, nor do I want to go to the inn."[88] Meanwhile, Jacob Sturm, who at age twenty-one in 1890, complained to his father about his assigned job in the Wagon Shop: "Father, I tell you if there is no other chance in Zoar than to be the Slave of Ben. Beiter [head of the Wagon Shop] I shall know some way to free myself after this winter is past. . . . I shall be inclined to look for a chance myself."[89] It should be noted that neither Sarah nor Jacob left the Society. Jacob Sturm remained with the Society through the dissolution, but not in the Wagon Shop. He became stationmaster of the Wheeling and Lake Erie railroad station.

The work habits of Zoar young people impressed outside visitors. A visitor named E. T. Stevenson of Cleveland asked if one Maria Rapp, who worked in the Dairy, might work as a domestic for them. He asked "whether she can wash and iron and clean. As to the cooking, Mrs. Stevenson would not object to teaching her. Can she speak English at all? . . . We should give her a dollar a week to begin with."[90]

Although boys were rarely allowed to court a girl in her parents' home,[91] working together at cornhusking bees, maple sugaring, hops pulling, and other group activities allowed them to get to know one another before marriage. John H. Haney, an outsider from Youngstown, obviously familiar with Zoar, wrote to David Sylvan in 1862 regarding what he saw as drawbacks to Zoar courtship: "It seems to me the Zoar folks do not cultivate the affections enough but they look too much to their own interest in every thing. I don't believe they have much affection for each other. And let me tell you they make a grand mistake in keeping such a strict watch over their youth. If they would let the boys & girls go together & have little social parties, they would do better. Now when they get together they are worse than if they were accustomed to being with each other. . . . If you were with females more you would learn to respect them."[92]

Pipsey Potts, a writer for *Arthur's Home Magazine* in 1882, agreed: "The young people of the Community need recreation. We were sorry for them. One evening a little party of them gathered at the hotel, and the two sitting-rooms were thrown open, and judging from the laughter and noise they were playing like a noisy lot of small children."[93]

An earlier letter from Zoarite Sarah Ott to her twin sister Rebecca Feucht at Economy speaks of the problem of choosing a marriage partner in such a small pool of eligible men: "You say that I should hurry and also get a husband [Rebecca has just married Benjamin Feucht]. A right one is not here and a bad one I don't want. If I can't get a good one, I would rather die. There are youths here I would not want. I'd rather hang from a tree than marry such a one."[94]

But youth and their hormones have a way of finding each other, and marriages took place nonetheless. It is worth noting that there are a surprising number of illegitimate births recorded with the father's name listed as "unknown" or taking place before a marriage was recorded.[95] Sarah

Ott mentions this fact in her 1866 letter: "Ludwig [Heid] married Salome Rauschenberger a bit late. She is just about due."[96]

Zoar couples had to obtain permission of the trustees (often a formality) and marriages took place before a justice of the peace, a Society member,[97] since, to the Separatists, marriage was strictly a legal ceremony. As marriage is a contract, Zoar marriages were recorded at the Tuscarawas County Courthouse in New Philadelphia as well as in a Copulation Book, kept after 1830 by the Separatists.[98] There is nothing in the record about marriage celebrations, but the Separatists' dim view of ceremonies of any kind, religious or otherwise, probably prevailed here as well, especially in the early years.

After marriage, the couple often moved in with either the bride's or, more often, the groom's family, as Nixon noted above. Work continued as before, with one household losing a member, and one household gaining one.

Views on work during pregnancy are also unknown, but presumably hands were not idle at that time either. Zoar families were average size for the period, with three to six children. Infant mortality was about the same as elsewhere in America. Sixty children under age two died in Zoar from 1834 when records began to the Society's end in 1898. Nineteen of these deaths were cholera victims of the 1834 epidemic: note that marriages had just been reinstated in 1829, and there were many susceptible infants and young children in the village at that time.[99]

POLITICAL LIFE

As previously mentioned, one of the first actions of the newly arrived Separatists was to walk to the county seat of New Philadelphia to declare their intentions to become citizens of the United States. Exactly how much these early Zoarites participated in politics is unclear. We know that a member served as justice of the peace and performed Society marriage ceremonies. Lewis Birk was a justice of the peace during from the 1830s until his death in 1851.[100]

Members often held various township offices, with any salary turned in to the Society (Simon Beuter, for instance, was paid $3.50 for "election and poll book" for the November 1852 election.) Nixon reports that there was "little interest taken in either state or national elections."[101]

In response to an 1852 inquiry from the German Sub-Committee of Whigs in Congress, Wiebel reported that more than half of the seventy-five Zoar [male] voters were Democrats, with about thirty Whigs. He replied that they preferred "civilian to a military character for the Presidential chair."[102] This is not surprising, given Zoar's pacifism.

The Separatists supported the Republican Party after its 1856 inception, and remained loyal Republicans for the rest of their history. One member, Jacob Kümmerle, a shoemaker, stubbornly voted Democratic until 1896, when the threat of going off the gold standard caused him to vote for McKinley.[103]

Simon Beuter's *Tag-Buch* gives clues to the Society's political beliefs, especially during the Civil War, when the Separatists' abhorrence of slaveholding made them pro-Union. Beuter recorded the national election results with few comments until the 1896 election of McKinley (he was disappointed when Democrat Grover Cleveland, "said to be a very immoral man," was elected in 1884). Nixon says even Beuter's handwriting gave away his excitement over the 1896 election of McKinley. "There has been no more important election since 1860. All the ignorant and vicious elements in all the parties united under the demagogic, anarchistic leader Bryan in an attempt to reduce by half the value of money, so that all creditors would have been cheated out of half of what was owing them."[104]

Beuter was not alone in his enthusiasm for nearby Canton, Ohio's native son, as McKinley's nomination earlier that year was cause for celebration in town. A Zoar correspondent described the scene in a column of "Zoar News" in the *Iron Valley Reporter:* "Mr. McKinley's nomination was duly celebrated here. When the news reached town Thursday evening, Mr. [Louis] Zimmerman got out the band. The band rendered all the patriotic airs and was much applauded. The spirit of patriotism took hold of young America who kept up the celebration til midnight."[105]

Nixon notes that, although the Society's investments may have fluctuated, none of the era's economic panics ever really influenced the Society's political life, as "the members were provided for just as well in the lean years as in the more prosperous times,"[106] living as they did under the protective umbrella of the Zoar Society.

ELDERLY

After the dangerous early years of childhood were over, Zoarites lived long lives. Nixon notes that in 1874, there were still about forty members who had made the initial trip from Germany. The number of the aged who still were actively working was remarkable: Gottfried Kappel still managed the

Woolen Mill at age eighty-six in 1876. Jacob Ackermann worked as a trustee and "performed the work of many a younger man" until his death in 1889 at age eighty-six. Michael Miller taught basket weaving at age eighty-five.[107]

The emigrant party of 1817 was composed of many older persons, especially older women. After all of their hard work to build the canal and keep the Society going, the trustees in 1835 decided to "reward" them by building them a dormitory, Number One House, much as they had built dormitories for the village children. Here they could live together and be waited on, thus saving the labor of attending to the infirm in their own homes. Wide hallways with openings in the wall for each room's heating stoves allowed others to care for the bedridden. However, this experiment was unsuccessful, as, unlike the children housed in the dormitories, the elderly had a voice, used it and refused to be segregated. It is not known just how long, or even if, the Number One House was used as a nursing home. This spacious Georgian Colonial mansion became, instead, the home of leader Joseph Bimeler, who, according to the 1850 census, shared it with eight other people, including his wife, Dorothea.

Elders, once they reached the age of sixty, could opt only to work at light tasks, but many continued to work much as they had before. Men who were no longer able to work in the fields made willow baskets, and women spun and plaited straw for hats.

The author has made a study of the causes of death in Zoar, as listed in the "Birth and Death Book." Lung diseases, such as consumption (tuberculosis), were the leading cause of death, with (in descending order) senility, cholera, fever, dropsy (heart failure), convulsions, cerebral hemorrhage, abdominal illness, and, tied for last place, liver disorders, cancer, heart conditions, and neck and throat disorders.[108] We must remember that these diagnoses were described by the compiler of the book, who was not a doctor. Today that list might be turned upside down, with cancer and heart disease being much higher on the list of fatal illnesses.

In addition to Bimeler's service as community physician, the Society hired outsiders to tend to the illnesses of members.[109] Bimeler was a self-taught practitioner of homeopathy, a medical philosophy that "like cures like," that small doses of an otherwise harmful substance would help cure disease. The Separatists subscribed to homeopathic journals purchased medicines from homeopathic drug suppliers, and Society practitioners of homeopathy, like John Petermann and Clemens Breil, were called "Doctor."[110] Anna Maria Beuter, wife of Simon, the Society gardener, was a midwife who delivered hundreds of children in her career for both Society members and outsiders, to whom she charged a fee of two dollars, with the cash turned into the Society's treasury.[111]

In 1895 one journalist described Zoar funerals like this: "Never was there a barer or colder form of funeral than the burial customs of the people of Zoar. At early dawn, with the first rays of the sun glinting over the hills and piercing the depths of the sombre valley, a little ghost-like group creep through the morning mist, bearing a coffin to the little cemetery. There, without service or ceremony, or words of prayer, they lay it quietly away, and creep back silently to the town, and, on the following Sunday the congregation are formally notified, in a few brief words, that one of the community had departed."[112]

Burials took place at the Zoar Cemetery at the end of West Seventh Street, still in use today. The funeral party followed the wagon with the casket on foot. The handmade coffin, often walnut, was taken from the wagon and lowered into the grave. Family members paid their respects, but, in keeping with Zoar custom, no religious ceremony was held. Remembrance of the departed member took place at the next Sunday's service. Bimeler would incorporate these tributes into his *Reden* (his weekly discourses); after his death, they were given by one of the trustees or cashier Christian Wiebel.

Some of these funeral discourses have survived. Here is part of one for Christina Ackermann (1800-1874). The sermon is dated December 12, 1874: "She and her older sister joined the Separatists when the group was forced to leave Germany for America. She arrived when Zoar was still a wilderness. When the community of goods was proposed, she willingly gave up her right to private property, as did the other older Separatists. She was a loyal and dependable member of the Society who was ever moving closer to her spiritual goal."[113]

Early graves were unmarked, as all were thought to be equal in death; even today, the southeastern section of the cemetery has no markers, except for that of Joseph Bimeler, whose grave was marked with a granite tombstone sometime in the 1930s. After the Civil War, graves were indicated with wooden, later limestone, headstones, many of which are now so weathered as to be unreadable. By the 1890s marble and granite stones were used.

LEISURE

Whether the early Separatists had what we now term "leisure" is debatable, but work rules relaxed as time passed and older Society members who remembered those hard early years passed on, so life in Zoar became a little more fun-filled.

In early Zoar, holidays were not celebrated, as one day was considered to be as holy as another, taking the word holiday, or *holy day,* literally. As noted, even Sunday could be used for work if urgent labor needed to be done, since "nature made no distinction" between days of the week.[114] Religious holidays reminded the Separatists too much of the established church back in Württemberg, although the day might be mentioned by Bimeler in his Sunday discourses. Interestingly, saints' days are indicated on the perpetual calendar painted by the Zoar Artist. Perhaps these yearly occasions helped mark the seasons, showing when to plant or harvest.

Easter was not specially celebrated until late in the Society's history, when Easter nests made of moss were filled with colored eggs and pretzels were baked on Good Friday. Nixon mentions that on Palm Sunday the entire town watched as the new lambs were turned out into the fields.[115]

Zoar legend tells us the Separatists began to celebrate Christmas when the clay horn, which they used to summon the workers, broke one frosty Christmas morning; they took this as a sign to no longer work on Christmas.[116] Other Zoar Christmas traditions, most celebrated late in the Society period, included baking gingerbread cookies, making a "broomstick tree" of evergreen branches stuck into a drilled broomstick "trunk," and having the *Krist Kind* (Christ Child), a veiled woman dressed in white, deliver treats to Zoar children.[117]

Independence Day was not observed until 1895. Gardener Simon Beuter complained in his *Tag-Buch,* "July 4, 1895: Our trustees ordered a holiday for the first time—what new mischief will be next? Everything for voluptuousness and mischief, but nothing for God."[118]

In many cases, the community disguised work as fun, as in maple sugaring, ice cutting, hops pulling, apple butter making, and cornhusking.[119] Quilting and making rag rugs were group activities for women and girls. Often young people were the prime participants in these work parties, but everyone pitched in when necessary, especially during the harvest. A celebration was held when the "Last Load" of grain came in from the fields to be stored.

Many chores were done in groups, making them social occasions, like "hops pull-ing," the annual fall harvest of hops vines, used to flavor beer. Hops also gave a distinctive flavor to yeast used at the Zoar Bakery. (Courtesy of the Ohio History Connection, Properties Collection, P365AV.)

Descendant Hilda Morhart described the event: "There was always a small celebration when the last load came in. Two or three teams were hitched to the wagon that contained the last sheaves. The horses were decorated with little American flags and the men on the load held a large American flag. The townspeople were told in advance they were near the village, and everyone, young and old, flocked to Main Street to cheer as they drove through town. The Zoar band, reputed to be the best in the state of Ohio at that time, met them at the outskirts of town and marched before them, playing their favorite marches."[120]

Which brings us to Zoar's most ubiquitous leisure-time activity: music. Hymns were sung during group activities as well as for Sunday church services. A brass band of twenty to thirty men was formed about 1840, and, according to Nixon, "played an important part in the life of the com-munity."[121] Existing music books in the Zoar collection include waltzes, marches, and airs from German composers. The band in later years played in nearby towns and entered band contests, including one in Columbus where, according to Hilda Morhart, they might have won first place, not second, if not for their homemade uniforms.[122] Band practice was on Monday nights, with concerts on Thursdays. Concerts were given in later years at the picnic grounds next to Zoar Lake in the western part of the village and on the flat porch roof of the Town Hall after it was built in 1884. The garden was also the scene of band concerts: "The young men have organized themselves into a band, and have good instruments. . . . During the summer evenings they . . . sit in the centre of the great garden and play until the bell rings for the hour of retirement."[123]

An orchestra, or string band, complemented the brass band and included some of the same players. Their music had a more classical bent. The band and orchestra plus instrumentalists and the church organist were featured in an ambitious 1892 New Year's Eve concert after which the band members "were feted to an oyster supper."[124]

A men's chorus, or *Männerchor,* was formed during the Society's last decade to sing familiar German folk songs like *Die Lorelei.*[125]

Bills for sheet music, pianos, and musical instruments abound in the records. Musical instruments were often purchased from the Harmonists at Economy, noted for their musical abilities. A melodeon (pump organ) was

Music was all-important to the Zoarites, from singing psalms at Sunday services to playing in the Zoar Band, which gave weekly concerts to visitors and residents alike. (Courtesy of the Ohio History Connection, Properties Collection, P365AV.)

purchased for the Meeting House in 1854, just after its completion.[126] Its present pipe organ was not bought until 1873. An 1854 tax bill states the Society had four pianos, including one in the Cabinet Shop. Some early pianos were hand built by Jacob Fritz, a cabinetmaker. Fritz, like Bimeler, a pianist, asked Bimeler's permission to build a piano . When the latter refused, Fritz persisted, building an instrument with available materials, including bone keys, instead of ivory. When Bimeler saw Fritz's handiwork, he relented and purchased the strings for him. A Fritz piano, one of several he built, is on display in Number One House.[127]

A clue to Zoar's musical tastes is the discovery of proof sheets dated 1859 from the Zoar Print Shop for the printing of Joseph Haydn's *Creation* (1798).[128] This oratorio, which uses the book of Genesis to show how God created the world, must have been appealing to the religious Separatists. It is not known if the piece was ever performed in Zoar.

Music was part of the school curriculum, but, for the most part, Zoar musicians were self-taught, with older members instructing the younger. We have seen in the previous chapter the case of Jacob Albert Beuter, son of the gardener Simon, who left Zoar for Economy to seek further musical education and became a music educator and composer.

Besides the musical groups, the Zoar Fire Department, founded in 1845, also acted as a social organization.[129] It held periodic meetings, elected officers, and even held parades through town.[130]

Each adult male had to periodically serve as night watchman. Two patrolled the village each night in two shifts, from eight o'clock to midnight and midnight to morning. Each watchman carried a stick with a lantern on the end. These sticks were passed from house to house as each took his turn. They checked each barn for sick animals, that each shop was secure and that no fires had broken out. The watchmen also guarded against transients, of which there were many.[131] After the town was incorporated in 1884, it had to have a jail to house miscreants, although no Separatist ever had a need to stay there.[132] Instead, this small log building, known as the "calaboose," housed tramps and those visitors who had imbibed too much Zoar beer.

Other pastimes included winter sports: ice skating on the fishpond and canal and sledding (there are numerous handmade sleds in the Zoar collection). Hilda Morhart tells of skating north to Bolivar and south to Zoar Station on the canal. Groups of young people would take horse-drawn sleigh rides on snowy roads.[133]

In summer, boats were rowed and picnics were held at Zoar Lake, although in the latter years, Zoarites had to compete with tourists for prime picnicking spots.

Mineral baths could be taken at the sulfur spring east of town: "Recently [1832] a mineral well was also discovered, about one mile away . . . , the water of which has a taste similar to that of the *Landstater Sauerwasser* [Landstat mineral water]. Since several female members of the Society who had suffered from rheumatism completely recovered by bathing in this water, a regular house has been built now for this purpose and they have made arrangement for a shower bath in the same building, as well as for several warm baths, in order to also be able to accommodate strangers who suffer from the same complaint and are willing to try the water."[134] Being sulfur water, it had a rotten-egg smell. Nixon says the bathhouse was discontinued by 1854. After the Society's dissolution, water from the spring was bottled and sold in a short-lived business as "Zoar Indian Springs Mineral Water."[135]

Some leisure pursuits were solitary endeavors, like raising dogs. Records show the Separatists sold dogs to outsiders, one in 1855 for three dollars and another in 1859 for two dollars—there is no indication of breed, but they may have been shepherd, or perhaps hunting, dogs. A dozen rifles, presumably used for hunting, were purchased in 1845. They also raised canary birds and sold both birds and birdhouses.[136]

The visual arts were represented by someone known today as the Zoar Artist. This is probably one Thomas Maier (1778-1851?), who traveled to America with the original group.[137] The 1850 census puts him working in the Woolen Mill. Perhaps he had a hand in designing the intricate coverlets made by the Separatists. The paintings of the artist, done in opaque watercolors, are primarily religious: illustrations of biblical parables, like the woman at the well, depictions of heaven and hell, and other religious subjects. Additional paintings are in the nature of keepsakes: illustrated poems and Bible verses. His distinctive style features floral garlands with a signature "cup-like" rose. The Zoar Artist also painted furniture and a perpetual calendar. Some of his pieces can be seen at Zoar Village State Memorial with others in private collections.

Photographs were banned by the Society as late as 1863,[138] presumably because of the biblical prohibition against "graven images." The earliest known photo of Society members is of the fire brigade in 1869.[139] Later Society members, including trustee Jacob Ackermann and Christina Petermann, the first child born in Zoar, had formal portraits taken. By the 1880s, visitors were snapping many photos, and the Society even posed for post-cards of harvesting scenes that were sold in the Zoar Store to tourists.

In 1854, the Society both exhibited and entered some of their products in the Tuscarawas County Fair. They won $10.75 in premiums and sold $47.31 worth of goods, including a wheel of cheese, bread, butter, socks, thread, flannel, linen, and a large amount of leather and calfskins.[140]

Zoar craftsmanship was becoming known to the wider community, and the Society was becoming less isolated. As the century wore on, contacts with outsiders at the hotel and through commercial dealings brought the world closer to Zoar. Individuals began to accumulate small amounts of cash, through tips from hotel visitors and selling eggs. Members began to collect keepsakes—some as gifts from hotel guests and others as trinkets bought at places like the county fair or from peddlers passing through town. These personal possessions were kept in special furniture pieces built in the Cabinet Shop called (in the Zoar vernacular) *glas kästlein* (little glass boxes).[141] Most were about two feet square, eight inches deep, with interior shelves and a glass-paneled door. Often lined with patterned wallpaper, the *kästlein* held precious objects that were not community property. Several *glas kästlein* can be seen in the Zoar museum buildings.

The trustees also would purchase specific items for members while on buying trips for the Zoar Store. Items on want lists often mentioned specific individuals, for instance, "a lead pencil for Christina Zimmermann" and a "needle case for Barbara Wagner."[142] The Clothing Register lists some of these personal items, including their price, under the recipient's name.

The Society purchased books of all kinds, including a volume of Shakespeare,[143] and subscribed to newspapers and magazines in both English and German. Some early members, all female, were illiterate, and signed the Articles of Agreement with an *X,* but reading the Bible and deciding for oneself what to believe were important to all of the Separatists. How much reading material was shared throughout the village is not known. In their testimony in the Supreme Court case, former members stated that Bimeler had a library, but no one was permitted access to it; books were taken from members and placed there; "only two German papers are ever allowed to Circulate among the other members, and then only after having been carefully examined by him [Bimeler]. . . . Many of the members have not even a Bible . . . besides, they are not allowed time to read, being often kept hard at work till the moment of retiring to rest."[144] There may be some truth to this, albeit exaggerated for the court case.

Any prohibitions against books and newspapers were probably very early, however. An examination of post office records shows lots of periodicals sent to Zoar to both members and outsiders by midcentury.[145] Most of these newspapers were in German, but by 1882, the editor of the local English-language newspaper in nearby Dover bragged about the number of subscribers from Zoar and that "we count the Zoar Society people among the staunchest friends of the *Iron Valley Reporter.*"[146]

RELATIONS WITH NEIGHBORS

Unlike some contemporary communal groups, notably the Perfectionists at Oneida or the Janssonists at Bishop Hill, the Zoar Society had cordial relations with its neighbors. It helped that the population of Tuscarawas County was predominantly of German descent during the nineteenth century.[147] The county was first settled in 1803 by Germans from western Pennsylvania and western Virginia.[148] The local Lawrence Township was also mostly German.[149] "Many of the Germans and Pennsylvania Germans who came to Tuscarawas County practiced non-Lutheran religions, some with a history of European religious persecution, Anabaptist sectors, including Mennonites and Amish, represent[ed] a particularly sizable proportion. Lawrence Township had an especially large settlement of Dunkards, who began to emigrate to Indiana in the 1830's."[150]

Upon arrival in 1817, the Separatists were given flour and potatoes by their neighbors and worked for these same neighbors to help feed themselves until the decision to become communal in 1819.[151] There is no extant record indicating that the newcomers were discriminated against because of their unorthodox religious beliefs or their later decision to become communal.

It seems that this shared cultural and language background allowed their neighbors in these early years to more readily accept these "different" people in their midst, people who were working just as hard as they were, trying to wrest a living out of the Ohio wilderness.

As seen in chapter 6, Zoar had relationships with all sorts of local farmers and other tradesmen during its history. Its communal nature was never mentioned in correspondence. It was, like the Ohio legislature had decreed in 1832, a corporation like any other, despite its different makeup.

By 1870, articles in local newspapers, much more common after that date, demonstrate that a familiar attitude had developed toward the Separatists by their neighbors. Zoar was by now more of a tourist destination—one that welcomed locals from Bolivar, Dover, and New Philadelphia as well as those from the big cities. Neighboring newspapers began including columns of "local news" by Zoar correspondents and references to outings to the Zoar Hotel for Sunday dinners. Susan Colpetzer, in her 1985 study of local attitudes toward Zoar, put it this way: "There is no indication in the local papers of outside pressure on the Zoar Society to abandon this system. Instead, the Society's communal system is consistently favorably described. For instance, rarely was 'strange' or any other negative term used to describe Zoarites' communal system; instead such terms as 'quaint' or 'refreshingly unconventional' were used." An attitude just short of ownership—"our Zoarites"—frequently was implied when the Society was mentioned in print.[152]

In sum, the Separatists were fortunate to find themselves in such a supportive environment, where they were accepted and even embraced.

CHAPTER 9

"To Enjoy the Advantages
Common to All"

Zoar, Communalism, and the Courts

If members separate themselves from the society, their interest in the property
ceases, and new members that may be admitted, under the articles, enjoy the
advantages common to all.

—US Supreme Court Justice John McLean, *Goesele v. Bimeler,* 1852

The legality of the communal relationships forged by the Zoar Society was
tested in the courts. Was the contract signed by the members valid? Did
they indeed give up any compensation for labor contributed when they
departed? What were the Society's responsibilities to former members
who either left on their own accord or who were dismissed?

The newly formed Zoar Society faced its first legal challenge in 1822.
Johann Gottfried Banzhoff, imprisoned for nine years in Württemberg, had
negotiated with the English Quakers and was once seen as one of Zoar's
leaders. He brought suit with several others, including Gottfried Bacher,
Johann Georg Platz, and one Feckenbush, first name unknown. Documents
for this case have been lost, but both Banzhoff and Bacher gave depositions in the Johannes Goesele case discussed below. Although Banzhoff
had signed the 1819 Articles of Association, he had little good to say about
the Society and Bimeler in particular. He related an incident at the port of
Antwerp before the voyage where he thought Bimeler acted "unbecoming
to a Christian" when he pocketed the proceeds of the sale of some "white
biscuit." Banzhoff declared that "if he [Bimeler] was opposed to anything,

137

that was the end of it." He was especially vocal about Bimeler's refusal to sign over the land to the group. "As soon as I learned Bimeler was the owner of the land, I became dissatisfied."[1]

The Society became celibate in 1822, and that decision entered into the suit as well. Bacher testified in 1851, "I gained my suit, but lost my wife. She remained with the society; she preferred remaining with Bimeler and the society she had signed [for] as a member."[2]

Although the Zoar Society prevailed in the lower court, it was appealed, and cash was awarded in arbitration to the complainants. Banzhoff received $1,000 while Bacher got $1,340. Bacher later sued for damages regarding the loss of his wife and claimed to have received $300.[3] Knowing how fragile the Society's finances were at this time, such payments must have created great hardship.

To create a sounder legal footing for itself, the Society became an Ohio corporation in 1832 in an act passed by the Ohio Legislature with all of the rights and responsibilities of a corporation.[4] A new Constitution was drawn up and signed by all full members on May 14, 1833, pledging they would abide by its rules and regulations. Article 10 explained, "Whosoever shall act contrary to this provision [the decisions of the trustees and Standing Committee] and will not be satisfied with their judgment loses and debars himself of all further enjoyment and rights of a member." Article 11 further detailed what happened when a member left or was dismissed for cause: "Neither the seceding members who leave the Society of their own accord nor those who are expelled therefrom can . . . in any wise make any demand or obtain, either upon property brought to the Society or for their labor or any other service which they may have rendered to the Society . . . any compensation whatever. . . . This constitution shall never in any wise be broken or annulled by dissatisfied or seceding members."[5]

On August 9, 1839, Bernhart Friedrich Sieber (also Siber), a second-class member since 1835 who was dismissed that winter,[6] sued the Society for reimbursement of the money and property he contributed, plus damages for alleged injuries he had suffered while a member. He claimed he was treated in a "harsh and oppressive manner, neglected in sickness." He said he was "supplied badly and scantily with provisions, and with those of a coarse and unwholesome kind." Sieber averred that Bimeler had "tried to sow disaffection and discord" between his wife, Catherine Maier Sieber, and himself "to seduce her affections," contributing to the miscarriage of her pregnancy.[7]

In answer to Sieber's petition, the Society claimed Sieber's labor was of "a very inferior nature," "light and easy labor which our women generally perform," "done with grumbling and dissatisfaction." Regarding Bimeler's treatment during Sieber's illness, the Society's reply stated that Bimeler "took a great deal of pains to do all for him that was in his power," and that seducing women "had never been in the character" of the agent general.

The Society's new legal status was not tested at this time, as the Sieber suit was withdrawn shortly after it was instituted, "without prejudice, at complainant's cost."[8]

Other cases, brought in the 1840s by former members Johann Georg Schande and Christian Weizhaar,[9] were dismissed by the courts. The definitive ruling on the legality of the Society's Constitution had to wait for yet another case that took almost a decade to reach a final opinion from the United States Supreme Court, causing the Society's leaders much anxiety, not to mention legal costs, in the meantime.

The instigator for much of this massive legal action was one Johannes (John) Goesele (or Gasely; the name is spelled innumerable ways in the records) and his wife,[10] Anna Maria Boehringer Goesele. Johannes was the nephew of Johannes Goesele Sr. (1761-1827), a respected member of the group, who had come to America in 1817 after suffering persecution for his religious beliefs by the government of Württemberg. Johannes Sr. had even been incarcerated by the authorities in the Fortress Asperg for seven years before his immigration.[11] Both men joined the fledgling Zoar Society; Johannes Sr. in 1819 with the first Articles of Agreement, his nephew in 1824, presumably after he was old enough.[12]

In 1832, after his uncle's death in 1827, Johannes Jr. became the landlord of the new Canal Tavern, an enterprise built along the Ohio & Erie Canal, about half a mile from the center of the village, but just far enough away from the prying eyes of the trustees. The canny Separatists saw the canal as a way to bring much-needed cash into its community. Not only did it bring cash, it brought the world and its temptations with it. These temptations proved to be too much for Johannes Jr. Rumors spread of drunkenness, secret caches of money, and hidden worldly goods at the tavern.[13]

Little did the Society know when they dismissed him on March 4, 1845, that Goesele would cost the Society almost twenty years of litigation and thousands of dollars in legal fees, and, in 1852, the case would set a precedent in the United States Supreme Court to be cited in similar cases by other communal groups, including the Harmony Society, the Oneida Community, and the Amana Society.[14]

Goesele's operation of the Canal Tavern was, according to one member, "a disgrace to a Civil Community." Another member testified that he saw Goesele "buying such Luxury Articles, to which no member was Entitled . . . to which Gasely replied, If you had the Chance as I had, you would do the same thing." The "luxury articles" included a clarinet, a music box, and a piece of velvet.[15]

Goesele took advantage of his location along the canal to travel three miles to Bolivar, ten miles to Massillon, or even the sixteen miles to Canton without the permission of the trustees. Even his wife, Anna Maria, was seen walking along the canal towpath to Bolivar. Peddlers and others were given room and board in exchange for luxury goods, which the Goeseles hoarded.[16]

Drunkenness and fighting were endemic at the tavern. One instance was tragic: two men, employees of the Society at the nearby Fairfield Furnace, who were "too drunk to stand," drowned in the Tuscarawas River on their way home.[17]

The instance that proved to be the last straw was when a hired hand became so drunk at the tavern on a wintry night in December 1844, he passed out in front of Peter (son of Joseph) Bimeler's home and had to be carried in a wheelbarrow back to the Canal Tavern to sleep it off. The place was closed three days after this incident.[18]

Goesele would not leave quietly. He told one witness, "This is my house and I will see who is Master of it, I or you."[19] When the Standing Committee convened to hear testimony regarding his dismissal from the Society, he refused to attend, saying, "[It is] your place first to defend me,"[20] and refused to leave the tavern for two months.

Society attorney J. C. Hance drew up an eviction notice, listing all of Goesele's transgressions, and invited him "to make known to said Society whatever you may have to offer in excuse or extenuation of your doings aforesaid and then and there to show cause . . . why you should not . . . be expelled from said Society."[21]

Instead, Goesele, his wife, his father-in-law (John George Boehringer), and disaffected members John George Jans (also Jaus), Conrad and Margaret Breymaier, and Matthew and Malinda Heilman,[22] filed suit against the Society in Tuscarawas County Court of Common Pleas on March 24, 1845. The focus of their suit was Bimeler. He was accused of "assuming to be their spiritual as well as temperal [*sic*] guide, and pretending to great sanctity, succeeded in acquiring their entire confidence, and in obtaining an almost unlimited influence over them, and by these means procured them to sign a Constitution or Articles of Association such as he desired." They blamed him for "oppression, debasement and slavery to which they and their Companions and Children have been long subjected."[23]

They claimed not to have understood the Articles of Agreement they signed surrendering their property rights: "They allege they never did, and they believe verry [*sic*] few of their associates ever did, fully and in all aspects, understand" what they had signed. Bimeler personally owned the land. The property was "acquired and accumulated" by "said Bimeler in his own name . . . without any Declaration of Trust . . . without ever using the name of said Society." Members were even refused the fruits of their labor: "[They] are for the most part denied them, being either sold, or even consumed at said Bimeler's own private Table." They accused Bimeler of living in extravagance, having a carriage when others walked, having a library when others "are not allowed time to read, being often kept hard at work till the moment of retiring to rest." To settle the suit, they asked that a full accounting be made of the Society's assets, that Bimeler be forced to testify and that "full and equal" shares be allotted to the petitioners, and that Goesele not be dismissed from the Society until their claim was adjusted.[24] Instead, the case was dismissed by the county court in November 1847.[25]

In the meantime, just as this suit was being dismissed, another one was being filed in the US District Court of Ohio. Interestingly, the complainants were not members of the Zoar Society but were citizens of Württemberg, cousins of the dismissed Johannes Goesele and children and grandchildren of the deceased Johannes Sr. Led by Johannes Sr.'s son, Johann Georg, they used their cousin's lawsuit as the basis for their own, including the attacks on Bimeler, but there was a twist: they implied that Johannes Sr. had substantially contributed to the purchase of the land before the instigation of communalism in 1819.[26]

The parties to the former Goesele suit, as well as the Weizhaar, Banzhoff, and Sieber cases adjudicated earlier, were called upon to give depositions and became part of the list of defendants, probably so no subsequent suit might endanger the complainants' envisioned gains.[27] Their testimony gives a glimpse into the workings of the Society under Bimeler and how, to certain individuals, his management might seem autocratic.

Christian Weizhaar, who had been a trustee, chafed under Bimeler's leadership. He told of an incident in which he was sent to plow an area he judged too dry. But "Bimeler insisted, and I obeyed." After an unsuccessful attempt at plowing, he abandoned the job at noon and that evening was chastised by the other trustees for not following orders. He then quit his job as trustee and later left the Society.[28]

Outsiders close to the Society also testified. One who was especially critical was Dr. Edward Caspari, who, in treating Society members, had heard their confidences. He testified that "married members complained that Bimeler instituted a system of espionage among families," that "those that still adhered to their primitive religious doctrine . . . considered Bimeler as a kind of divinely commissioned leader." Caspari thought that "about half of the members would very gladly dissolve their connection with Bimeler if they were only sure they could recover what they consider their rightful property." Former members such as Matthew Heilman weren't above insinuating that Bimeler had fathered an illegitimate child then living in the latter's home. "I think the child favors Bimeler a little in appearance," he testified.[29]

As this case wound its way through the legal system, the former members (called *Widerwärtige,* or "repugnant adversaries," by the Separatists) attempted to convince those still in the community to join them in the most forceful way. On May 7, 1849, the community found itself "invaded" by these cast-off members and their attorney, David Quinn, who occupied the Meeting House and issued a proclamation, written on broadsides, which they posted throughout the village.[30]

This manifesto, addressed to "Brothers and Sisters," claimed that they had "now returned to take possession of our property." Bimeler was still considered the foe: "Our religion has taught us that all men were equal . . . and for this cause we stood with coverd [*sic*] heads before kings. But what is now the situation of our society? One man is all—the others are naught."[31]

In a most interesting reference, these recent German immigrants refer to the overthrow of tyranny during the American Revolution: "Take for instance, the example set by the american [*sic*] colonists in the year 1776, and behold the flame which grew out of a small fire."[32] What had these dissidents learned that their fellow Society members had not? Or perhaps this was the influence of their attorney Quinn.

But economics was the real reason for their visit. These disgruntled former members wanted payment for what they considered they had contributed to the success of the Society: "After a long life of uncommon toil and labour, we have securd [*sic*] ourselves an estate of nearly half a million value. These are sufficient to make all of us rich, enabling us to spend the remainder of our days in ease and comfort, and why should we not all of us do this?" The document suggested two ways: to liquidate and divide up the assets equally or to liquidate and distribute fifty-dollar shares "in just proportion to services renderd [*sic*]."[33]

The remaining members of the community would have none of it. They passed a resolution, stating that "the aforesaid fallen-away ones cannot, nor will not, be recognized as our Brothers and Sisters as long as they continue to pursue the way of persecution that they have begun." They further resolved that "we under no circumstances intend to accept any of the offers that they are making to us." This reply ended with a support of the community of goods and the vow to leave the matter up to the courts, "the same authorities before whom they have summoned us."[34]

With that, the case wound its way through the courts, with at least three continuances. The Society spared no expense in retaining its attorneys. The lead, Thomas Ewing (1789-1871), was from a pioneer Ohio family. He served as secretary of the treasury under William Henry Harrison, organized the Department of the Interior for Zachary Taylor, and served as US senator from Ohio twice, the second time right as this case was being heard in 1850-51. His co-counsel, Henry Stanberry (1803-1881), was just as notable; he served as Ohio attorney general from 1846 until just prior to this case when he resigned. Later he served as President Andrew Johnson's attorney general and then his defense attorney in his impeachment. At the time of this case, he was in the midst of helping revise the Ohio Constitution. When not working together, Ewing and Stanberry were often rivals in the courtroom.[35] The two lawyers were paid more than two thousand five hundred dollars in legal fees over the length of the case.[36]

The case was heard in the United States Circuit Court of the Seventh District of Ohio on April 15, 1851. In those days, "the circuit courts were given no judges of their own. Instead, each circuit court had three part-time members, a district judge and two Supreme Court judges assigned to 'circuit riding' in addition to their high-court duties. Circuit courts met twice a year at each district court in their circuits. In practice, this required eight or nine sessions a year in several different states, forcing the Supreme Court Justices to spend inordinate periods of time on the road."[37]

Because of this, the Society was fortunate to have the same justice hear its case in the US Circuit Court and later in the US Supreme Court. Justice John McLean (1785-1861), an Ohioan, had been appointed to the high court in 1830. Before that, he was a congressman, the postmaster general under

John Quincy Adams, and earlier a justice on the Ohio Supreme Court.[38] He heard the circuit court case with Ohio District Court Judge Humphrey H. Leavitt.[39]

Their decision can be summarized as follows: Bimeler can hold the land in trust for the Society without a legal document; each member has an interest in the land, paid for by his or her labor; the Articles of Agreement are a contract to relinquish individual interest in the property; members have no right to alter the contract, as signing divests members of their individual right, and heirs (the folks in Germany who brought the suit) have no title, except as members; and the court may not decree a forfeiture or void the contract.[40]

Regarding the central allegation that Goesele Sr. had contributed funds to the initial purchase of the land, McLean said, "No facts are proved which authorize this conclusion. On the contrary it appears that the only money paid for the lands, shortly after their arrival at Zoar, was a pittance, which some of the members had saved of the eighteen dollars which they had each received, as a charity, in Philadelphia."[41]

He declared the communal society was a "universal partnership, known to the common law, and is not in violation of any of its principles. . . . The society is peculiar in its organization. Its members seem to have been influenced by a high sense of religious duty—and they evince a determination to reach 'a better inheritance.'" He deplored the impeachment of Bimeler's character, that it was not, in his judgment, sustained by the evidence:

> The jealousy of the human heart often finds sources of discontent in the ordinary intercourse of life . . . and many other things are considered as evidence of neglect, or intentional offense, when the person charged is innocent of the motive attributed to him. . . . This is generally the conduct of narrow minds. . . .
>
> Upon a deliberate consideration of this case, I am brought to [the] conclusion, that the complainants are not entitled to relief against the contract of their ancestor. . . . I think the agreement by the members, giving up their individual interest in the property for a common interest in the whole of it, so long as they shall remain members, is not void in law, and consequently, the bill of the complainants is dismissed.[42]

The complainants immediately appealed to the United States Supreme Court on July 18, 1851. The decision, rendered in the December term, 1852,

---

SUPREME COURT OF THE UNITED STATES.

No. 209.

JOHN G. GOESELE ET AL., APPELLANTS,

vs.

JOSEPH M. BIMELER ET AL.

APPEAL FROM THE CIRCUIT COURT OF THE UNITED STATES, FOR THE
DISTRICT OF OHIO.

The Separatists' US Supreme Court case *Goesele v. Bimeler* demonstrated that the Society's membership contract was valid, providing a precedent for other communal groups. (Title page, US Supreme Court testimony, *Goesele v. Bimeler.*)

was essentially the same as that of the circuit court, and, not surprisingly, McLean also wrote the majority opinion. As to the central question of inheritance, he declared that Goesele Sr. "had no individual right, and could transmit none to his heirs."[43]

Regarding partition of the property to provide relief to the complainants: since the Society's wealth had increased over 700 percent since Goesele Sr.'s death in 1827, "there is not a shadow of evidence to sustain the right." McLean described why seceding members could claim no interest: "If members separate themselves from the society, their interest in the property ceases, and new members that may be admitted, under the articles, enjoy the advantages common to all." He reiterated his disdain for Bimeler's detractors who claimed the leader held the land for himself, not the Society: "In this matter, the conduct of Bimeler is not only not fraudulent, but it was above reproach. It was wise and most judicious to secure the best interests of the association."[44]

But the crux of the matter was the communal nature of the organization itself:

This argument [by the complainants] does not seem to comprehend the principles of the association. . . . This is a benevolent scheme, and from its character might be properly denominated a charity. . . . It is clear the individual members could have no rights to the property, except its use, under the restrictions imposed by the articles. . . . Such an [individual] ownership would defeat the great object in view, by necessarily giving to the association a temporary character. If the interests of the members could be transferred, or pass by descent, the maintenance of the community would be impossible. [It would eventually] . . . pass out of the community into the hands of strangers, and thereby defeat the object in view.[45]

With the publication of this soon-to-be landmark decision, the Society rejoiced, even sharing the good news with their fellow communitarians, the Harmonists, who were suffering through a similar court case.[46]

But the respite was short-lived. John and Anna Maria Goesele, the former Canal Tavern landlords, having been prohibited in the previous case from furthering their suit by their relatives,[47] were now living in nearby Dover, in a state of poverty. The Society even went so far as to give these former members supplies during the summer and fall of 1852.[48] But this generosity did not stop the Goeseles from bringing suit against the Society for a second time on November 14, 1853.[49]

This time, the case focused on the fact that Anna Maria was "forced" to leave the Society when her husband was dismissed. After the ejection of her husband on March 5, 1845, the Society expressly sent her a note (which they carefully preserved in the records, perhaps knowing they might need it eight years later), telling her that the "duty as a wife and a mother being paramount to your duty as a member of said Society" gave "assurance that if now or hereafter you shall ask support from the Society your rights as a member thereof will be respected."[50] But to be supported, she would have to hold up her end of the bargain by living and working in Zoar, and that she was apparently unwilling to do.

The case in the county court was dismissed on February 3, 1854, due to the following grounds: the contract she signed when she became a member in 1833 was valid, the said contract bars such claims, the Society's liability is only to members in their employ, and the Society has complied with its contract with Anna Maria.[51]

Even with this defeat in the local court, the Goeseles doggedly appealed to the district court and then, finally, after both John and Anna Maria had died, to the state's supreme court, this time by their "heirs and assigns."

In the December term, 1862, nine long years after it was originally filed, the case was decided by the court in a dismissal delivered by Justice J. Peck: he reiterated the reasons given by the lower courts and added, "Mrs. Gasely contracted for only a qualified interest in the property to be accumulated by their joint labors, and so long as she maintained her connection with the society, she, in common with her associates, had the use and benefit of all of it, and thereby received all the compensation she had stipulated to obtain." She did "not show any present legal or equitable right to the property in which they claim to participate."[52] The "heirs and assigns" appealed the case no further.

No other suits were brought until right after the Society's dissolution in 1898, when a very few former members sued to share in the distribution of property.[53] All were dismissed.

After the Goesele case was settled in 1852, Zoar members and trustees could return to the business of being a communal society in the midst of a capitalist world, with the secure knowledge that their rights, different though they might be from their fellow citizens, were protected by the highest courts in the land—so long as they had the funds to employ an attorney or two.

CHAPTER 10

"Tested the Conviction"

Zoar and the Civil War

The Civil War tested the conviction of the community in respect of war and showed a clear line of cleavage. The older members, consistent with the principles and early belief of the Separatists [in pacifism] . . . but the younger men enthusiastically offered to go as soldiers.
　—George B. Landis, "The Society of Separatists of Zoar, Ohio," 1899

Pacifism was a bedrock tenet of the Separatist creed, as shown in Zoar Principle 11: "We cannot serve the state as bodily soldiers, since a Christian cannot murder his enemy, much less his friend."[1] How much of this belief came from their experiences in Württemberg during the Napoleonic wars, having soldiers quartered in their homes or being conscripted into King Friedrich II's army, is not known.[2]

By 1860 the friction between North and South and feelings about the institution of slavery began to affect the citizens of Zoar. Simon Beuter's diary reflects the increasing tensions. This daybook (*Tag-Buch*) is the only source we have of Zoar's contemporary thought. Here is a rundown of his diary entries for the months preceding secession:

> January 1860: Congress has been in Washington for six weeks but cannot get organized. Seemingly all that appears certain is that slavery is a blot of shame (*ein Schandfleck*) that cannot be allowed to stay.

June 1860: In both Europe and America, the fires of war are ready to burst into flames. The Society of Separatists at Zoar is faring no better than others: everyone finds fault with others, but not with oneself.

November 1860: On November 6, the presidential election passes without incident; Republican candidate Abraham Lincoln wins by "an enormous majority" (*eine ungeheure Mehrheit*).

January 1861: Only the sword appears capable of settling the dispute between North and South over the issue of slavery. The insanity of the slave-holders (*die Verrücktheit der Sklavenhalter*) leaves no room for compromise, and "the North is not going to give up any of its rights, nor should it."[3]

Zoar's young men, those born in the 1840s, composed its second genera-tion and were thus removed from the memory of the persecutions expe-rienced by their parents and grandparents in Germany. These men only knew life in tranquil Zoar and felt Americanized enough to have a patriotic urge to serve their country. In a rare instance of political commentary in their correspondence, these tensions were discussed by gardener Simon Beuter in a letter to trustee R. L. Baker of the Harmony Society in Janu-ary 1861: "What will happen now with regard to the southern states? At first everyone thought it would soon be over, but it now appears that the breach is becoming ever greater and the bitterness worse and worse. In our opinion, it would be better for the secession to take place without a war, for the long established superiority in strength of the southern states will overcome the north anyhow, and Congress does nothing but scold and quarrel. But we will have to await what comes. Only no war."[4]

The summary of Beuter's diary continues:

February 1861: South Carolina, Georgia, Florida, Alabama, and Louisi-ana secede from the Union. From the South comes nothing but violence and betrayal. The journal keeper rebukes President Buchanan's perceived ineptitude.

April 1861: Despite looming war in the South and abroad, the outlook for the Zoar fruit crop remains favorable. In the face of war between the government and the rebel slaveholders, the prospect of revolution raises its head. Virginia has seceded from the Union. Later in the month, Beuter offers various comments on Alexander II of Russia, the papacy, and Napo-leon III. The president has requested three hundred thousand troops.

May 1861: To date, eighty-one thousand volunteer troops have enlisted in Ohio.

July 1861: On Independence Day, Congress meets to discuss the war. For a week or so prior to that time, a comet has been seen in the northern heavens. Later in the month, the president requests $400 million and 400,000 troops to put down the conspiracy (*um die Verschwörung zu unterdrücken*); it is noted later in the month that Congress has in fact granted the president $500 million and 500,000 troops. "How blessed is the Union and how sad the state of the South!" Losses are reported for the First Battle of Bull Run.[5]

These entries and the number of publications subscribed to by the Separatists suggest they were well informed about current political events. It was only a matter of time before "a conflict would emerge between the Separatists' conscientious objection to war, and their ideological impulse toward conscientious participation in what they considered to be the just cause of the Union."[6]

In September 1861 Beuter noted that "seven of our youth, some of them still underage lads, have allowed themselves to be recruited. This is in direct opposition to our principles, and shows that they have not yet made [them] their own. . . . Three of these volunteers were taken back because they had not reached the necessary age, one withdrew of his own accord, and one . . . took off; there are two still in the army who came directly from our Society."[7] The Society account book gives only the family names of the recruits: "Beeler [Bühler], Kücherer, Kern, Miller, Rieker, Knöpfle" (the seventh was Simon Breil) and notes that each recruit was given two dollars in cash, so some foreknowledge of the enlistments must have occurred.

Those who returned to Zoar gave back their two dollars, but Christian Miller (who was probably the one who "took off") instead used his money to go to Economy, accompanied by a letter from his father, Michael, who wrote to Economy trustee Baker: "He committed an error in my absence by becoming a volunteer soldier, along with others. They were all not yet adults, and could get free from the recruiters, who have no right to recruit minors. . . . So his mother and I have given him the advice to go to you, which he willingly accepted, though he wishes that none would know where he is. I gladly agreed to this, for my conscience does not [allow me to] permit him to become a solider if he regrets [having taken that step]." Miller returned to Zoar in April 1862, but, according the Zoar trustee Sylvan, was "probably a lost cause" and "devoted himself to military affairs" rather than his job of printing books.[8]

Simon Breil and Samuel Knöpfle remained enlisted in Company B of the 51st Ohio Volunteer Regiment, and both returned to Zoar after the war, became members of the Society, and worked (Breil as a tanner and Knöpfle as a tailor).[9] Unfortunately, we have none of their letters home from the field in the Zoar Papers, so we are unable to know more about their war experiences.

For those remaining in Zoar, the next year saw more questioning by its young men. Was it their duty to serve? An unsigned essay asks, "Do you consider yourself a patriot? . . . Let us now decide by what means we can best contribute to this cause. We must act, for God has richly supplied us with the means necessary to do so. . . . Let us send ourselves into the unavoidable fray, be it ever so arduous, and offer our every power to suppress this terrible rebellion in the shortest time possible."[10]

It was only a month later until, in the summer of 1862, that the following notice was given:

> The undersigned wish to let you know herewith that they intend soon to leave for Cleveland, Ohio in order to enter the German Regiment there . . . [though] we would not have decided to take this step if it could have been avoided. However, since soon there will be a lottery, we wish to enlist now. We know that it is contrary to the Principles of the Separatists to go to war, but now, in this present crisis, in order to contend for freedom and human rights, we feel it our duty to unite our forces with those who, at the first call, sacrifice all, indeed their most precious lives, in order to contend on behalf of those who cannot fight for posterity and for a free home. We await an approval or rejection of our appeal.
>
> Signed with greatest amicability,
>
> [no signatures on the extant copy][11]

Did the trustees know about this beforehand? What was the "appeal" referred to in the last line? Did the boys steal away in the night, as Zoar legend has it? If so, it was an open secret, as mothers, sisters, and sweethearts made copies of Psalm 91 for each to carry with them.[12] ("A thousand shall fall at thy side, and ten thousand at thy right hand; but it shall not come nigh thee." [Verse 7] and "For he shall give his angels charge over thee, to keep thee in all thy ways." [Verse 11]) for each to carry with them.

These volunteers were John Brunny, age 22; Anton (Anthony) Burkhart, age 22; John Geissler, age 21; Gottfried Kappel, age 22; Leo Kern, age 20; John Kücherer, age 19; Christian Rieker, age 20; Franz (Frank) Strobel, age

22; Daniel Unsöld, age 25; Eugene B. Wright, age 20; and Adam Zeib, age 18. They were assigned to Company I of the 107th Ohio Volunteer Infantry, officially entered the armed forces on August 22, 1862, were mustered in on September 9 of that year, and, except for death or incapacity, were mustered out on July 10, 1865.

Subsequent Zoar histories state that fourteen young men joined the Union Army. With the addition of the two from 1861, the above make only thirteen; the fourteenth is Jacob Thumm, age 18, whose parents were not Zoar members, but hired laborers. In addition, there are more men with Zoar connections who joined during 1862-64, making a total of as many as 24: John Breil, age 23; Magnus Burkhart, age 20; John Jähle (age uncertain); Frederick Kücherer, age 21; George Kümmerle, age 21; Jacob Kümmerle, age 23; John Kuemmerle, age 18; Huldereich Langlotz (age uncertain); John Smith, age 24; and Lucas Strobel, age 19.

The 107th Ohio Volunteer Infantry (OVI) was a regiment whose members were primarily of German descent.[13] The Zoar volunteers probably joined it so they could be with others who spoke the same language.

The Society trustees were in a quandary. Did they forsake their core belief in pacifism at the risk of being seen as unpatriotic? Already they had donated clothing and money to the Soldiers' Aid Society in nearby Dover,[14] and were truly sympathetic to the Union cause and the abolition of slavery. But were they to lose all of their eligible young men to the draft? An explanation of their case and a plea for assistance was sent to Ohio governor David Tod, dated September 23, 1862:

> In consequence of their views held sacred by their fathers, and now by them, living there under the despotic Government of King Fredrick the 2d of Württemberg, they suffered imprisonment, confiscation of property, and had to endure numerous other personal tortures for a period of from 12 to 16 years, until at last the king became convinced, that no change could be wrought upon their minds and resolutions, satisfied himself that they would rather suffer death, than violate the convictions of their consciences. . . .
>
> The present unhappy and unfortunate condition of our country, however, by the late conscription act of Congress requires of them such services, which they for the reasons stated conscientiously and most earnestly have to protest against. . . .
>
> [This paragraph, with the exception of the last sentence, appears in the German version only.] Because our members are unbound in every respect

(*in jeder Beziehung ungebunden*) and—according to our Constitution—can only be asked to render voluntary but never forced services, they can take charge of their persons as they wish. Therefore, if by entering the army they have disregarded our principles and have not fully acknowledged them, such action cannot be assumed to be normative (*deßwegen ist es nicht als Richtschnur anzunehmen*). The Society as a whole still maintains the same principles as in the beginning. Twenty eight between the ages of 18 and 45, including some not fit for service, still remain. . . .

That they are ready, prepared, and willing, in lieu of any military services, to make such a pecuniary sacrifice, as the proper authority may assess against them, and trust and pray, that through your kind attention, assistance, power and influence, the object of their wishes may be accomplished and truly relieve them from the discharge of a service, which, by the teachings of divine law and the promptings of their consciences they can and dare not perform.[15]

This petition was signed by the three trustees and more than two dozen other men, many of whom were too old to serve. The German version, tellingly titled "Reasons Why the Separatists Should Not Perform Any War Duties,"[16] with its addition of a statement absolving the Society from the responsibility of the actions of the volunteers, was more for the eyes of its own members than those of the Ohio governor.

The Society, at the same time, did not forget those who had volunteered and who were now stationed in Cleveland. The Zoar account books show a visit to the recruits by John Brunny Sr., father of one of them, on September 5 with a "Box [of] Sundries for Volunteers."[17] An unsigned letter of thanks, addressed to "Esteemed Friends," followed: "Since we have no opportunity just now to thank you in person for your kind sharing, we wish to express, through these few lines, our most heartfelt gratitude for all the acts of friendship that you showed us earlier, and now again recently."[18] This was the first of many boxes sent to Zoar soldiers in the field during the course of the war.

Cleveland industrialist Charles J. Woolson, who frequently visited the Zoar Hotel with his family and developed a close relationship with the Separatists, took the opportunity to visit the recruits and wrote to Christian Wiebel: "I went several times to see your young men who have enlisted, to ascertain that they were comfortable. At first, some of them appeared a little homesick, but afterwards they were in better spirits. I think they will do their duty, and prove themselves good soldiers."[19]

From the many letters sent home, we can follow the lives of a few of these Zoar soldiers. On September 25, John Brunny, while stationed at Camp Wallace, near Covington, Kentucky, was getting to know the sometimes inane life as a soldier. He reports on an all-day "march to nowhere": "To our greatest dismay, we only then realized that the entire march was an exemplary masterpiece of stupidity and inability on the part of our leaders, for the place where we now are located is barely two miles away from our previous camp, and could have been reached in one hour."[20]

Back at Zoar, the trustees were granted just part of their request to Governor Tod. Instead of total exemption from service, they had to pay a two-hundred-dollar penalty for those who were subject to the draft. Two young men from Zoar, Levi Bimeler and Christian Ruof, were selected in the Tuscarawas County draft lottery and their penalties duly paid.[21]

One of that summer's volunteers, Eugene B. Wright, was not faring well. He became ill with diphtheria and rheumatism soon after enlistment.[22] From Camp Delaware (near Columbus) on October 16, he wrote to his commanding officer requesting leave: "I am taking the liberty of directing my lines to you and therein laying forth my wish, namely to request a leave from you until I am again capable of serving. For, I believe, my illness could be healed sooner if I were at home, since I would not be exposed to all the various harsh weather such as we have here. In my present condition I cannot be of use to my fatherland, but much rather a hindrance, if I need to be fed and clothed by the government when I cannot render any service in return."[23]

A few words should be said here about Wright. He was brought to Zoar as an infant and brought up "as one of their own" in the household of David Sylvan, son of trustee Jacob, and David's wife, Jacobina. He was not exactly an orphan (his father made occasional appearances during his life) and was an intelligent and introspective young man who was given, in addition to his regular schooling, "two hours of instruction in the evening from my good friend J. M. Bäumler, preacher and leader of the community." Philip Webber, in his book *Zoar in the Civil War,* speculates that Wright may have been groomed for community leadership by Bimeler.[24] Wright was raised with the Sylvans' son, David Jr., who is the recipient of many of Wright's letters.

Happily, the Zoar manuscript collection contains a treasure-trove of Wright's writings. Included is an incomplete autobiography, wherein Wright shows both his gratitude and ambivalence regarding his Zoar upbringing, decrying Zoar's "narrow-mindedness in religious and political matters."[25] He felt both "of Zoar" and "not of Zoar" and chafed at the

Society's rules and regulations for young people. His writings show a naive patriotism, a professed faith in God, and much self-criticism. In a prewar statement of principles dated January 1861, the eighteen-year-old Wright wrote: "In the present political crisis, if necessary, I would join my countrymen and fellow-citizens to serve for my beloved country and liberty, as liberty is a great blessing of our God; happy must anybody, or a whole nation, be in the enjoyment of that blessing (bestowed to the American nation by kind Providence), if only it would not be misused!"[26] The realities of soldiering in a disease-ridden camp changed Wright's youthful goals.

On October 22, 1862, Christian Rieker writes to his family from Camp Delaware on the occasion of his twenty-first birthday. He speculates on his future: "How long I shall live or shall yet spend in this state, is something that I do not know. There is One who knows all that, as you yourselves realize, and we shall just allow Him to take care of the matter. . . . And now, we must once more move along. Yesterday we received marching orders, and we don't even know just when we need to get moving, or where we are headed. Some say we are going to Washington . . . For my part, I believe we are going to join the troops commanded by Siegel."[27]

Rieker was correct. The "Siegel" mentioned was German-born Maj. Gen. Franz Siegel (also Sigel; 1824–1902), commander of the 11th Corps, of which the 107th OVI was to become a part. Siegel was noted for his ability to recruit and motivate German immigrant troops, who often sang "I'm going to fight mit Siegel" to the tune of "The Girl I Left Behind Me." By the time the 107th saw much action, Siegel had been succeeded in command of the 11th Corps by General O. O. Howard. It's not known if Siegel's German background had any influence on the Zoar enlistees.

Eugene Wright, who by this time had returned to the regiment, wrote to David Sylvan on November 22, 1862, from Fairfax Courthouse, Virginia: "I soon found my comrades, who are all healthy, safe and sound as ever. It appears that Leo [Kern] enjoyed good times in the hospital, because when he came out, he weighed 166 lbs., which doesn't indicate any great [weight] loss. . . . The box is not yet here, but we have apprised the quartermaster so that he will deliver it to us. . . . General Siegel also visited this regiment and told the officers and soldiers how they should act, and that right and justice should prevail, which in any case would be of paramount importance in such a situation."[28]

John Brunny, writing from Stafford Courthouse, Virginia, on December 22, 1862, commented on the regiment's reduced troop strength and, echoing the lament of all soldiers about the lack of quality food: "The regiments near us are all reduced, most of them consisting of only 200 to 300 men. . . . As for food, we really have enough. I'll remain quiet about the quality, since the very word 'Crackers' sickens me. Yesterday again we received two potatoes per man, something we'd not had in some time."[29]

Eugene Wright had been demoted from sergeant to private on December 1, 1862.[30] It's conceivable his inability to serve may have had a role, as did his agitating to try to obtain conscientious objector status or petitioning the Zoar trustees to find a substitute for him. On January 20, 1863, the trustees wrote to Wright:

> As we now see from your letter, you have no prospect of being freed or released from military service because of Biblical scruples, and have found yourself moved by a certain inner drive to decline all military service as entirely against true spirituality, the teachings of our Lord and Master, and against the Principles of Separation.
>
> Now concerning the possibility mentioned in your letter of obtaining a substitute for you, and that that might be easier achieved here, such is not the case. We would never be able to come to peace with ourselves for going against our conscience. Also, you can no doubt judge, or might know, into what a position we [you?] put the Trustees in such a case, and that we cannot lightly do such a thing without subjecting ourselves to sure reproach, or without arousing dissatisfaction if we were to pay a certain sum of money on your behalf. . . .
>
> Moreover, we have been informed by persons who know for certain that it is very difficult, if not impossible, to find a man who would voluntarily enlist in the place of another. . . .
>
> It may seem unexpectedly harsh to receive such news, but that is all we can do at this time, and under the present circumstances. We commend you to the special protection of God and his grace, that he may soon again lead you back into our midst, safe and sound.[31]

As Philip Webber notes, Wright's request had put the trustees in an awkward position. Unlike those potential draftees for whom the Society had paid penalties, Wright had enlisted voluntarily. In a subsequent letter, dated February 19, trustee Jacob Ackermann suggested that Wright might volunteer for an officer's commission, serve for a time, and then resign. This was something the moralistic Wright was unwilling to do. In a second letter, dated March 13, 1863, an exasperated Ackermann urges Wright to accept a noncombatant role instead, as the ends would justify the means: "Many others take advantage of such an opportunity in order to be free of the repulsive state of serving as a soldier."[32]

Ignoring Ackermann's advice, Wright remained a soldier in the field. He grew impatient with his status, writing David Sylvan on March 27, 1863, from Brooks Station, Virginia: "Up until now, there has been no change in my fate, for which I am really wishing, as I am fatigued by uncertainty. Still, the Almighty knows why it is going this way."[33] When the 107th left Brooks Station in late April 1863, Wright was not among the troops—he was on his way back to Zoar, a deserter.

Christian Rieker wrote to his sister, Maria Ruof, from Brooks Station on April 12 of a special visitor, a visit he and the other Zoar soldiers would remember all their lives: "Abraham Lincoln and his wife . . . visited the entire Potomac Army. . . . He visited each corps [*corps* appears in English] individually, and the generals were with him. The soldiers had to pass in review there in front of him, each corps in turn, especially the artillery and cavalry and infantry. It was quite something to see. . . . I believe that if we go at it again, they will get *hell* [*hell* appears in English] from us; but will we get none?"[34]

And "go at it" they did, at the Battle of Chancellorsville, beginning April 30, 1863. Rieker wrote to his sister on May 11, 1863. In the letter he refers to Psalm 91:7-9, copies of which were given to the Zoar soldiers:

Dear Sister! With greatest joy I take up the pen, in order to let you know again how I am doing, and that I am still alive, and this is indeed a very great miracle. However, for God all things are possible. Just as is written in the Psalm, though a thousand fall on your left and a thousand on your right, it shall not strike you, for it is God who stands by your side to help you [*dir beisteht*], as I myself have now seen.

Many fell on my right and on my left, yet it did not harm me in the least. The bullets just whistled by [my] head like a true hailstorm; they simply whistled a little worse, as you can imagine for yourselves. Still, I sprang through it all like a rabbit, though I left my knapsack behind for the rebels.[35]

Those at Zoar observed Lincoln's call for a "Day of National Humiliation, Fasting and Prayer" on April 30. A statement, which was probably written by the newly arrived deserter Eugene Wright, reaffirmed the Society's principles and patriotism. It reads, in part:

Their Principles are entirely according to the teachings of the Gospel, among which is: in no instance to avenge oneself in a warlike manner or to practice the use of murderous weapons, but to suffer death rather than to murder one's fellow-human or even one's greatest enemy. Hence, these their Principles forbid them to go to war, even to fight for their own rights. Because their trust is placed in God, they heed God's proclamation: "Vengeance is mine, I shall repay." In this they are therefore doing what their Principles allow, something that no one can deny them in a free country. Moreover the Society, made up of Separatists, is absolutely for preservation of the Union, and the compassion for the fallen and wounded in the service of our fatherland is widespread whenever reports of such incidents are received. In order to keep abreast of such reports, one and one half times as many newspapers are currently received as were earlier. These are read with the greatest attention to the latest reports received by *mail and telegraph*.[36]

Being in the same unit, the Zoar soldiers kept track of one another. Christian Rieker in his letter to his sister Maria on May 30, 1863, reports on fellow enlistee Gottfried Kappel, asks about Eugene Wright, and relates more about his battle experiences:

I was so glad to read that you are all still healthy, as I myself still am, and as are the others, with the exception of Gottfried Kappel, who has been sick just about the whole time since we returned from our last battle. He has nervous fever [*Nervenfieber:* neurasthenia?] and is very sick. He is unaware of what is happening around him. Often he wants to leave, and when we ask him where, he says to Zoar. I don't have much confidence in his recovery, but we want to hope for the best. In general, quite a few are dying from the same illness in our regiment.

You also wrote me that you had to laugh when you heard that we had to run so much [when under attack]. True, it is funny to hear about, but it wasn't funny anymore for me when I had to run. I just had to pay attention to the bombs being shot at me. I pulled in my bulging [i.e., pack-laden] back whenever one came toward me.

I also let my backpack fly away, though I don't know how far it flew. Perhaps it is already in Tennessee with some rebel. I regret very much letting go of it, but at the same time, my life was dearer to me than my backpack.

And now I would like to know where our honest and loyal Eugene [B. Wright] is. He once said that it would not be right if he were a lieutenant,

The Civil War was a watershed event in Zoar, with many of its young men enlisting, despite the community's pacifism. Stenciled on this American flag are the names of some of the enlistees. (Courtesy of the Ohio History Connection, Properties Collection, P365AV.)

and then went home. As we once said to him, he should become an officer and then he could resign and return home. But he did not think that it was right to do things that way, though it would have been better than breaking his oath and deserting, as he now has done. That shows his piety for what it really is. When he was here among us, he said it was a sin to kill, and so on and so forth. But he is not at all what I thought he was. He didn't even say goodbye to us. He just indicated that he didn't know if he would see us again.

In short: I must close now. I remain your Brother

Christian Rieker

[top margin, last page] I have lost my respect for Eugene. He is not a man.[37]

In June, the Society received word that Kappel had died on June 12. Simon Beuter reacted to it in this way: "Gottfried Kappel is reported to have died in the army hospital, the first to have forfeited his life in this rash undertaking [*diese voreilige Unternehmung*]."[38] The exact meaning of "rash undertaking" is not clear—did he mean the war itself, or the fact that Zoar boys enlisted in it?

Soldiers' pay was often enclosed in letters for safekeeping. Franz Strobel sent fifty dollars home to David Sylvan on June 6, 1863:

Friend David!
Divide the enclosed as follows:
from G[ottfried] Kappel $30 to his father,
Leo Kern $15.00 to Levi Beumler [Bimeler]
J. Kücherer $5.00 to John Breimeyer[39]

Such cash was duly kept on account in the Society coffers for each soldier. Family members could, with the soldier's permission, withdraw cash when needed.

The 107th participated in the battle of Gettysburg, July 1-3, 1863. Two Zoar soldiers, Leo Kern, who subsequently spent time at the notorious Andersonville Prison, and Christian Rieker, were both captured. According to Hilda Morhart, Kern was captured because he returned to the battlefield to retrieve his backpack.[40] Maria Ruof, Rieker's sister, to whom he had written so many letters, sent a package of food to him in prison, accompanied by a letter, on December 5, 1863, and cautions: "I am so afraid that when you receive your *box* you will eat too much [before your system adjusts to a normal diet], and everyone says that then there is nothing more that can be done to help you. I plead with you, dear brother, do not eat too much, and thank God from your heart that he has helped you thus far." In the box was a bag of *Riwele* or dry noodles, to which she gives preparation instructions, to boil them in a little bit of water or broth. "You don't need many to make a full kettle."[41]

Morgan's Raid in the summer of 1863 brought the war home to Ohio. Gen. John Hunt Morgan and his cavalry spread terror through Indiana and Kentucky as well as the Buckeye State. In late July, after several skirmishes, including the Battle of Buffington's Island on the Ohio River, his troops veered north to nearby Carroll and Columbiana Counties, putting locals, including the Zoarites, on edge. When word spread that Morgan might be close, Jacob Lubold, a Zoar hired hand, took his rifle and stood in the doorway of the hotel, determined to shoot any who dared to enter. When horsemen were heard galloping into town, Lubold ran into the road shooting his rifle in the air, not at Morgan's raiders, but at pranksters from Bolivar, out to scare the Separatists.[42]

The trustees were still attempting to find a way to keep the Society's remaining men from having to serve. A document, signed by twenty-four young men and dated July 10, 1863, states in English, "We the undersigned, do hereby declare, that we can not conscientiously perform militia or military duty, as required by the late militia law of the State of Ohio, but instead are willing to pay such fine, to which we, as citizens of the state and of the United States may reasonably and equitably be subjected to." A sheaf of receipts for two-dollar fines for nonperformance at the September 29, 1863, Lawrence Township military muster are labeled with names almost identical to the signers. Yet another petition was sent, this time to the Ohio General Assembly, asking if labor on public works could be substituted for the fines.[43]

This nonperformance of military duty did not prevent the Society from assisting the families of others who were serving. An 1863 article in the New Philadelphia *Ohio Democrat* listed the Society as lending over $8,000 to the county for "the relief of families of volunteers." A study of the Society's cash books shows it was more like $10,900 in loans at interest rates of 8 percent and 6 percent between 1862 and 1863. They also bought US bonds to fund the war effort, gaining $5,225 in bond interest in 1864.[44]

Not all Zoar soldiers served in the infantry. John Geissler, after somehow injuring his feet and spending time as a hospital patient, served as a nurse. He writes from Mount Pleasant General Hospital in Washington, DC, on October 4, 1863: "I was transferred last week to Ward 6 as a nurse. I am no longer in the tents, we have it harder here, and we have a lot of work. There are thirty-two beds in each ward, with five nurses [per ward?]. I need to stay up all night long, but still, it is better than in the field. I could have been transferred to a Band if I were in an invalid choir, but that is not possible."[45]

His comrades John Brunny and Huldreich Langlotz did serve as musicians. Brunny writes on December 25-29, 1863, from Folly Island, South Carolina, near Charleston, where the 107th had been transferred after the battle of Gettysburg: "Our band consists of twenty men. Since only two of us blow the lead part [*da wir aber nur zum zweit Lead blasen*], you can understand that it is not so very easy, with uniform on, parading around [*herumstolzieren*], until the lips are sore. That, at least, is past, because the skin becomes thick as leather if one does nothing for a year and a half but blow. Earlier, however, it was terribly bothersome [*plagend übel*]."[46]

Langlotz, a nonmember who was married to Friedrika Rieker, Christian's sister, wrote his father-in-law, Jacob, on January 31, 1864: "Because all our musical instruments were broken during the battle at Chickamauga and we have not played since then, our commanding officer has decided to send us back to Camp Thomas, which he will probably do in February."[47]

John Geissler, in a letter dated March 3, 1864, upon his arrival from Folly Island to Jacksonville, Florida, wrote to his family about his culinary experiences in the field: "I just wish you could have seen how we baked cake for ourselves. One fellow had an old shovel and another a rusted can and some put the dough on pieces of bread and held it to the fire. In the beginning, we didn't even have salt. That was quite a story. If one is hungry, one can make do with anything; this is especially so for the soldier. When I come home, I'll be able to eat everything."[48]

On March 19, 1864, Eugene Wright died of tuberculosis at Zoar at age twenty-one. Two undated and unsigned items are attributed to him and seem to have been written just before his death. In the first, a draft of a letter to his comrades, he appears to urge them to follow his example, that of desertion of duty: "I can only wish that you yourself might experience such a great evidence of God's love, grace, and compassion, and that he might also lead you out of the slavery of the military as he has done for me, which no one thought possible. . . . All things are possible to him who believes."[49]

Although undated, this second item may have been written by Wright as a farewell: "My God, you have protected me in such a fatherly manner up to this point, kept me in the face of many a physical and spiritual danger, and since I can do nothing of myself, I ask you at the beginning of this year that you would further protect me from sin and other attacks; that you would bless my heart with wisdom, understanding, and the recognition of good and evil so that I may live my life to please you and benefit my fellow-man; and that you would not take me, in my sinful state, from this earth into speedy judgment. This I pray of you kind Father, for you alone are in a position to grant this to me. Amen."[50]

Simon Beuter continued to follow the progress of the war in his diary. Webber notes, "If there is one trend that is consistent in Beuter's journal for the Civil War years, it is this: he did not want to fight the war, but delighted in cheering for his favored side in the conflict."[51] At the end of August 1864, Beuter traveled to Cincinnati, attempting to hire substitutes for the Zoar men, and comments on the conditions in "the world" as compared to those in isolated Zoar:

Esteemed Friend,

I am herewith letting you know how the prospects are for volunteers here. Today we worked as much as we could from morning until now; the success was not altogether bad, we have enlisted two men, and have the pledge of nine men until tomorrow at 9:00, but the price is high: we cannot get them for less than the $450 reported yesterday, and the costs for Haly and Stout, though I just saw a man who demanded the same amount and no more. If he can do something, we can get through the matter that much quicker. If we do not offer the above sum, there are others who are glad to pay it, and I am even more afraid because people are still coming who are looking for recruits. The city is almost full.

Now you [plural] should write to us right away whether we should proceed or not; naturally, it will cost our Society some of the $1,000 that was last promised; at first I thought we could get by without using it, but at the above-mentioned price that won't be the case. But if I could advise, I would not consider the matter of money, since the people at home have absolutely no idea what a soldier's life is like. Just in the camps, those who have just come from their homes are almost all sick, since they get nothing but hard crackers and stinking bacon. And, if our people would actually come into the hospitals, Zoar would be a paradise by comparison. Folks who have lived so long in Zoar don't have any notion what a desolate world it is, despite the small passing inconveniences [at Zoar].[52]

A penciled note on the envelope containing this letter indicates acceptance of the $450 price.

As the conflict continued, the Separatists paid $1,200 on January 25, 1865, into the Lawrence Township volunteer fund as Lincoln asked for additional troops.[53]

The end of the war, Lincoln's assassination, and the execution of the assassins were all noted in Beuter's diary. In December he states that all of the Zoar soldiers, save the deceased Gottfried Kappel and Eugene Wright, had returned home.

And it was in Zoar that some, but not all of them, stayed. Early enlistees Simon Breil and Samuel Knopfle became members and remained in Zoar for the rest of their lives. Anton Burkhart, Leo Kern, John Kuecherer, and Christian Rieker of the 107th did the same. John Brunny, Franz Strobel, Daniel Unsöld, and Magnus Burkhart stayed in the area but never became members. John Geissler, who had already become a probationary member before his enlistment, did not stay. An extant letter shows him in Marysville, Ohio, northwest of Columbus, in 1869.[54]

Interestingly, the Society was still paying militia fines ("Commutation & Millage") to John Willard, deputy treasurer (presumably of Tuscarawas County) on October 4, 1865—$30 each for Salmon Rauschenberger, Jacob Brunny, John Ruof, Christian Ruof, and William Ansbacher. This was nearly six months after the war's end on April 12, 1865.[55]

In researching this book, the author came across one of the Zoar financial ledger books. In it, under "Domestic [i.e., Society members'] Bills Payable," are entries for the pay received by the soldiers who had returned to the Society, Kuemmerle and Knöpfle among them, as well as those funds deposited for Gottfried Kappel just prior to his death. Entries also included money received for their Civil War pensions. There is no indication that any of these former soldiers ever drew upon these funds, although it probably was paid out to them or their heirs at the 1898 dissolution. Somehow, this says much about just how strong the communal bond still was among those who had served—the money they had earned by laying their lives on the line belonged not to them, but to the Society.[56]

The strain put on the Society by the Civil War was a lasting one. No longer did the beliefs brought from Württemberg hold sway over the entire community. The trustees wrestled with the question of how "patriotic" and Americanized the Society should become. They realized that no lofty principle, no matter how noble, would exempt their young men from the draft. For those who returned after the war to its welcoming arms, the Society was again a place of refuge, but the outside world was brought ever closer to Zoar through their wartime experiences.

CHAPTER 11

"Applicants of Good Character"

Membership in the Zoar Society

We have accepted new members up to the present time, and I think we will keep on doing so; but our doors are only open to applicants of good character.

—Zoar interviewee to William Alfred Hinds, *American Communities*, 1878

"Jacob Ackermann: Dear sir: I would rather say brother, but as I am a stranger to you I will waite untill we are better acquainted, *which I hope will soon be;* I have been a communist at heart for two years and trying by *God's Grace* to prepair myself for the great work which I faithfully believe he has called me to, namely to live in and work for a *Christian Community.*"[1]

Thus begins a typical letter to the Separatist Society of Zoar requesting membership. Although this letter is undated, it probably was written soon after the 1878 publication of William A. Hinds's *American Communities,* which is mentioned in the letter. Both this book, and more prevalently, Charles F. Nordhoff's *Communistic Societies of the United States,* occasioned numerous written requests for admission as members of this German communal society.

After the decision to become communal in 1819, as the Zoar Society prospered, newcomers from Germany, most with ties, either familial or religious, to current members, arrived frequently during these early years. So many wanted to join that the trustees insisted new members sign a contract as early as 1820.[2] Signing this trial contract, or *probe-kontrekt,* gave them all the rights of members except voting or holding office and they need not surrender their property. They also promised to "obey the orders of the Trustees as long as their strength and health would permit." The trustees, in turn, promised to furnish the probationary members with housing, food, and "not less than two suits" of clothing. This provision did not become a part of their governing document until the 1833 Constitution, when a year's probationary period was specified for new members and a new probationary membership category (first class) was formally instituted.[3]

The prospective probationary member had to apply to and be accepted by the trustees for a trial period of at least one year, "without exception, even if born and educated in the Society." Males had to reach the age of twenty-one, and females had to be age eighteen to be first-class members. Probationers pledged "to use all their industry and skill in behalf of the exclusive benefit of the said Separatist Society of Zoar;" and to put their minor children under the exclusive guardianship and care of the trustees.[4] After probation, prospective members, "by their own free will and accord," would again apply to the trustees, "who shall make it known to the Society, at least thirty days previous" to allow for any objections by the entire membership before signing the contract for second-class, or full, membership.

The conduct of members was spelled out. Article 4 forbade "profane language, immoral words or acts" and called for all "to endeavor to set good examples and to cherish general and mutual love." "Good and moral behavior" based on "the principles of holy writ" were to be observed by both members and officers.

Article 6 obligated members to place all money in their possession with the trustees, but they could withdraw sums for "extra necessities." First-class members could, if still probationers, withdraw the entire sum without penalty upon leaving the Society. There were always many more first-class members than second, with a primary reason being they could take out this money if they left the group. In later years, a potential member might work for wages instead of immediately entering the probationary class.[5]

New members were expected to reveal any debts and absolve the Society for such indebtedness. Concealment of debts was grounds for dismissal. The time to transition from being a first-class member to a second-class member varied but averaged about four years. William A. Hinds of the Oneida Community, came to Zoar in the 1870s to do research for his book *American Communities*. He received this reply to a question about the two classes of membership: "Some are perfectly satisfied with their present position and don't care to enter the higher class. This may in a few cases be owing to the fact, that so long as a person remains in the first class he can withdraw any money he put into the common fund on joining the Community, and use it as he likes; but on joining the second class there is an entire surrender of all property rights."[6] During the latter years of the Society, some probationers never became second-class members but remained in the first class, enjoying the benefits of membership, but never fully committing to it. Some of these long-time first-class members quickly joined the second class when the decision was made to dissolve the Society so they could claim a full share in the proceeds.[7]

The greatest increase in membership was from 1830 to 1834, when at least 170 persons were taken into the community. Hinds was told by his Society informant that the membership reached its highest population, "never quite five hundred," by 1834, the year of the cholera epidemic.[8]

Hinds's interviewee continues:

> We generally pay wages for a year or more to applicants, so that they may have time and opportunity to get acquainted with us and we with them. If the acquaintance proves mutually satisfactory, and they again apply for admission to the Community, they are admitted as probationary members and sign the Articles of the First Class. If during the next year they commend themselves they may make application for admission to the second class, and if there is no good ground of rejection will be admitted; when they give up their property forever. Rich people seldom apply for membership, and we are glad of it. We would rather take poor people, half naked though they may be, provided they have the right character.[9]

Some of these new members, as noted, heard about the group through relatives still living in Germany.[10] In these early years, the Society needed labor, and still felt the close ties to the motherland. Such affiliated immigration seems to have ceased by about 1850, although Hinds's interviewee claims they were still accepting new members in 1878: "Our doors are only open to applicants of good character."[11]

World events were the cause of later petitions to join the Society, especially Germans caught in the great wave of immigration to the United States after the 1848 German Revolution. Many, like potter Roman Blaser of New Braunfels, Texas, still did not feel at home here, as he wrote in 1852: "It is certain that Texas does not suit me, because . . . it is too hot . . . and the people have no money. . . . So, I would like to ask you, if there would not be something in my trade . . . whereby I could support myself."[12]

But the great majority of extant letters of application to the Zoar Society date from the 1870s and early 1880s, coinciding with the 1875 publication of Charles Nordhoff's *The Communistic Societies of the United States*. Nordhoff (1830–1901), was born in Prussia and came to Cincinnati to live at age five. As a youth, he was apprenticed to a printer but enlisted in the navy at age fourteen and worked on ships around the world until age twenty-three when he took up journalism, eventually becoming an editor at the *New York Post*. He left the *Post* in 1871 to travel and write what became his best-known work.

This book, in the words of one reviewer, "is not historical, except incidentally, but aims to show what is the present condition, material and moral, now existing" and "is chiefly a detailed account of the mode of life."[13] Its detail is something we contemporary historians are forever grateful for.

Its publication coincides with the Panic of 1873, the contraction of the world economy after the Civil War, which began with the failure of many railroads, including Jay Cooke's Northern Pacific, and resulted in tight credit, bank failures, and factory closings. This disruption in the economy left many looking for an alternate way out of "this wicked and uncharitable struggle," as one petitioner put it.[14]

Nordhoff's treatment of Zoar is fairly accurate, but not flattering. He calls the Separatists "unintellectual" and "dull and lethargic" and says that Joseph Bimeler left "no marks to show he strove for or desired a higher life here, . . . or valued beauty, or . . . comfort." However, Nordhoff noted that "the amount of ingenuity and business skill which they have developed is quite remarkable," and ended his chapter with the statement, "when I saw how much roughness there is in the life of the country people, I concluded that . . . [Zoar] was perhaps still a step higher . . . than the average life of the surrounding country."[15]

With such a mixed review, it is perhaps surprising that Zoar received so many requests for membership and information. The extant letters received

Facing page: Despite his lukewarm appraisal of the Zoar community, the publishers of Charles Nordhoff's 1875 book, *Communistic Societies of the United States,* chose this compilation of Zoar scenes as the frontispiece of the volume. Zoar's inclusion in this review of nineteenth-century American communalism brought Zoar many applications for membership as well as unwanted publicity. (Frontispiece, *Communistic Societies of the United States,* by Charles Nordhoff, 1874.)

OLD CHURCH. THE MILL.

BAUMELER'S RESIDENCE.

LOG HUTS. STREET VIEW.

between the publication of Nordhoff's book in 1875 and the year 1880 will be considered here, but so many letters were received by the Separatists in the last years of the Society that they had a form letter of rejection drawn up to send.[16] The letter writers can be divided into six distinct groups, with some overlap. The first are those from unhappy Germans, longing for a taste of home. Next, and most prevalent, are seekers of religious truth, who, after reading Nordhoff's (as well as William A. Hinds's) cursory look at the Separatist religion, felt they had found a spiritual home. Freethinkers and self-proclaimed Socialists were another group. The dismal economy brought letters from those looking for jobs and security as well as former Civil War soldiers seeking refuge. Lastly are several letters from Shakers or former Shakers, who knew communal life, but wanted a change.

Julius Ulmer, writing in broken English from Philadelphia, calls himself a "lost sheep looking for a harbor" who "couldn't find a place where really peace is at home." He comes not empty-handed, but with "small capital" he would like to "place it in the way to secure me a home forever, where I could tend to the soul by doing not too rough Work besides. . . . I am a native German, and I don't feel happy till yet in this country. I am looking for peace and I am sure their [*sic*] is a place for me where I find some."[17]

T. H. Rose of Marietta, Ohio, wrote "I have been reading . . . Nordhoff's book and have been captured by it. . . . Of all the communes I have read about, yours meets my unqualified approval. . . . I was born in Vermont—do not speak German—but have always had a great respect for the German people. . . . I have no means, but long for just such a home as yours—away from the idle, swearing and wicked world. . . . You would find me a steady, quiet, industrious man with good moral habits—and a desire to be good and do good."[18]

A couple from Illinois asked to become members so they could "rear their children near devout people." Rudolph Hoffman of Newark, New Jersey, asked if he could become a "spiritual member." K. Codman of Massachusetts, an illiterate thirty-year-old painter, professed in a dictated letter that he "has some knollege of your faith and accepts it. . . . My faith is strong and I am willing to work. We all want to do what we think is right and I think if I could join your Community I could be a benefit to you and myself." W. P. Carter, a merchant from Montgomery, Alabama, stated he had embraced the Separatist faith. After he was refused admission, he wrote again, remonstrating that he thought "every good citizen 'possessed of principle' was accepted."[19]

Those professing to be Socialists or Communists include the aforementioned George Biggars, who claimed to have "read very carefully the *American Socialist*,"[20] the newspaper edited by William A. Hinds that discussed communal living, and one H. Cadwallader of Wilmington, Delaware, who wrote, "Having read something of communities of late in general and of yours in particular. . . . I think I like your mode of living rather better that the others, as it seems to be more liberal than the Shakers, Inspirationists or Harmonists. . . . I think the life of a Communist is pre-eminently the best life to lead." Carl Archut of Philadelphia asked to visit Zoar; he said he had read about Amana in a newspaper, and had read Nordhoff's book.[21] These writers may have thought that community life was the solution to life's problems, especially in this period of economic uncertainty. Nordhoff's and Hinds's books, superficial as they might be, made the comparative study of these groups rather easy.

The hard times of the late 1870s gave a plaintive quality to some letters. A. Edwins of Columbia Cross Roads (Ohio?) asked for membership and stated simply, "I have work [*sic*] as a machinist until the Panic." Charles Flynn of Columbus, Ohio, said he had "no particular trade," but "no intemperate habits."[22]

Equally touching are letters from former Civil War soldiers, most living at the National Soldiers' Home in Dayton, about two hundred miles away.[23] One, although written in 1873, before the publication of Nordhoff's book, deserves mention. Benjamin Roesstle wrote on behalf of a fellow German living at the facility, "He is not clever enough to get along in the world. He has had no education, and is very shy and tells me he would remain with you all his life, if you would take care of him, for he has no one to look after him, and left to himself he will go to the dogs."[24] The idea of Zoar as a nursing home or way station for ex-soldiers is seen in George Schmidt's letter of October 1880, in which he wrote that although he didn't think he could meet the entrance requirements, he wished to know if he could live in Zoar for a month or two until his pension came and he prepared for a civil service examination.[25]

Perhaps most interesting to students of communalism are the letters from former and current Shakers. A. W. Birkbeck of Enfield, New Hampshire, representing a group of applicants, said he read Nordhoff's book and "desire[d] to live a retired life. We would have [in Zoar] the protection of the temptations of the world."[26]

Sylvester Brewer, of Lewisburg, Kentucky, a former Shaker, states, "I have been reading Nordhoff's book . . . [and] I have been looking at the growing difficulties between Capital and Labor and I can see no way for Labor to successfully compete with Capital but by combining together in communities." He also gives his reason for leaving Shakerism, that he "could not accept the Second Coming of Christ in the person of Ann Lee."[27]

Karl Gustav Andler, a former Shaker who had lived at South Union, Kentucky, for three years, said he still had "a thirst within me for something higher. Christian unity is and shall be my motto." This native of Calw, Württemberg, also offered to contribute "several hundred dollars" if accepted.[28]

Another Shaker of German background, Mary Dotterer of the Watervliet community near Dayton, complained that her two daughters had been taken away from her. "I want to have them under my care during the night at least. . . . I would like to have my children better taught in German, and also, I would like to embrace your religion." She inquired about Zoar's mode of dress, "Would our plain dresses do?"[29]

It is interesting to note that only one adult non-German was ever taken in by the Separatists. Amasa Blodgett (ca. 1784–1877), was a former Shaker. He left the community at Enfield, New Hampshire, becoming a Zoarite in 1841. He worked in Zoar's iron industry and as a farm laborer. He was still living at the time of Nordhoff's visit and his background was duly noted: "A number of members have lived to past eighty—the oldest now is ninety-one; and he, strangely enough, is an American, a native of New Hampshire, who, after a roving life in the West, at last, when past fifty, became a Shaker, and after eleven years among that people, came to Zoar twenty-eight years ago, and has lived here ever since. The old fellow showed the shrewd intelligence of the Yankee."[30]

How did the Separatists respond to these pleas? For the most part, the Society cashier replied with a boilerplate letter, curtly and unemotionally rejecting the correspondents' notions of becoming a member. One extant draft reads in part, "The undersigned, cannot, under no conditions whatever, receive, for the time being, any further new-comers to membership of this society, and thus deem it superfluous to enter into a disquisition of the present rules and regulations, religious or otherwise, of this establishment."[31] Another rejection letter told the recipient "that the present situation and arrangem[en]ts of this establishm[en]t forbid he reception of any new-comers whatsoever."[32] Many inquiries had the words "Replied Negatively" written in large letters across them.[33]

Even those with German backgrounds who might have been accepted in earlier times were rejected. In his study of Zoar's applicants for membership, Edgar Nixon theorizes that by the 1870s, Zoar's population had become constant, and new members were a destabilizing force, and newcomers would have had to work hard to learn the concept of community.[34]

The Zoar Society's Simon Beuter wrote in 1878 to the trustees of the Harmony Society about a new member just accepted by the Society: "I cannot decide whether the man is sincere or not, but he does not appeal to me. I don't like to be a pessimist, would much rather be an optimist, but the communistic revival of these times has given rise to so many marvelous theories, that one has to be especially careful."[35]

The publication of Charles Nordhoff's *Communistic Societies* shed an unwelcome light on the Zoar Society, as well as making much work for the cashier who had to respond to the many inquiries the book engendered. The cloistered village of Zoar at this point in its history did not need to bring in outsiders, however sincere, who were influenced by this book and unacquainted with Zoar's history, its trials in Germany and its communal spirit. It was this spirit, after all, that had held the village together for more than fifty years. In all, this was just unwanted publicity for the Separatists, but invaluable knowledge for future historians.

CHAPTER 12

"Thy Delights, Enchanting Zoar"

The World Comes to Zoar

But we declare, another day,
We'll come again and make a stay,
When in this way we won't be tore,
From thy delights, enchanting Zoar.
　—Constance Fenimore Woolson, untitled poem, ca. 1863

The tiny bit of Germany that is Zoar has always been attractive to visitors. The 1829 diary of George Washington Hayward's trip from his home in Easton, Massachusetts, to Zanesville, Ohio, included walking the distance from Canton to Zoar: "We dined at Zoar 14 miles from Canton. Zoar is a German settlement containing about 20 to 30 houses. The inhabitance [*sic*] are a singular people. Their property is one common stock; Their affairs are regulated by one man who allots to each individual his particular employment. He also delivers discourses to them on the Sabbath. The inhabitants are said to be industrious; they are employed in agriculture and in various mechanical arts. This place is situated on the east bank of the Tuscarawas river; it contains a saw-mill a brewery, a public house [Canal Tavern] and 1 store."[1] Hayward goes on to be the first of many to describe the symbolic Zoar Garden and its "hot house."

The canal brought numerous early visitors and journalists whose impressions are valuable first glimpses into Zoar life. As the Separatists, apart from gardener Beuter, were not diarists, and few wrote personal letters—having no need, as they rarely traveled out of Zoar—these accounts are most helpful to the historian's understanding of Zoar life, or at least what Zoar life appeared to those living in the outside world.

Below are a few descriptions from the 1830s and '40s. The first, one of only a handful of contemporary descriptions of Joseph Bimeler, is from Moses Quinby, a beekeeper of upstate New York in 1831:

> Just before we took our leave the next morning we went to see Mr. Bimenir the priest ~~He lives in houses not at all superior to any of the rest~~. He received us very kindly was quite sociable He speaks English very well He invited us into his Garden which was decked with flowers and srubs of very different kinds and some few trees On the North side is his bee house containing more than 40 hives These he does not kill to get the honey, but places boxes on them not ruining it in that way. His house is nothing more than any of the rest and his dress was nothing superior He is also their only physician.[2]

This writer for the English *Penny Magazine* in 1837 tells about the new bridge over the Tuscarawas. There is no extant photo of this bridge, so we would not know much about it if not for this description:

> They have likewise built, by their own unaided efforts, a large, handsome and substantial bridge across the Tuscarawa [*sic*], as well as one over the canal, which are open, free of all expense, for the largest carriages. Upon the banks of the canal they have erected a handsome and roomy house [Canal Mill?] as a depôt for their own produce as well as for that of their neighbours; which yields them considerable profit. An inn upon the canal is no less lucrative, as nearly every article of consumption is of their own growing.[3]

New England transcendentalist Sophia Dana Ripley's account of her visit in 1838, published three years later, is the only contemporary look at the children's nurseries, perhaps a more lighthearted view than that of Zoar children who actually lived there:

> The women here are as much at leisure so far as household affairs and tending children, as the most fashionable lady could desire . . . their children are taken from them at three and put under the care of matrons, the boys in one house and the girls in another, until they are old enough to be of use, when they tend cattle, mow, reap or do any other kind of field work. . . . The gardener

consigned us to the care of the weaver, who devoted the whole morning to the care of us. We found him a very intelligent man who spoke English well and gave us all the information we desired. He first took us to the boys' dwelling, where we found fifteen to twenty happy little urchins braiding coarse straw hats; for they have no school in summer, and I think receive very little education at any season. We went up to their sleeping apartment, a large airy room with clean beds, and a furnace by which it can be heated in winter. [After lunch], we then went to the house of the little girls, where there seemed to be more play going on than work, and where I was particularly charmed with their clean and abundant wardrobes, arranged in partitions against the walls of their sleeping rooms, with a closet full of little colored muslin, and white linen caps with white linen frills for their Sunday wear.[4]

By 1841, travel around the state was becoming somewhat easier with the addition of the canal and post roads between major towns. Zoar was included in Warren Jenkins's *Ohio Gazetteer,* essentially a tour book describing Ohio's towns and byways. Not only has he included a vivid description of the town ("[you] enter upon a street that has the appearance of having been swept"), but he also attempts to describe Zoar's unusual governance:

They are tenants in common, and each member of the community thinks of advancing his own interest only by furthering that of the whole. They are called to a particular stand every morning, and to each are assigned their respective labors for the day, by their director. Their perfect harmony of feeling, unity of interest, simplicity of manner, universal frugality, and uniting industry, directed by an able financier, have enriched the whole, and have brought their premises into the highest state of cultivation.[5]

Who wouldn't want to visit such a utopian place?

And, in increasing numbers, people did, some for just a stay overnight while traveling through on the canal, others to stay a week or more in the summer to escape the dirt and smoke of nearby cities like Cleveland and Pittsburgh. The Zoar Hotel, built in 1833 to house such travelers, brought in a total of $2,218.53 for the year 1841, the same year as the *Ohio Gazetteer* was published. Money came in even during the winter months when the canal was closed to traffic—twenty-two dollars was turned in to cashier Bimeler on January 6, 1841.[6]

Tourists flocked to Zoar to escape the grime of the cities, to stay at the Zoar Hotel, to sample the hearty food, and to stroll in the Zoar Garden. (Courtesy of the Ohio History Connection, Properties Collection, P365AV.)

Essayist and nonmember P. F. D. has this to say about early Zoar tourism: "Many people stay here several days, to study the institutions and organization of the community of Zoar and at the same time enjoy a sojourn in pleasant rural surroundings. A pleasure garden situated right next to the inn affords much pleasure to one who loves the beauties of nature. Most guests staying at the inn are pleased by the cleanliness and the friendly landlady's excellent service and by the reasonable charges."[7] What those "reasonable charges" were in the 1830s is not known, but in 1864 they were $4 per week for an adult and $2 a week for a child; by 1870, it was $5 a week or $1.25 a day for an adult. This amount presumably included meals.[8] It also may have included wine—for an extra charge. Hotelier Johann Georg Gretzinger (Grötzinger) advertised in the June 23, 1835, *Tuscarawas Advocate* that the Zoar Hotel had "FRENCH WINES FOR SALE—The subscriber wishes to inform his friends and the public generally that he has now on hand, at the Zoar Hotel, a good assortment of FRENCH WINES which he offers for sale on very reasonable terms for cash, either by the gallon or the bottle."[9]

The attitude of Zoar residents toward these strangers in their midst is mixed: writers of first-person accounts invariably remark on the kindness of everyone they meet (see Ripley's comment above); students of communal groups, like Charles Nordhoff and William A. Hinds, were easily able to interview Zoar leaders to obtain information. By midcentury, the Zoar Hotel, with its twenty rooms, was not able to handle the influx of summer visitors, so some were housed in the Garden House and the Cobbler Shop (across from the hotel),[10] in the same dwellings as Zoar families, which may have made for some interesting, if potentially awkward, interactions.

By all accounts, the Separatists were ambivalent about tourism: they liked the income it brought, may have appreciated the kindnesses the visitors imparted, including tips and small gifts, but it says a lot that Zoar children were forbidden to speak to hotel guests for many years.[11] In April 1864 Johan Georg Ruof, proprietor of the hotel, published a notice in the *Tuscarawas Advocate* that the hotel would no longer "extend any accommodations to transient parties and visitors" on Sundays, "travelers excepted," considering "Sunday (the first day of the week) [is] a day of rest, worship, and meditation." Such a notice, reflecting back on the Separatists' earlier insistence that needed work should be performed on Sundays, as it was just another day, shows the disruption that tourism brought to Zoar.

This prohibition did not last long. By 1874 Zoar was again welcoming guests on Sundays, as this article from the Dover newspaper testifies: "Zoar is getting to be quite a resort again for pleasure seekers. For some time they had shut down on entertaining Sunday visitors, but the dollars were too great an inducement, and now strangers come in flocks on the Lord's day. Numbers go from our town, weekly; church members, Sabbath-school scholars, and all. They, perhaps, consider it a Sabbath days' journey toward the promised land."[12]

The Society did refrain from serving alcohol on Sundays, although serving it on other days sometimes brought criticism: "The excursion over the Marietta road to Zoar, Sunday, was a huge affair. People turned out in multitudes. . . . To the credit of the Society . . . not a drop of beer, wine, or liquor could be had at any price. Zoar had a crowd yesterday from the old Forest City [Cleveland]; but the law was trampled in the dust. Beer was sold boldly without respect to age or sex."[13]

An A. R. Gould of Carrollton and New Cumberland asked on May 11, 1874, if he could set up a photo studio in Zoar during the "flower and strawberry season." There is a one-word reply, *Abgelehnt* (declined), written on the back in German. It is polite, but firm, a hairbreadth more courteous than outright "rejected."[14] Whether this refusal was due to the Separatists' dislike of "graven images" (although a photo of the Zoar fire brigade had been taken five years earlier),[15] or if the Separatists were dismayed at what such a commercial enterprise would do to Zoar's tranquil atmosphere, is not known.

Increasingly, recreational facilities were built to accommodate visitors— the damming of an old "ox-bow" of the Tuscarawas River to create Zoar Lake and the erection of a boat dock and a picnic grounds on its shoreline. Of course, when not competing with the tourists, the locals could use them, too, when they had time away from their chores.

The Woolson family of Cleveland made numerous visits to Zoar during the 1840s through the 1860s. Their experiences, although not typical, illustrate the lure of what daughter Constance Fenimore Woolson called "The Happy Valley." As a girl, Constance accompanied her father on summer trips. A letter in the Zoar manuscripts gives details of one of these excursions. Dated July 3, 1856, Charles Woolson inquired about the rates at the Zoar Hotel and wondered if it would be all right to bring his wife, three daughters, granddaughter, and nurse to visit. Christian Wiebel, the Society treasurer, replied that the rate for that many would be forty-five dollars per week, but that he preferred that they not bring the granddaughter and nurse, as they "may render it difficult to bestow the necessary attention and comfort to all."[16]

Charles Woolson's daughter Constance was educated as a well-bred Victorian young lady in Cleveland's finishing schools. She was a great-niece of the famed American author James Fenimore Cooper; her mother was the daughter of one his older sisters. Her father, a businessman with the iron foundry Woolson, Hitchcock & Carter in the Cleveland Flats along the Cuyahoga River, had once been a journalist and publisher. According to her biographer, "Literary expression was a normal part of Miss Woolson's childhood activities."[17]

In preparation for an 1862 visit to Zoar, Charles Woolson asked about the price for keeping horses (answer: two dollars) and if the Society had sidesaddles, "I mean such saddles as Ladies use to ride on. Please let me know! My daughters wish to ride on horseback when they go into the country, but to do that they must have saddles!" On this letter's reverse, Wiebel indicated his reply on the boarding of horses, but not on the availability of sidesaddles.[18]

That fall, at the Civil War camp in Cleveland, where Zoar's enlistees were billeted, Charles Woolson took a paternal interest in the Zoar boys, visited them in camp, and wrote to reassure the Separatists that they were in good spirits (see chapter 10).[19]

The next year, as part of the Woolson family's plan to return to Zoar, Charles Woolson, now a familiar guest and a bit demanding as such, wrote in February and again in March to inquire about building a boat for his daughter Constance in time for her visit. She had asked a sawmill worker about such a boat the year before. It's not clear if the worker promised to actually make her a boat or if such a boat could be made. Nevertheless, Charles Woolson sought to satisfy his daughter's wish:

> My daughter wishes me to write you and say that she hopes you have not forgotten the promise you made to build her a Boat.
>
> She says she shall be *very much disappointed* if you do not have it finished and ready for her use when she comes to Zoar, as she expects to do so on the *23rd of May!*
>
> She has *set her heart on the Boat,* and I hope you will not fail to have it ready for her.
>
> We think we shall stay 3 or 4 weeks at Zoar, and then, perhaps, we may have the boat sent up to Cleveland by Canal: or we may decide to let it remain under your care at Zoar until we come there again.[20]

The Woolson daughters made a second trip to Zoar that fall of 1863. Their solicitous father asked if he could ship a coal-burning Franklin stove—of his own manufacture—to Zoar, so "when they go down there, in a few weeks, [the girls] may have a pleasant bright fire to sit by in the Evening."[21] In 1865 Woolson traded four of his stoves to pay for part of his hotel bill for that season. Until Charles Woolson's death, the family continued to visit Zoar, even purchasing Zoar butter and eggs to be shipped north to them on the canal. Woolson, in the barter economy of the day, even paid for the Society's subscription to the *Cleveland Herald* newspaper and took the amount off his bill.[22]

Filed in the Zoar manuscripts with the above letters of 1863 regarding the boat and stove is a poem in the hand of Constance Fenimore Woolson conveying her feelings about Zoar:

> Our hearts bleed fresh at every pore
> At leaving thee, beloved Zoar,
> Your meads so green, and hills so gay,

Fade sadly from our sights away.
Your bretzels [pretzels] and your soft green cheese,
Your happy days of lazy ease,
The miller's boat above the fall,
It breaks our hearts to leave you all.
We've "been and gone" and come away,
Whence we should dearly love to stay,
Thy shady streams we see no more,
Alas, "We've left thee, happy Zoar."
No more sweet songs at evening hour,
Will charm us by thy magic power,
And all such joys, which we adore,
We've left behind at lovely Zoar.
But we declare, another day,
We'll come again and make a stay,
When in this way we won't be tore,
From thy delights, enchanting Zoar.[23]

A final letter from Charles Woolson, dated 1866, is addressed to Christian Ruof, "Landlord at the Zoar Hotel," and shows an easy familiarity between the family and the Society. He comments that a jug of wine was missing in their luggage after their arrival home, as was a set of harness. He asks that both be sent by canal boat. Apparently he gave a pair of white horses to the Society. "I hope the white horses please you? and that the change of masters pleases them."[24]

Constance grew close to her father on these trips and later remarked in a letter, "As I look back now, I see it was the romantic side of my father's nature that was pleased with the little Tuscarawas community; father had so much romance. It had but little to feed upon in Ohio."[25]

After Charles Woolson's death in 1869, his family left Cleveland never to return, and Constance, unmarried, embarked on her literary career. Her first published story was "The Happy Valley," printed in *Harpers Monthly* in July 1870. She was thirty years old. She had moved with her mother to St. Augustine, Florida. Perhaps this four-page, first-person account brought back pleasant memories of summer visits to Zoar with her father. Although she never mentions the name "Zoar," the place is obvious from the context. The narrator, her father, and her sister Sadie drive a carriage down from Cleveland (a three-day trip), noting the changes in landscape from the flat

Lake Erie shore to the Appalachian foothills surrounding Zoar. The hills are seen as a device protecting the "Happy Valley."

The story gives wonderfully detailed descriptions of everyday life in Zoar, from the "hieroglyphic sign" (i.e., the house number) on the milk pails, to the "bretzels [pretzels], queen of cakes." She describes a church service and its music: "The singers were accompanied by a band , . . . a collection of quaint wooden pipes, flageolets, flutes and violins, whose patterns came from the old country half a century before, and, like every thing else in the Happy Valley remained unchanged."[26]

Although the narrator mentions how "rich" the community is, how much land they have, how their "morality is without a flaw," she doesn't detail why the Separatists came here and why they prospered in America. Zoar is admired for its picturesqueness, its embodiment of the pastoral ideal, not its utopian vision. For whatever reason, she does admire it. The story concludes: "Happy little Valley; our ways are not as thy ways, but who can say that thou hast not chosen the better part?"[27]

Probably most Zoar visitors, like Woolson, never took the time to reflect on just why the community lived the way it did and how it became so successful; they just liked visiting there, enjoying the tranquil atmosphere, eating the wholesome food, boating on the river, and being out of the city.

A republication of "The Happy Valley" in the regional *Cleveland Herald* newspaper later that year caused somewhat of an uproar in Zoar, where inhabitants objected to some of the characterizations. Word got back to Woolson, then living in Cooperstown, New York, who wrote to David Sylvan. She explained that "if I had wished to write a 'History of Zoar,' I should have called it by that name and endeavored to collect the exact facts on the subject." She called the piece a "fancy sketch" and explained she was describing Zoar as it appeared to her parents when they first visited in 1845. She thought the readers of *Harper's* would not care for "how it [Zoar] is now, almost entirely Americanized." She apologized that some descriptions were edited out of the story, how she did not mean for the German expressions used by characters to be disrespectful, and concluded that she had "no intention of saying anything against a place I like so much as Zoar."[28]

Publication of "The Happy Valley" began Woolson's literary career. As far as can be determined, she never returned to Zoar but used it as a setting in two more stories, "Solomon," published in the *Atlantic Monthly* in 1873, and "Wilhelmina," printed in the same magazine in 1875. Both use Zoar as just a backdrop and are not as evocative of the community as "The Happy Valley." Both use female narrators to relate a story that happens to someone else. "Solomon," a young artist who grew up in the "community," but worked as an outsider in a coal mine, was never able to achieve his artistic potential until he, after being injured in a mining accident and on his deathbed, produces a realistic charcoal portrait of his wife, Dorcas. The insular life of Zoar offers a stark contrast to what might have been the life of Solomon.

"Wilhelmina" is set during the Civil War, as Zoar's enlistees are returning. Wilhelmina, the sweetheart of returning soldier Gustav, is rejected by her suitor. Gustav decides to leave the Society "with all its rules and bells." Wilhelmina, disconsolate, but a practical Zoarite, decides instead to marry the baker, whom she does not love, despite the narrator's advice to leave the community and follow Gustav. "No, I'se better here," she says.[29] Tragically, she dies soon after her marriage.

This story is more descriptive, even using similar phrases copied from "The Happy Valley." It, too, is a romanticized picture, placing Zoar much more isolated than it really was and giving the impression that the Separatists were forced to send their young men to war, when, instead, the enlistees left voluntarily and exemptions were purchased for others.

"Wilhelmina" was printed in its entirety in the January 1, 1875, issue of the *Tuscarawas Advocate,* published in nearby New Philadelphia.[30] Its publication caused a letter to the editor to appear in the January 22 issue criticizing the article and its author.

Written by one "N.," presumably a close neighbor to the Separatists and one who knew intimately of their lives, the letter uses strong language to correct some of the assumptions made by Miss Woolson in the story: "She would try and make the world believe that . . . the whole Society was as ignorant as the Fejee [*sic*] Islanders." N. states correctly that newspapers were allowed in Zoar. In regard to the Civil War, his view is that Woolson "would seem to call in question the loyalty of the Society, by asserting that not until the war threatened with hanging could they be induced to hang out the flag. Now, that assertion might have been dropped in to spice and adorn the tale, but has no foundation in truth."[31]

He is most incensed regarding Woolson's description of the gardener's wife, Wilhelmina's mother, who is referred to several times as "leather-colored," reflecting the time she spent in the sun gardening. N. is indignant that such a "modest lady" should be called such a derogatory term. "Now,

Mr. Editor, I am acquainted with the gardener's wife, and have seen the authoress, Miss Woolson, and so far as comeliness is concerned, the odds is in favor of the gardener's wife, if not in gab and gaudy plumage."[32]

Constance Woolson received a copy of this letter to the editor, and in correspondence to her friend Samuel Mather, she acknowledged that the publication of "Wilhelmina" disturbed some at the community. "Someone sent me a New Philadelphia paper containing a savage article on 'Wilhelmina,' based upon the idea that my characters were all from life, and consequently 'the leathery woman' was the good Mrs. [Simon] Beiter [Beuter], the gardener's wife, etc., etc. Of course the article in the country paper was of no consequence, but I was distressed to think that perhaps the Beiters, always good friends of mine, thought so, too. I therefore wrote to Mr. Beiter telling him it was but a fancy sketch."[33]

Other reviewers were not so unkind to Miss Woolson. In his review of *Castle Nowhere: Lake-Country Sketches* (1875) in which both "Solomon" and "Wilhelmina" were reprinted in an anthology, William Dean Howells, Ohio-born editor of the *Atlantic Monthly,* thought that "Solomon" was "a triumph of its kind. . . . The Zoar Community . . . has had the fortune to find an artist [as] the first who introduces us to its life. Solomon's character is studied with a delicate and courageous sympathy . . . and keenly touches us with his pathetic history. An even greater success of the literary art is his poor, complaining wife. . . . It is a very complete and beautiful story."[34]

Howells thought "Wilhelmina" "not quite so good" as "Solomon." Rayburn S. Moore, author of a book on Woolson and her work, writes that the character of Wilhelmina "fails to come alive" and that "the emotional attachment to her lover Gustav never seems quite real."[35]

After leaving Ohio, Woolson traveled with her mother and sister, Clara, to St. Augustine, Florida, which also became a setting for her stories. They spent time in other resort towns, especially Asheville, North Carolina, and Mackinac Island, Michigan. After her mother's death in 1879, Woolson traveled to Europe to write and live out the rest of her life. She died after an influenza attack in 1894.

Today, with her books out of print, Woolson is known mainly to literary scholars. Her reputation is now as a pioneer in the "local-color movement"— using and describing her surroundings in the background of her stories. Other scholars note her treatment of Americans in Europe (a prevalent theme in her later work) and her ability to describe accurately small-town life.

These three stories, "descriptive articles in the guise of fiction," serve as eyewitness accounts of someone who really cared about Zoar and its people and help to show Zoar life as it appeared to "a highly conscious writer, careful, skillful, subtle, with a sensitive clairvoyant feeling for human nature, with the gift of discriminating observation."[36]

Tourism continued after the Civil War, aided by numerous articles in newspapers and magazines. The railroad began to promote the idea that locals take day trips to Zoar, as in this 1874 advertisement in a New Philadelphia paper: "Parties of half a dozen or less, desiring even one days recreation, have a nice opportunity now by taking the 7 A.M. train on the C. and P. [Cleveland & Pittsburgh] to Zoar Station, (fare 35 cts.) thence . . . to Zoar, where the day may be pleasantly whiled away, and return . . . arriving at New Philadelphia by the 9 P.M. train."[37]

Zoar began to receive national attention. Pipsey Potts (Rosella Rice), in a series of three articles in *Arthur's Home Magazine* in 1882, showed the community in all of its guises. She, like all writers, loved its picturesqueness, how it reminded her of her childhood. She worried that her worldly ways and dress would embarrass or anger the Separatists—"They gave no sign of disapproval, nor did they compare the modern styles with their own, and looked at us with a pleased interest that made their shy, modest faces a study for the artist. . . . Some of the dear girls seemed to think the visible horizon bounded the world."[38]

Asking to see "something we don't see at home—something unusual," she is directed to view "da milking" of the cows, which she describes in great detail. After meeting an aged female Separatist, she wondered just what the secret of their contentedness was. She attends a church service, with "the music . . . like a chant, a rising and falling and swelling of sweet sounds." She visited the cemetery, boated down the river, and wondered "what will be the future of this quaint German community? And yet it is not hard to foresee." She bemoaned the fact that a railroad station would soon be built and how that would change everything for "these honest, simple and kind people."[39]

Potts saw the future—the coming of the Wheeling & Lake Erie Railroad into town did change much in the village. Now came the day-trippers, Sunday school classes from Canton and Massillon, German-American clubs from Cleveland, and crowds of merrymakers from as close as Bolivar: "They arrived at Zoar about 1:00 where they found the land flowing with milk and

Tourism increased further when the Wheeling & Lake Erie Railroad built its station right at the edge of the village in 1882, bringing day-trippers from Cleveland and other cities. (Courtesy of the Ohio History Connection, Mavis Kathrein Collection, AV5.)

honey—no, lemonade and beer, we mean. After serving a delicious repast of ginger cake and cheese, the crowds dispersed to the pea-nut stands. They started on their homeward journey about 4:30 and arrived at 5:30."[40]

An advertisement in the *Tuscarawas Advocate* in July 1883, shortly after the railroad began its Zoar service read, "The village of Zoar, or the dominion of the Separatists . . . is a spot no one should fail to visit. A quaint town of about 300 quaint people with quaint customs . . . with natural scenery rivaling the most beautiful that Ohio produces, forms one of the finest picnic grounds known to pleasure seekers."

Tourists begat more and more visitors, or, as one observer put it, "The traveling guests at Zoar are continually growing in number, for everyone who has spent one summer there, becomes a voluntary agent of the colony."[41]

Zoar was noted for its wholesome food. One account describes how picnickers, who arrived not just by rail, but also by bicycle and "tally-ho" wagon, were served: "The Zoar Hotel put 20 articles of food on the table all at the same time and everybody helped himself to as much as he wanted. The charge was 60 cents for adults and 40 cents for children."[42]

Not exactly tourists were the Benedictine sisters of St. Joseph's Convent in St. Marys, Pennsylvania. No one is sure exactly how the sisters became known to the Separatists, but the Separatists gave them Zoar-manufactured goods like flour and fabric; one time, they even donated a cow and calf. The sisters stayed in the Assembly House, and in return for the Separatists' generosity, they bestowed beaded keepsakes and Catholic religious lithographs, the latter certainly not in keeping with the Separatists' beliefs, but are still part of the Zoar museum collections.[43]

Another notable visitor to Zoar was Alexander Gunn. Born in New England in 1837, he came to Cleveland around 1850, working for the George Worthington Hardware Company and eventually becoming a part owner. (Known in the late twentieth century as Sentry Hardware, the company dissolved in 1991.)[44] He first visited Zoar in the late 1870s, falling in love with its peacefulness. His visits increased though the 1880s. His favorite room at the hotel was room 7, under the cupola, which he called "the bridal chamber."[45] Eventually, the Separatists rented him the Hermitage, one of the original log cabins on the eastern edge of the village, for eighteen dollars a year. This, he used as a clubhouse and retreat, although he continued to sleep at the hotel.

Although such a visitor himself, Gunn came to resent the "summer boarder:" "The hotel is crowded to-day with cheap merrymakers, who come in buggies with their girls and have dinner, roam about the village, and drive home in the evening. Tanned reapers, awkward in Sunday clothes, with table manners unspeakable." Retiring from the pressures of business, Gunn began a transient existence between Zoar and travel. He began a journal, the *Hermitage-Zoar Note-Book* in 1889, chronicling his observations, an invaluable source of what Zoar was like, to a semi-outsider at least, during its last years. The book was privately printed, along with a companion volume, *Journal of Travel,* by his wealthy friend and traveling companion, financier William C. Whitney, after Gunn's 1901 death in Germany. Whitney served as secretary of the navy in the first Cleveland administration beginning in 1885.[46]

Although not a German, Gunn felt an affinity to the community's leadership and a few members of the orchestra, whom he called his "amiable junta,"[47] widening an already existing gulf between the governed and those governing. The trustees were invited to private musical soirees and drinking parties. Not just a typical visitor, he often helped out, in his own way, with the harvest, as he noted in his *Note-Book* on November 7, 1891: "I go to the field and husk corn; have dinner in the field, and work until night. Then the band plays. We have a keg of . . . beer, and all get mellow thereon."

Much mention is made of wine, beer and drinking: "The community consumes three thousand dollars' worth of beer alone a year, to say nothing of [hard] cider; and every household has a private stock of wine, made from everything conceivable—blackberries, currants, grapes, and even elder-flowers. An insatiable thirst is the strongest sentiment at Zoar" (June 4, 1892).[48] How much, if any, of this "insatiable thirst" was due to Gunn's influence is impossible to say.

Gardening was Gunn's passion, with his magnificent Hermitage garden containing 174 varieties of roses and an orchard of 170 apple, pear, crabapple, and plum trees. "All the earth again is green. Flowers and music of birds. Distances soften in the humid haze; each day it seems as if nature has a new face," Gunn enthused in May 1898.[49]

Although offered two different diplomatic positions in the Cleveland administration,[50] Gunn truly preferred the conviviality of his Zoar "junta" and relished his solitude, surrounded by his many sculptures, paintings, and books, which lined the walls of the Hermitage. He wrote in his *Note-Book* on September 12, 1898: "After dinner, Jim Hoyt came in and marveled that I cooked my own food, and how I could endure to dine alone. I have great company at dinner. Sometimes Shakspere [*sic*], at others Balzac, and the great people who have left books. Thoreau and Emerson dine often with me, nor in the airy, spiritual sense make any inroad on my larder. I drink for all the immortals gathered at my board." The charm of Zoar never left him, even during his travels to Europe, Egypt, and California.

How must it have appeared to the older Society members to have the Zoar leadership consorting with such a cosmopolitan outsider? Edgar Nixon, in his 1933 dissertation, put it this way: "The ideal of life which Gunn portrayed to his Zoar friends was delightful, but it was an ideal foreign to the fundamental purposes of the Society. Gunn's hedonism was an exotic growth in the Separatism of Zoar. . . . Those excluded from the inner circle resented the presence of such a group within the Society. This resentment was aggravated by the fact that Gunn made no effort to cultivate the liking of those who had nothing to offer him socially. The result was a widening of the breech which had been gradually growing between the members of the Society, and those entrusted with its government."[51]

The old guard was indeed changing, and a new generation was moving into leadership positions. Jacob Ackermann, a trustee since 1832, died in 1889, and no longer could the Society "move on the energy supplied by its founders." Ackermann's successor as cashier, Louis Zimmermann (1858-1912), felt that capitalizing on tourism would be the answer to increasing the Society's revenue, in his words, "a gold mine."[52]

To boost revenue, the cash-strapped Zoar Society decided to double the size of the hotel with a Queen Anne-style addition in 1892. Instead, the increased visitation was a major reason for the Society's 1898 dissolution. (Courtesy of the Ohio History Connection, Properties Collection, P365AV.)

On November 2, 1891, the trustees and Standing Committee adopted the following resolution: "That circumstances demand and make it necessary to build an addition to the present hotel. The building shall contain about 50 rooms, and shall not cost over $5,000. It is further resolved that an architect be engaged to draw up complete plans, and to supervise its erection."[53] Gunn, not surprisingly, voiced his disapproval in his diary: "The new hotel is, between drenchings, approaching completion. There is much to criticize. The plumbing is ill placed and the carpentry scamped. . . . There has been a series of pitched battles between the old and the new ideas of color, fitness, etc., in its finish and furnishings. Christian [Ruof], the landlord, would not be considered an arbiter in matters of taste, but he has a pertinacity which carries things generally his way."[54]

This new "stick-style" Queen Anne addition was built of wood. Two large, shingled dormers with a central four-sided dome spanned the wide front porch. It adjoined the old hotel on the south side. This "up-to-date" style structure was wildly out of place in the old German village. At its completion, an advertisement was placed in the local *Iron Valley Reporter* newspaper, soliciting guests: "Zoar Hotel. The undersigned are pleased to announce that their new hotel will be completed and ready for guests on July 1st. The new house is furnished with all modern conveniences, including hot and cold baths. The village has long been noted for its picturesqueness and beauty. For further information, address the Zoar Society, Zoar, O."[55]

The hotel served some notable guests, including Ohio governor Myron T. Herrick, financier Marcus Hanna and governor and later US president William McKinley, who had visited the village several times before his 1896 election, and paid a notable visit in 1901 while president, just before his assassination.[56]

In the late 1890s, Zoar was the scene for several "Schwabenfests," a musical gathering of bands and singers who came on special trains from all over northeast Ohio and western Pennsylvania. All participants had their roots in Swabia, the area in southwest Germany from which most the Separatists came. The star attraction was the Harmony Band of Economy, Pennsylvania, led by John Duss. A reporter from the *Tuscarawas Advocate* described the scene at the 1897 Schwabenfest: "Zoar had never been so crowded with people as it was on this occasion, and it is estimated that over two thousand people were in the village. Large crowds from all the surrounding towns were present to view the festivities both Sunday and Monday."[57]

The scene for the Schwabenfest was the picnic grounds near Zoar Lake, which boasted a shelter with picnic tables and a bandstand. The male bandsmen and singers were housed overnight in the barns, while their families stayed in private homes.[58] Naturally, the event was the occasion for lots of beer drinking, causing this lament in the local newspaper: "The Schwabe are great beer imbibers, and last year when they were here, they drank out the brewery. Hope they will not be quite so thirsty this year. We want some beer too."[59] These Schwabenfests were discontinued after the Society's 1898 dissolution.

The 1890s brought another type of visitor: the artist. Frederick Carl Gottwald, an instructor at the Cleveland School of Art, and fellow artist Ora Coltman opened the Zoar Summer School, lasting over twenty years and training many young artists of the Cleveland School. They persuaded the Separatists to remodel the old log meeting house into artists' studios, with north-facing dormer windows on the second floor. Other area artists, such as Cullen Yates, also brought students to Zoar. Many of these artists were friends of Alexander Gunn (Gottwald painted a fine portrait of Gunn), who encouraged their study. Zoar's picturesqueness is reflected in their works, which vividly document Zoar's appearance during this period. Young Zoar boys were paid a quarter by the artists to carry their canvases and paints, adding just that much more cash to the communal economy.[60]

The new hotel proved attractive to regular visitors as well, as those who once stayed a few days now stayed a week or more. But at what cost to Zoar's communal endeavor? This we will explore in the next chapter.

CHAPTER 13

"Vanish Like a Light Morning Mist"

The Zoar Society Dissolves

We may form the best resolves, and aim to live according to the rules laid down by the founders of this Community, but all of these vanish like a light morning mist, when we see the total corruptness of our whole system.

—Levi Bimeler, *The Nugitna,* December 30, 1895

Karl Knortz was a German who had come to America in 1863. He wrote many books for the German market, acquainting his former countrymen with American literature, including the works of Whitman and Longfellow. A teacher and German-language newspaper editor, he visited Zoar in 1893. A description of his visit was included in the book, *Aus der Mappe eines Deutsch-Amerikaners (From the Notebook of a German American)*, published in Bamberg, Germany, that same year. Much of the article was a detailed discussion of the Separatist religion, but he also described the village and its people. After a sentence about tourism, one remark seems quite perceptive about the Society in the 1890s: "Through this intercourse with strangers, the Separatists are brought into contact with the outer world. And, as they see only the favorable side of it, it incites in many of them a desire for independence. They begin to feel, that in a communistic colony the individual is absorbed by the whole and must work for it. Therefore many of the people who have grown up there leave their quiet, peaceful home to seek the happiness afar of which they are dreaming. . . . Besides, the young people lack the religious faith of the first settlers."[1]

In that comment, Knortz puts his finger on two of the major reasons for the end of the Zoar Society—tourism and lack of religious fervor. In addition, the Separatists no longer were able to keep pace with the booming technological advances in their craft industries. Related to this were losses in their investments—there was no longer enough free capital to improve these businesses and keep them up to date. Perhaps the most important reason was time—this third generation did not have firsthand knowledge of religious persecution in Germany—nor did they experience the cohesion created by carving a town out of the wilderness. Why should they have to make the sacrifices required to be a member of the Zoar Society, when they could just as easily (or easier!) go out and make a better life on their own? "Just look at what those hotel visitors have! Why can't I have a fast horse, a smart buggy, and fashionable clothes?"

Visits by outsiders to Zoar have been detailed in the preceding chapter, but not how they affected the workings of the Zoar Society. The divisiveness caused by reliance on tourism was even seen by reporters. Robert Shackleton, writing for *Godey's Magazine* in 1896, observed, "But when they recently built a new and large hotel they began to be more like other people. . . . It has been the summer crowding of tourists that has brought unrest and worldliness into the community, and that has made the younger generation ill content with a quiet and uneventful life."[2]

George B. Landis, in his report for the American Historical Association, saw that "the visitors at the summer hotel, by flashy dress, free use of money and marvelous tales of another world, unintentionally aroused discontent in the younger generation of Zoarites."[3]

Even Alexander Gunn, seen by some as the main cause of this dissatisfaction, had nothing good to say about visitors to the hotel: "The village is infested with the annual swarm of boarders. This is a cheap Newport for the small aristocracy of the neighboring towns."[4]

It seemed to some that their own lives were subordinate to those of their visitors. In the words of Edgar Nixon: "The community appeared to exist for the hotel. The first fruits of the season, the first vegetables, cream and butter, were sent to the hotel for the enjoyment of the guests, or were sold. It was admitted that this practice had served a valid purpose during the early years of the community. But many members felt that the time was past for the frugal living and rigid self-denial of the earlier period."[5] When would they, the members who had worked so hard over so many years, get to enjoy the fruits of their labors?

The hotel visitors introduced another disruptive element into the Society—cash. Hotel maids and waitresses, livery stable boys, and those who carried canvases for artists all received tips. This money allowed the young people to buy trinkets unavailable to ordinary Zoarites. Sales of excess eggs and produce to visitors brought in even more money. Former members sent funds back home to their Zoar relatives. There was nothing the trustees could do to stop this underground economy.

The ability to worship together freely was the reason why Zoar was founded. Joseph Bimeler promulgated a religion of the heart, where all believers would try to be born again in Christ. Bimeler's teachings helped to hold the community together, motivating them to make the sacrifices a communal society required. As Nixon states, "They made these sacrifices for a religious, not a social, ideal."[6] After Bimeler's death, no one in the Society had the ability to inspire the membership as he had done, and their religious services became routine, with favorite Bimeler discourses read again and again.

This decline in religious fervor had been noted as early as 1863 by David Sylvan, a young leader of the Society, in a letter to his friend Eugene Wright, the Civil War enlistee: "On the hill stands the chapel, whose little bell faithfully rings, sending afar its full, melodic tones to admonish the people to bring the almighty a loving song in his assembly hall. But alas! It calls out almost in vain. The benches are so empty; hardly any are there. The gray heads are only weakly, or not even at all, represented. . . . in the song, youthful voices are barely audible, and one asks: Where have they gone, who once filled and still should fill this room in the house of the Lord? And so the hollow echo answers: Gone away! Away! Away!"[7]

By the 1890s, less than a third of the members regularly attended church. Simon Beuter, who by this time was directing the services, laments this fact in a diary entry for August 1894: "It has now come so far that the Meetings will soon have to cease entirely because more than two-thirds of the people no longer go where bread and water of life may still be received by these poor souls. This is an unmistakable sign of the times! What was once the chosen people is now become a Babylon that no longer wishes to hear of God. Oh Lord! Let thy light shine once again in these darkened hearts, so that they may be awakened before it is too late, and before it will be said, 'And the door was locked. Amen.'"[8]

He further vented his feelings in a letter to the Harmonist leader John Duss: "What is going to become of us? The young ones are running away on a massive scale, leaving the old, the crippled and the lame behind. . . . Nobody wants to acknowledge what is going to happen; the faith has completely died, which is the worst thing that can happen to a Society founded on God. The world cannot prevail much longer, and it appears that it has been started with the communist societies because they are most of all in Satan's way, because they [the communist societies] have introduced, even though imperfectly, what is necessary for the whole world."[9]

The young were indeed leaving. Alexander Gunn notes one such departure in his diary: "The band is crippled by the departure of Otto [Seitz], the clarinet player, who left last week to try his fortune in the world."[10] Seitz, as did the others who left, departed without any compensation from the Society, just his personal possessions. The Society's workforce was thus reduced, further hastening the Society's end. Such leave-takings were noted in the "Zoar News" section of the *Iron Valley Reporter* of nearby Dover with a mixture of sadness and pride:

> Mr. and Mrs. David Harr . . . have decided to leave the Society next fall and will make their home in Cleveland. Mr. Harr was Superintendent of the Zoar Woolen Mills and had a reputation as manufacturer of the best allwool blankets in the state. . . . We are sorry that the family leaves us as it is one of the best families in Zoar. . . . John Barkhart [Burkhart] has left the Society and has secured a place in the tin mills of Dover. We are well acquainted with John and assure you that he will be a faithful workman, a profit to his employers, and withall an honest fellow. It is significant that the best element leaves the Society. We never heard any of the town loafers express the wish to assume an independent station in life.[11]

Nixon declares that "it is evident that the Society was never free from a discontented element."[12] The early lawsuits aside, it stands to reason that with so many people living in such proximity, with such dependence on one another for their livelihood, that there would be at least occasional discord. A communal society is just one large family, with all the squabbles that living in a large family entails. But these complaints became much more numerous and acrimonious during the decade of the 1890s.

It was economic factors that ultimately forced the Society's dissolution, says Nixon. He speculates that the first generation might have overcome these obstacles, but not this present one. The members' loyalty to the Separatist ideal was no longer evident. This lack of loyalty showed most outwardly in members' attitudes toward its businesses. No one cared any more—Nixon cites an example of workers at the Woolen Mill turning on the machinery after lunch to give the impression of working hard, but not really working at all. One former member, Levi Bimeler, reported that the shops in the winter were mere "loafing places," with petty graft, say a bottle of wine, given to the craftsperson to get special work done.[13]

The trustees did not want to spend scarce funds to update machinery in places like the Woolen Mill,[14] saying that it "served well before; it will have to serve now." In the words of Alexander Gunn: "Every innovation is met with a clamorous resistance from the hide-bound fogies who would still use the flail and reaping-hook."[15] Modern farming methods were not employed. Nixon writes that, unlike earlier in the century, profits were not reinvested in the industries, but, as we have seen, the leadership instead bought stocks and bonds and gave loans and mortgages to locals. These investments often proved disastrous, with large sums of money lost. None of the Society's later leaders had Bimeler's business acumen, nor were they up to the challenges of a changing economic order.[16]

Nixon reports that when he interviewed surviving members in the early 1930s, there was a widespread belief that fraud was somehow involved in the financial losses. With the extant business records so fragmented, it is impossible for a modern researcher to tell. No system of auditing by a neutral party was employed; each industry supervisor kept his own books. Nixon speculates that if the position of agent general, abandoned after Bimeler's death, had been kept, having one person supervise all aspects of the Zoar economic picture might have been more effective.[17]

It was a great-grandson of Bimeler, Levi, the village schoolteacher, who brought all of these matters to a head in a series of three newsletters in the winter of 1895-96. Called *The Nugitna* ("Anti-Gun[n]" backwards), the publication called for the dissolution of the Society, which he deemed too corrupt to continue—an eerie parallel to the early Separatists' similar feeling against the established Lutheran church.

The Nugitna, the only newspaper published in Zoar, was a legal-size sheet, printed on a duplicating machine at the Sewing House, where Bimeler then was living. Besides an editorial, it contained newsy items about town residents. Its name alone suggested one reason for the editor's ire. The paper was (ironically) *sold* to members for ten cents per copy.[18]

In his first editorial in the December 30, 1895 issue, Bimeler revises the preamble to the US Declaration of Independence that "whenever any form of government becomes destructive of the ends for which it was instituted, it is the right of the governed to amend or abolish it." He adds, "This Society has for a long time back become destructive of the ends for which it was instituted" and goes on to list the reasons why the Society was formed: to execute Christian principles, to strive for peace and unity, to unite individual interests into one common stock, to abolish distinctions of rank and fortune, and, lastly, "to live as brethren and sisters of one common family." He asks his readers to examine their lives to see if they are living up to these principles: "We may form the best resolves, and aim to live according to the rules laid down by the founders of this Community, but all of these vanish like a light morning mist, when we see the total corruptness of our whole system."[19]

The second issue of *The Nugitna,* dated January 27, 1896, a month later, covered a similar theme—"Where is the "Spirit of Love" now? Where is the bond of peace and unity? Where are the planters and fosterers of this Spirit? Gone, forever"—and discussed the reception of the previous issue by the membership: "Some went so far as to express themselves thus: This act is enough to expel the publisher from the Society; but when the cool, second thought came, the impracticability of such expulsion made itself manifest. . . . *The Nugitna* created more stir than anything we can think of in the history of this Society. . . ." Bimeler then refers to the *Widerwärtige,* who occupied the Meeting House in 1849. (See chapter 9.) "We are not seeking to throw anybody from and putting ourselves in the place as those petitioners. . . . No! We simply desire that receding members shall receive a proper share of the Society's property."[20]

In the third issue, February 24, 1896, Bimeler discussed equality and the Society's leadership: "There was equality of fortune among the first settlers. But let us look at the conditions of things as they exist now. Is there a union of individual interests now? . . . All this has been brought about by time, intercourse with the outside world. . . . There has always been, and to a certain extent still is a tendency to keep the affairs of the Society from the knowledge of the members. Is it because those in office are the wise men of the Society? Or, are the members too ignorant to be trusted with the knowledge of the Society's affairs. Which?"[21]

This final remark may have been the last straw for the trustees. The editor was asked to appear before them. After securing legal counsel and discovering his words and actions could be grounds for dismissal, he sent a statement via his brother John Bimeler, who happened to be one of the

The team of surveyors hired by the Society did an admirable job of dividing the over seven thousand acres into parcels, taking into consideration land use, road access, and other factors. (Courtesy of the Ohio History Connection, Properties Collection, P365AV.)

trustees, that he would cease publication. Cashier Louis Zimmerman demanded an apology, but none was forthcoming.[22] An editorial for a fourth edition of *The Nugitna* was written but never published. In it, Bimeler condemns communism as idealistic but impractical ("It deadens all push, energy and ambition").[23]

In the end, financial considerations did what subversive literature could not. The Society was rapidly depleting its capital. Nixon records that a total of fifty-five thousand dollars in securities were sold between 1884 and 1897.[24] The trustees were finally convinced that a division of the Society property was a better alternative than bankruptcy, although one trustee, Christian Ruof, the hotelkeeper, continued to oppose the dissolution, supported by members Simon Beuter and John Sturm.

A formal declaration to disband the Society was made at a meeting of the members on March 10, 1898. A resolution, giving reasons for such action, was adopted:

Among the causes for this conclusion are the following:

(1) For a period of forty years past the financial condition of the Society has
     been and is such that its annual income has not and does not now pay
     its annual expenses, by large sums each year, and is becoming worse in
     that respect each year under the best and most economical management
     which the Society could bring into requisition.

(2) The union by religious sentiment and faith among the members of the
     Society has become abandoned, each member having his or her own
     religious faith, and a great majority of them decline and refuse to be
     bound thereby either in theory or in practice.

(3) The industrial and economic habits of a great majority of the members
     of the Society have become greatly changed, so as no longer to conform
     to the articles of the Constitution which they respectively subscribed
     when they became members, to the great financial detriment of the
     Society.

(4) Many of the members have become and are progressive in sentiment,
     opposed to a community of property in theory, and believe and advocate
     individual ownership of property, self-control, and all the personal and
     property rights of American citizens, and are not content with less. For
     these reasons, and others which might be truthfully enumerated, we . . .
     being members and the only members of the second class . . . believ-
     ing and being thoroughly convinced, that the objects and purposes for
     which said Society was originally founded and afterward incorporated
     have proved a failure, and that the interest of each of us can no longer be
     promoted or protected by the continuance of a community of property,
     but to the contrary thereof, require a dissolution of said corporation and
     a division of its net property and assets among us, to hold absolutely in
     our own respective rights, to ourselves and to our respective heirs and
     assigns forever . . . excepting the following tracts and parcels.[25]

Those parcels excepted included the Meeting House, the cemetery, the
Town Hall, and the Canal Mill with forty-seven adjoining acres for the
"purpose of donating the same to induce the construction, maintaining
and operating at that place a Manufactory or Manufactories, if such can be
done within two years of this date."[26] Two parcels of land were sold to the
Wheeling & Lake Erie Railroad adjacent to its right of way.[27] Each family
would keep its furniture, clothing and household goods, except pianos

and organs. In the case where two families shared a house, the kitchen goods would be divided by the appointed commissioners "except in cases in which two families make such division amicably."²⁸

The three commissioners—Samuel Foltz (Zoar's present Foltz Street is named for him), Henry Fisher, and William Becker—were appointed to make the division. George E. Hayward was the surveyor. The 7,300 acres owned in 1898 were valued at $340,820, with personal property listed at $16,250. The Society included a total of 222 men women and children, with 135 of those classified as full members and 11 as first-class probationary members.²⁹

Alexander Gunn observed the goings-on with a mixture of resignation and sadness: "The partition of Zoar is being prepared. The brethren ever more carelessly respond to the bell for labor."³⁰ And this, "The surveyors and arbitrators are making ready for the division of the Zoar property. The great woods are sold for fifteen thousand dollars. I shall not dare to wander in the profaned and mangled woods again."³¹

E. O. Randall, the secretary of the Ohio State Archaeological and Historical Society (now the Ohio History Connection) made a visit to Zoar right before the division and again less than a year afterward. His monograph, "History of the Zoar Society," originally printed in 1899 as part of the Ohio Archaeological and Historical Society *Quarterly,* later as a stand-alone volume in 1904, is an invaluable resource in gauging the mood of the Society during this time of upheaval.

> The patriarch . . . did not wish to give up the Zoarite scheme. Communism with him had been and still was a success. This was the sentiment of many of the older members—it was too late for them to launch out into the world on an untried experience for themselves; many of them succumbed reluctantly and apprehensively to the will of the great majority—in the decision to disband. To them it was a life free from care, worry and excessive work. They literally took no thought for the morrow. They lay down in comfortable homes at night, in certain and satisfactory knowledge that they would be equally well provided for.³²

He met younger folks who were of a different opinion: "The blacksmith, a stalwart six footer, testified he had worked hard all his life with an indefinite undivided property interest as his reward. 'Think how much I would have now had I worked and saved for myself—some in the Society have

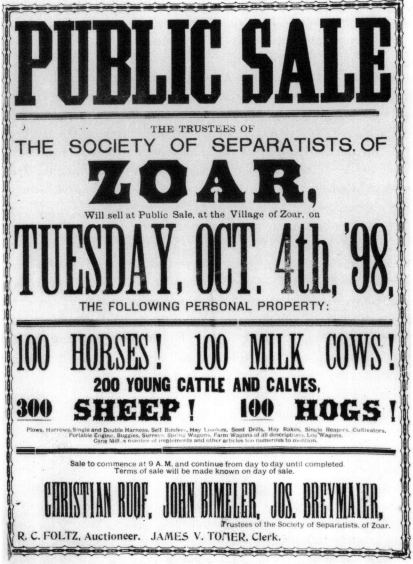

PUBLIC SALE

THE TRUSTEES OF

THE SOCIETY OF SEPARATISTS. OF

ZOAR,

Will sell at Public Sale, at the Village of Zoar, on

TUESDAY, OCT. 4th, '98,

THE FOLLOWING PERSONAL PROPERTY:

100 HORSES! 100 MILK COWS!

200 YOUNG CATTLE AND CALVES,

300 SHEEP! 100 HOGS!

Plows, Harrows, Single and Double Harness, Self Binders, Hay Loaders, Seed Drills, Hay Rakes, Single Reapers, Cultivators, Portable Engine, Buggies, Surreys, Spring Wagons, Farm Wagons of all descriptions, Log Wagons, Cane Mill, a number of implements and other articles too numerous to mention.

Sale to commence at 9 A. M. and continue from day to day until completed.
Terms of sale will be made known on day of sale.

CHRISTIAN RUOF, JOHN BIMELER, JOS. BREYMAIER,

Trustees of the Society of Separatists, of Zoar.

R. C. FOLTZ, Auctioneer.   JAMES V. TOMER, Clerk.

A huge auction was held to sell communally owned property. Members received about two hundred dollars each from the auction proceeds, plus their clothing, furniture, other personal possessions, and the home (or portion of a home) they lived in. Those with occupations received the place where they had worked (the tinsmith, the Tin Shop, for instance); others were awarded a plot of land outside the village. (Courtesy of the Ohio History Connection, Zoar Photographic Collection, AV9.)

done hardly any work, but will get the same that I do. This way of doing business is not natural, nor right,' he added."[33]

A huge auction of community property was held in October—livestock, farm implements, and other equipment. Gunn observed the scene: "The sale of Zoar chattels continues. A crowd of country people, only a few of whom have any idea of purchase—they eye me curiously. . . . The field opposite my house is filled with implements—wagons, cider-tanks, and every kind of rustic gear. The auctioneer, with incredible fluency, urges the rustics to bid. His gestures would make a stump orator frantic that he could not equal them. He talks in every fiber of his organization. Some women linger about, draggled in the wet grass. Some of the old members move about, dazed to see the ancient objects scattered."[34]

The value of a full share was about two thousand dollars, with probationary members receiving half shares, and children who had worked for the Society for at least a year each receiving forty dollars. Each family received a home (or a portion of one) in the village, farm land, and a cash dividend of about two hundred dollars.[35] The commissioners attempted to pair the home or property with the occupation of the member—the tinsmith received the Tin Shop, for example. Some thought the larger enterprises, like the hotel, store and Custom Mill, ought to have been sold and the proceeds divided, as those who acquired shares in these ready-made businesses, on the whole, fared better than their counterparts. Some larger homes were divided in shares—Number One House, for example, was owned by three families, the Sewing House by two. Some received buildings that were not homes at all—like the Magazine and Dairy—and had to remodel them to make them livable (much to the dismay of the historians and architects who later had to restore them back to their original configurations).

Not everyone was happy. After the members received their assigned dwellings on September 20, 1898, the following appeared in the "Zoar News" column of the September 29 edition of the *Iron Valley Reporter:* "How three such esteemed men as the allotting commissioners are could divide homes in such a quixotic way is inconceivable to our mind. Where two or three families lived together like cat and dog in one house, they were left there to continue said manner of living. In some instances a party got only two halls of the dwelling, in others one family controls kitchen, cellar, washhouse and staircases, while the other has the remainder."[36]

The surveyor and commissioners did a laudable job in parceling out the farmland, taking into consideration whether the acreage was cleared or wooded, and whether it was close to a road or water. The map created by the surveyor, still in use today by the Tuscarawas County recorder, shows a crazy-quilt pattern of irregularly shaped lots, each labeled with the names of the new owners.

Remarkably, there was little contention among the members about the partition; they accepted the fact that the division was "as just as . . . was possible under the circumstances."[37] There were a few lawsuits from former members wanting a share in return for what they felt they had previously contributed, but these cases were all dismissed on the grounds that, by leaving, the former member had broken their contract with the Society.

The dissolution was big news, even in Cleveland. The *Plain Dealer* ran a two-page illustrated spread, even speculating on the reasons behind the division: "The younger generation are in the majority at present and it is they who are arranging for the separation. They want to branch out and make money as rapidly as the people who visit the town every summer."[38]

Editorials and the "Zoar News" column in Dover's *Iron Valley Reporter* gave local readers an up-close look at the nearby goings-on. The editor was sanguine in his initial appraisal of the situation: "But a year ago the last man of the original comers, Michael Miller, passed over to the other world; and his departure seemed to release many from the restraint of the old covenant: and ideas that had been held in abeyance sprang into prominence, and there is no doubt in our mind but that these ideas will gain strength till a dissolution of the old methods will prevail."[39]

A rumor, promulgated in the *Plain Dealer* and other papers, and reported in the Dover paper, was that "two-thirds of the members of the Zoar Society, most of them older" will return to their "old way of living immediately after the division" because "in their declining years, they would rather be communistic than adopt a system of living about which they know nothing." The editor of the *Iron Valley Reporter* asked "Mr. Zoar Correspondent" (Orthoford Kappel) to clarify. Kappel called the reports "hallucinations" and "really very marvelous." He says that "any one of us who would be so bigoted to assert that any of us would go back to the old plan of living after going to such enormous trouble and necessary expense is simply maddening." He suggests that the writer of such a rumor might find space in "the asylum for the insane nearing completion at Massillon."[40]

It had to be a difficult changeover, not only for the elderly, but for everyone. Kappel shared his feelings with the readers of the *Iron Valley Reporter:*

Some say we are an ungrateful one for writing things for publication which should remain with us dear fools only, that the world may think everything was smooth sailing and immensely just and satisfactory. And they may be right, for why should we say anything when we only lose the cherry tree which our great-grandfather planted; and when only two-thirds of our wash-house and wood-shed and accessories go to our neighbor; and when our coal-house is cut in two; and when we have to spend $60 this week for a new roof in order to save the ceiling from falling on us while we sleep, etc. And for all these blessings we are called ungrateful.[41]

But some were positively giddy, exploring the new world of private possessions, as Randall saw on his second visit in 1899:

The baker and his wife had hung over the door the sign "Bakery," and had converted their front room into a sale shop with counters and cases, the latter filled with cookies and pies, tidily displayed to tempt the appetite. As a fellow visitor and myself stood upon the porch the husband of the woman drove up with a new buggy and dapper horse. "Where did your husband get that fine rig?" I shall never forget the tone of self-satisfaction with which she promptly replied,—"That is OURS—we bought it. Isn't it nice to have your own horse?" This innate propensity for personal proprietorship is a factor in human nature that the advocate of universal communism fails to properly appreciate or consider.[42]

A problem still remained—what to do with the Zoar Meeting House, which had been exempted from the division. Gunn, above the fray, drily observed: "The brotherhood is rent in two factions over the possession of the meeting-house; one, under the restless schoolmaster, favors complete occupation, with a settled Lutheran preacher; the other refuses to yield all right."[43]

Said schoolmaster, the indefatigable Levi Bimeler, even took to the pages of the newspaper to plead his cause.[44] No provision had been made as to what denomination to make the church in the division, just that a "Meeting House Association" be formed. Bimeler headed a minority that insisted a Lutheran minister be hired—the others were firmly opposed to Lutheranism, the faith they had renounced almost a hundred years before. The question was settled when Dr. Theodore J. Merten,[45] of the German Evangelical Church (now St. John's United Church of Christ) of Bolivar, offered to serve both churches. The fact he could give sermons in German was a plus. Church and Sunday school services were given in German until 1925.[46] The congregation, now the Zoar United Church of Christ, still meets there today.

Not everyone easily gave up the faith that was so uniquely Zoar. Simon Beuter, for one, was sorrowful at the passing of the Zoar religion that had persisted for almost a century. His entry for September 1898, at the end of the long summer of change, sums up his feelings: "I had no desire to write anything this entire summer because of the great event of the dissolution of the communistic Society of the Separatists of Zoar. This Society was founded in the name of the Trinity, and dissolved in a spirit other than godly. . . . The *Geistliche Lieder* are sung no more, and our harps hang on the willows of Babylon. When will they be taken up again? Most of the members are happy and laugh, and Satan laughs too, for he has conquered, he has succeeded in destroying the Nursery of the Lord. But the angels will weep, and I with them."[47]

Was the Society's end unavoidable? It would seem so, as members became more and more acquainted with and accustomed to the outside world, be it through tourism, business, or contact with former members who had already made the leap into the unknown. There are so many "what-ifs": what if its financial situation not been as dire; if Zoar had kept its technology up to date or found new income sources; if the exodus of so many of its young people had not been so great; if its religion was still the cohesive force it was in the beginning; if Bimeler had trained a successor or if there would have been someone else with his skills as both business and religious leader to carry on. Whether any of these changes would have helped, or just prolonged the inevitable, is anyone's guess.

It's tempting to say that the Zoar Society went into a steep decline after Bimeler's death and never recovered. The author hopes this book proves once and for all that was not the case. No, Sylvan and Ackermann and the other later trustees were not Bimeler, but they kept the Society working together and thriving for more years after Bimeler's death than the number of years before it. Not all communal societies have such a successful climax—Zoar ended with almost as many people as it began. The society they formed allowed them to worship as they pleased, live together as they liked, and succeed for seventy-nine years, "the life-span of a man," as prophesized by the visionary Barbara Grubermann back in Germany.[48] A legacy of which to be proud.

CHAPTER 14

"Possesses National Significance"

Zoar Since 1898

The community of Zoar, 1817–1898, possesses national significance as a successful utopian communal society founded by German religious dissenters, where
all shared equally. Zoar's architecture and landscape clearly illustrate its German
heritage and convey its historic evolution from founding to eventual dissolution.
—Plaque designating Zoar as a National Historic Landmark, 2016

After the thrilling, albeit disquieting, changes brought about by the dissolution, the dawn of the twentieth century saw Zoar settle into normalcy.
Heads of households had to scramble to figure out how to make a living now
that the Zoar Society was no longer providing one for them. A descendant,
Howard Sarbaugh, put it this way, "The people after the division had a
difficult task in earning a living and learning how to live."[1] Some pursued
their former occupations and learned about real-world competition: "The
cheery master cobbler had established himself in the ancient log church
[the Bimeler Cabin] which dated back to the early years of the colony,
and was probably the oldest structure in the village, and for many years
had been used as a storage room. He told me one of his two assistants had
abandoned the leather bench for the farmer's plow. The other 'help hand'
opened a new and rival establishment. It was the first, and indeed, the only
case of competition ever experienced in Zoar."[2]

Others commuted to the nearby towns of Canton, Dover, or New Philadelphia to work. Still others sold their shares and departed Zoar for good,

often leaving their aged parents. Many of the children of those remaining later left Zoar in the 1910s and '20s to make their way in the world. This first non-communal generation seemed a bit ashamed to be from Zoar and many couldn't wait to get away.[3]

As described, those who had received shares in income-producing properties, like the Zoar Hotel and the Custom Mill, fared better. Farmers still brought their grain to the mill, and tourists still flocked to the hotel, with both long-term visitors and day-trippers coming in by rail, and subsequently by automobile. Artists still arrived in summer to paint the quaint buildings and pastoral landscapes. Some homeowners sold their red clay tile roofs to outsiders, replacing them with slate. Those who wanted "modern" homes with central heat (central heating was difficult to install due to the arched stone cellars of most Zoar houses) moved away.[4]

Twentieth-century progress came to the village, with named streets, paved roads, and modern conveniences. Zoar had its own electric plant as early as 1902,[5] with a generator at the old sawmill providing the power.

Most of the large farming and industrial buildings surrounding the town lay empty. The animals were gone, the industries shuttered. E. O. Randall observed in 1899 that "the huge horse stables, cow stable and sheep stable were like great banquet halls deserted."[6]

Soon after the dissolution, Alexander Gunn bought the Hermitage (which he had formerly rented) and the huge Brewery, which he turned into a clubhouse and gallery for his artwork. Unfortunately, he did not live much longer to enjoy his Zoar abodes, as he died on a trip to Germany in 1901. He was subsequently buried in Zoar. A huge stone boulder today marks his grave, located between the cemetery and brewery. The Brewery was refurbished at a cost of forty thousand dollars in 1922 to create "Keller's Tavern" and turned into a dance hall with a "modern dancing pavilion." The building burned in 1959, but its foundation still remains.[7]

"Taking the waters" for health purposes was all the rage in the early twentieth century in places like Hot Springs, Arkansas, and Warm Springs, Georgia. In 1912, to capitalize on Zoar's reputation as a resort and to exploit the use of its own mineral springs, the Zoar Mineral Springs Sanitarium Co. was incorporated. A slick promotional brochure was printed, featuring an architectural rendering of a very Floridian-looking hotel structure, and listing the spring water's benefits ("help for Bright's Disease, Nervous Troubles, Rheumatism and Gout, and Catarrhal conditions"), and even including the water's mineral content (concentrations of sodium carbonate and potassium sulfate were the highest). Capitalized at one hundred thousand dollars and backed by Dr. W. A. McConkey of Canton and other investors, including Zoarites John and August Bimeler, whose family owned the site of the springs, the brochure extoled Zoar's "quaintness, cleanliness, and quietude [that] appeal to the seeker of health or rest."[8] Sadly, nothing became of the plan, although the Bimeler family sold bottled water from the mineral springs through the 1910s.[9]

The year 1913 saw a devastating flood on the Ohio River and its tributaries, including the Tuscarawas, which killed over four hundred people and destroyed over twenty thousand homes, ending any further use of the Ohio & Erie Canal. In 1921 the State of Ohio, still owners of the canal lands, constructed "State Fish Farm No. 12," a fish hatchery, on the remains of Lock 10, close to Zoar. Never very successful—its waters were too warm and too polluted—the hatchery closed in 1935.[10]

Zoar celebrated the centennial of its founding in 1917. Articles appeared in the newspapers and a banner was strung over (the still unpaved) Main Street near the hotel. The festivities, held at the Zoar picnic grounds, were to be "quiet, simple and dignified . . . in keeping with the principles of the village founders." On August 17, 1917, just a few days after the hundredth anniversary of the Separatists' arrival in Philadelphia on August 14, speeches were given in German and English and the Massillon Band was on hand to provide music. The printed program in the New Philadelphia *Daily Times* promised "General good times and fellowship."[11]

The celebration of the centennial showed that people in Zoar had not completely forgotten their heritage, but it was not until rumors of a gigantic flood control project and its possible dire consequences for Zoar reached the ears of townspeople that the town really began to awaken from its slumber. Additionally, a historical perspective of Zoar's importance had been gained during those thirty years.

The year 1923 saw another proposal to entice visitors to Zoar. Levi Bimeler and other investors from Massillon and Canton offered water-side lots for sale near Zoar Lake ("The lake will be stocked with plenty of fish."). An even glossier brochure than that for the sanitarium was produced,[12] with idyllic photographs illustrating the tranquil beauty of Zoar. Alas, this scheme produced nothing but phantom concrete streets that can still be seen near the Zoar Guard Lock.

Even before anyone knew just what would happen with flood control, the townspeople and others got together in 1929 to restore the Zoar Garden,

Gaining a sense of their history, former Zoar Society members and their children restored the neglected central garden in 1929. The tiny Norway spruce shown here is the same tree that towers over the garden's center today. (Courtesy of the Ohio History Connection, Louis Baus Collection, P223AV.)

which had been sadly neglected in the interim. Early on, vegetables had been grown in its beds to sell to tourists, and grass tennis courts were laid out for hotel visitors. In 1929, led by descendant Paul Rieker, who later would help preserve the village log cabins, the residents got together to replant the garden, replanting the center tree and laying out the beds and pathways. "EVERYONE IN ZOAR HELPED! Not only that, they continued to care for the Garden for about a decade until the Ohio State [*sic*] Historical Society took over this responsibility."[13] It again became "the Garden of Happiness."

This successful cooperation led to the formation of the Zoar Historical Society in 1930, and its successor, the Zoar Foundation, in 1936. Former Zoar members and their descendants raided attics for furniture and other Zoar-made artifacts to create a museum in Number One House, formerly home to Joseph Bimeler and later trustees. These items are the core of the collections currently on display at Zoar Village State Memorial. The townspeople sought the advice and assistance of the Ohio Archaeological and Historical Society (OSAHS, later the Ohio Historical Society and now the Ohio History Connection) in the formation and operation of the museum, and in 1941, Number One House and the Garden, including the unrestored Garden House, were purchased by the state of Ohio to be operated by the OSAHS as a State Memorial. In 1942 Lillian Ruof Bimeler Sturm, whose family had operated the Hotel, donated her home and its contents to the OSAHS, further enlarging the site. The state also acquired the sites of the dilapidated Tin Shop, Wagon Shop and Blacksmith Shop in the 1940s with an eye for future restoration.

Wanting to document Zoar's history, descendant Edgar Burkhardt Nixon, a great-grandson of Simon Beuter, wrote his doctoral dissertation on Zoar for the Ohio State University in 1933, which has been liberally quoted in this volume. Nixon spoke German and was able to interview former members, which added immeasurably to his account. For over seventy-five years, Nixon's dissertation has been the core of all subsequent scholarly research about Zoar. Dr. Nixon spent his career as an archivist at the Franklin Delano Roosevelt Library at Hyde Park, New York. In 1980 he and his brother Richard donated manuscripts which he had used in his dissertation to the Ohio Historical Society. Once called the "Coleman Papers," for their then owner, a Dr. Coleman, and now called the "Nixon Family Papers," the collection is valuable in documenting Zoar's history and has also been quoted frequently herein.

Zoar structures were documented by the Historic American Buildings Survey in 1936. This Depression-era project, begun in 1933, gave employment to out-of-work architects and photographers. The resultant drawings and photos detail the site, and have been used extensively in later restorations. Zoar furniture and decorative arts were documented by artists from two other WPA-era programs, the *Index of American Design* and the Federal Art Project.[14]

The 1930s saw an avid interest in Zoar "antiques," with outside collectors purchasing items from descendants. Four of the five extant log cabins (the Bimeler Cabin, the Zeeb Cabin [Number 9 House], the Print Shop, and the Hermitage) were restored by Paul Rieker (1898-1977), the last child born during the Society; a fifth cabin was rehabilitated in the 1980s. Their red tile roofs were removed, with modern rolled roofing placed beneath and the tile replaced. The clay chinking between the logs was exchanged for modern materials.

The town was now beginning to hear more and more about the rumored flood control project. Since the 1913 flood, several studies had been conducted regarding what should be done to slow subsequent floodwaters from draining into the larger rivers. A series of dams on the Tuscarawas and Muskingum was proposed, one to be located between Zoar and Dover. The US Army Corps of Engineers (USACE), in charge of the project, looked for ways to create a flood plain, where water could be impounded when dam gates were closed during heavy rains. One proposal, thankfully discarded, was to move Zoar to higher ground, as was planned for other nearby towns (Zoarville [formerly Zoar Station], Sandyville, Magnolia), so that any large debris (like parts of dwellings) floating downstream from flooding would not damage the dam. The idea of moving Zoar certainly got the attention of residents, the Ohio State Archaeological and Historical Society, and many others. The irony was that Zoar had never flooded, as it was on high ground, but possibly would now, if the dam gates were closed and water was impounded behind them. Finally a compromise was reached;[15] an earthen levee and diversion dam would be constructed.

In 1933, the Public Works Administration (PWA) awarded a grant of $22,090,000.00 to the USACE to construct the proposed plan. In 1934, the Federal Government executed a contract with the Muskingum Watershed Conservancy District [MWCD] to allow the USACE to conduct investigations and draft a final plan. This official plan for the basin was approved by the MWCD on 19 November 1934. Construction of the project began in 1935 and the completed system was turned over to the MWCD in 1938. The Flood Control Act of 1939 returned the dams to the federal government and flood control operations back to USACE. Today the USACE Huntington District manages these projects.[16]

Construction of the levee necessitated the destruction of Zoar's industrial buildings, the three-story Woolen Mill, the Machine Shop, the Planing Mill and others, which were vacant and had fallen into disrepair since 1898. The Custom Mill was moved two miles south to Zoarville and became Ehlers' General Store, open through the 1980s. The rear half of the huge Cow Barn was dismantled to make way for the levee footprint (the remainder of the barn was damaged in a windstorm in 1980 and torn down in 1984). The Wheeling & Lake Erie railroad line and the highway out of town (Main Street had become State Route 212) were rerouted.

The levee, although protecting the residential area, cut off the view of the nearby river and canal. Hemmed in as it is now by the levee, today's visitors have a skewed impression of the size of Zoar's land holdings, not understanding that the Separatists owned land two miles in all directions from the town center.

The Depression fairly eliminated what tourist trade still remained at the hotel. Young people still left their families for jobs in other places, and Zoar slowly became a village of elderly descendants and younger outsiders who purchased the empty houses of older Zoar residents, who had died, a process that continued through the early 1980s.

In 1947, the Victorian addition to the hotel was razed, as it was no longer used and had not been built in the same sturdy manner as the original. In the 1950s the hotel experienced a renaissance, not as a place to stay, but as a place to eat. Postwar Sunday drivers made the Zoar Hotel a destination for hearty chicken dinners. Later hotel proprietors turned its vast vaulted cellar into a rathskeller bar, complete with nightly entertainment. But these owners couldn't make a go of it and the hotel closed in 1984 and remained vacant.

Townspeople celebrated the centennial of the Meeting House in 1953 with the performance of a play about Zoar history written by descendant Hilda Dischinger Morhart. Unlike some of her generation, Hilda (1899-1978) listened to the stories told by the older residents and began writing them down. With the help of others, these became the play and later a book, *The Zoar Story,* written for Zoar's sesquicentennial in 1967. It was illustrated with drawings by Zoar descendant Edna Bimeler Leuking.[17] The sesquicentennial was a month-long celebration and included a reprise of the play, an art show, a music festival, a visit by Ohio governor James A. Rhodes and more.[18]

The success of the anniversary led to the formation of a new organization, the Zoar Community Association (ZCA), that same year. They decided to prioritize the restoration of the Zoar School House, empty since 1953 and given back to the village. The ZCA leased it from the village in 1971 and restoration was completed in 1985. The ZCA has since restored the Zoar Town Hall (2001).

In 1968 the ZCA began a yearly celebration with some of the same features as the 150th anniversary. This was Separatists Days, later called the Zoar Harvest Festival, and marked its fiftieth year in 2018. Although the event has gone through changes, it still features an antiques show, art show, and craftspeople demonstrating their skills.

In 1965 and again in 1967, Ohio voters passed bond issues that allowed restoration to begin on the vacant Garden House, the recently acquired

Bakery and the sites of the Tin Shop, Wagon Shop, and Blacksmith Shop. After these buildings opened in 1970 and 1972, the Ohio Historical Society employed costumed interpreters who told visitors about the site. The Zoar Store was acquired in 1970 and restoration began soon after but was not completed until May 1980. In 1990 restoration began with state capital funds on the Dairy, behind the Store, with the Kitchen-Magazine complex located behind Number One House following in 1992. These restorations, which richly illustrate Zoar's daily life, opened in April 1995.

In 1965 the state of Ohio began to dispose of the canal lands it owned, selling or giving them to nearby landowners or donating them to local governments. The Tuscarawas County Commissioners received the seven-mile stretch of canal from Bolivar to Zoarville, which the Separatists had helped to create in the 1820s. This part of the canal is no longer watered, and its four locks were mostly forgotten until a movement began in 1989 to designate the entire canal towpath from Cleveland south to Zoar (later New Philadelphia) a National Heritage Corridor. This program, a part of the National Park Service, recognizes linear resources like trails, railbeds, and towpaths for their historic significance. After a lot of hard work, a report was written and Congress approved the Ohio & Erie Canalway National Heritage Corridor in 1995.[19] Since then, the towpath has become a popular hiking and biking trail, bringing visitors to Zoar from all over northeast Ohio and beyond. The Canalway has also reemphasized the importance of the canal to Zoar's story, since the levee now completely divorces the village from the river and canal.

Other Zoar buildings owned by the state of Ohio remain to be restored. The Sewing House, built in 1830 and purchased in 1965, is now used for storage but may be restored to illustrate Zoar's extensive textile industry. The Zoar Hotel, acquired in 1996, underwent exterior restoration in 2002, but as of this writing its interior remains unrestored and its future use is undetermined.

The winter of 2005 saw a severe test of the Zoar levee. A winter flood closed Dover Dam and floodwaters backed up to the levee for days. This "record high water event resulted in Dover Dam's impoundment reaching a record pool elevation."[20] Water permeated the levee, creating "pin boils" on the inside where the water seeped beneath it, carrying soil. The water flooded many town cellars on the west side of the village, knocking out electrical and heating systems in many buildings. The town was also practically surrounded by water for several days.

The seepage destabilized the base of the levee and the diversion dam, and in 2007, the Corps of Engineers declared it as "Urgent—Failure Initiation Foreseen," or Dam Safety Action Class (DSAC) II. Following another flood in the spring of 2008, even more boils were noticed. This resulted in a DSAC I, or "Urgent and Compelling—Critically Near Failure," classification.[21] To determine what to do, the Corps commissioned a thorough study of the levee and the surrounding town to determine if the project warranted the millions of dollars it would take to rehabilitate the levee. To prepare the public for the worst, it also gave residents (and other lovers of Zoar) three possible options that the study *might* conclude: to fix the levee, to move the town to higher ground, or, worst case scenario, to destroy the town and take down the levee.

Obviously, the last two options were unacceptable. The levee must be fixed. Zoar mayor Larry Bell and Community Association president Jon Elsasser mobilized forces to "Save Historic Zoar." Newspaper stories, support letters, postcards, visits from congressmen, posters, word of mouth—all were employed in working to persuade the Corps to fix the levee, not move or destroy the town. After a lot of work, meetings, money, and publicity, the study concluded in 2013 that the levee should be repaired. At this writing, preliminary work has begun.

An additional consequence of the study done by the Corps of Engineers was to apply to the National Park Service to become a National Historic Landmark. This designation would demonstrate to both governmental officials and the public Zoar's impact on the nation's history. Zoar's Historic District had been listed on the National Register of Historic Places since 1969, but it had never applied for this higher classification, which implies outstanding historical significance. Using some of the information gathered for the levee study, plus much additional research, the application was approved by the secretary of the interior in November 2016.

Another result of the 2005 flood was that the cellar of the 1868 Bimeler Museum on Third Street was filled with water. Its foundation had been built on a deposit of highly porous sand almost twenty feet deep.[22] The extreme saturation of the sand from the flood caused the walls to shift, the foundation to crack, and doors, windows, and floors to buckle, destabilizing the entire structure. Heating and electrical service were destroyed and the building was soon filled with black mold. Museum collections were moved and the building closed. Engineering studies were undertaken, and the building was placed on jacks, a concrete mat laid underneath to eliminate

Today the village center has been preserved through actions of the state of Ohio and its partner, the Ohio History Connection, which have maintained, restored, and reconstructed many Separatist-era buildings. The Zoar Community Association and private individuals have also restored and rehabilitated structures that contribute to the village ambiance. Number One House, seen here, along with eleven other museum buildings, can be toured seasonally by the public. (Courtesy Zoar Village State Memorial.)

future subsidence, and the foundation and cellar rebuilt. Using both public and private funds, the structure was restored, including a new porch to resemble the original (it had been remodeled in 1922 by owners Lillian and William Bimeler), and the removal of many layers of white paint. In May 2017 the building was rededicated as a decorative arts museum.

In addition to Zoar buildings, furnishings, and decorative arts, the Ohio History Connection has a wealth of material about Zoar at its Archives-Library in Columbus. Included are manuscripts, photographs, and books. In 2000 the Ohio Historical Society purchased a large collection of Zoar manuscripts from local collectors Jack and Pat Adamson, further expanding its holdings. Some, but not all, of the manuscripts in the different collections are either translated or summarized from the original German. Some Zoar photos and manuscript materials can be found online at www. OhioMemory.org.

In 2009 the Ohio Historical Society turned over day-to-day manage-ment of Zoar Village State Memorial to the Zoar Community Association as part of a statewide program of leasing its state memorials to local sup-port groups. General maintenance of the site is the responsibility of the ZCA, but the state of Ohio still performs capital improvements and larger maintenance projects. The ZCA receives a small yearly subsidy payment, keeps ticket and gift shop revenues, and employs staff to run the site.

Since the mid-1970s, private individuals have restored or rehabilitated their homes in the village, adding to town ambiance. Zoar is unique among historic sites in Ohio, as it is an integral part of a real town, with historic structures privately and publicly owned standing side by side. Many of the privately owned buildings contain shops, restaurants and bed-and-breakfast inns that make a visit to Zoar complete.

CONCLUSION

Would you be reading about a small group of nineteenth-century German immigrants with a unique religious perspective if they had *not* decided to form a communal society? It is doubtful. The Separatists were not evangeli-cal—they did not seek to convert others to their beliefs, so their religion had no great national reach. Their beliefs were extremely personal—they were between themselves and God, with each person on his or her own quest toward sanctification. That is not to say it was not a strong religious attitude—it was strong enough to withstand years of persecution and prison and to bring them halfway around the world to allow the Separatists to worship in their own way.

Their religion was resilient enough for them to carve out a settlement in the wilds of Ohio, enduring enough to withstand the privations of those early years, strong enough to tolerate eight years of celibacy, hardy enough to dig a canal by hand, and durable enough to see the Society through seventy-nine years. One can truthfully say that as the Separatist religion declined, so did the Society—not a steep decline, but an extremely slow, inexorable one.

It's unlikely that the Separatists would have combined together com-munally if they had not desired to continue to worship as one body, but they found the communal form suited their needs, and they were blessed to have such a multi-talented figure as Joseph Bimeler to lead them, both in a religious and a business sense. Whether an early leader like Johann Gott-fried Banzhaff (see chapter 2), had he stayed with the group, would have had the organizational qualities of Bimeler is anyone's guess. Bimeler was a polarizing figure, even to his contemporaries. One gets the impression that later leaders, like Jacob Sylvan and Jacob Ackermann, were continu-ally looking over their shoulders and asking themselves, when faced with a difficult situation, "What would Joseph have done?" And when they did innovate, like entering the financial markets in the 1880s, the Society did not fare well.

Did communalism "work" in Zoar? Did the members have the commit-ment needed to make it work? Yes and yes. The fact that the Society ended with almost as many members as it had when it began, despite the exodus of many of its younger folk, says volumes. Was it the security of being taken care of that kept the members together? Was it just tradition? Was it fear of making a living for one's self? This writer thinks it was something else; it was the shared experience of working together for a common purpose, and when this waned, so did the Society.

Part of Zoar's importance to the present day is its longevity, since it is one of the longest-lived communal societies in the United States. But perhaps Zoar's greatest contribution is its clear illustration of two concepts held dear to all Americans: religious freedom and toleration of differences.

Probably nowhere else in the world could a group of former prisoners and lawbreakers be allowed to come and set up their own religion with an economy contrary to the prevailing capitalistic system—and then be allowed to be successful within that system. No one came and said, "You can't do that here." No one marched or protested against them; in fact, as we have seen, their neighbors looked on them fondly and possessively.

The Separatists, despite their different lifestyle, were accepted by main-stream America, used the American system to succeed and put their own particular German stamp on life in nineteenth-century America.

They also created their own German-flavored architecture, furniture, textiles, frakturs, and other artifacts, which delighted nineteenth-century visitors as well as today's.

Often, when this writer worked in Zoar, she could be heard responding to a question from a visitor to which the answer was not known, by say-ing, "The Separatists just didn't write everything down about their lives. They never thought they would someday be famous." I hope this volume helps, in some small way, to increase their fame.

Daniel Ulrich Huber's 1833 Poem

Daniel Huber's Poem
By Daniel Ulrich Huber (1768-1840), 1833. Translated by Philip Webber, 2017.

A Song about the course of the Separatists, in which is composed [compiled] something of their persecutions that they suffered for the honor God and the truth in the Kingdom of Württemberg.

Secondly, the departure and trip, [accomplished] by God's leading and direction, from their fatherland to North America.

[in a different hand] August Bäumler [perhaps a later possessor of the manuscript]

Verse 1
My heart, soul and spirit [*Gemüt*]
[Give] laud and praise, day and night;
God's grace, loyalty and goodness
Has brought us this far,
Into a land where calm and quiet [prevail]
And addition, noble freedom.

Daniel Huber's poem resides in the Zoar Papers, box 93, folder 3.

Translator's note: I have tried to balance the need for fidelity to the original text with the requirement of producing readable English. Occasionally, the order of lines within a stanza was changed to achieve better clarity in English. Philip Webber, May 2017.

Verse 2
Yes, how could I hope for more,
Yes, how could I thank more
That this way stood open to me,
That after my fall
I might also come here,
To all the Separatists.

Verse 3
Still, out of the depths,
For a second time, the Lord,
Out of sheer grace called to me:
Stand up from your fall,
Stand up and do not tarry,
See, judgment hastens.

Verse 4
Noble freedom, noble fortune
Here in the liberated land,
Yes, when I think back now,
To the sorrowful condition
Where the countryman's goods and blood
Belonged to the brood of tyrants.

Verse 5
If a father had four of five sons,
And they were forced [to enlist],
Father, son and marriages were told:
Don't you know that are mine,
Take the sword and rifle
And protect my [the ruler's] honor.

Verse 6
Even as the Separatists
Perceived the tyranny,
And wished to live as Christians
And speak the truth freely,
The war and battle raged
Far and wide throughout the land.

Verse 7
This battle continued long,
Yes, it lasted many years,
One recognized its fierceness,

It put the clergy in danger,
Who believed and were fearful
Another kingdom might arise.[1]

Verse 8
The officials and the priests,
Came forth in total anger.
It was decreed that [the Separatists] should be punished
Until they took off their cap and hat.
Troops would be sent to them
Until they gave [the authorities] honor.

Verse 9
The people were not compensated.
The [troops] destroyed our country
With flags, weapons and drums,
And marched [resisters] off,
To execution quarters,
Thirty men and officers.

Verse 10
But also for this scourge,
Its days were determined—
How long it should last—
It lasted probably a month,
And then despite all effort,
They withdrew without a victory.

Verse 11
How often they tried:
They searched outside the house,
To discover some hiding place,
They looked in every corner,
Searched for what a blind man
Is unable to find.

Verse 12
Owing to an awful event,
The evil brood quickly found us,
And delivered hard blows
Venting their wrath upon us,
Breaking down the door of the house,
And fiercely bringing the people out.

Verse 13
Children were violently abducted
And placed into the orphanage
In order to direct their souls
Away from their inner foundation;
They were forcefully taught
Ceremonies and hypocrisy.

Verse 14
Just like murderers and thieves
Many were arrested,
Pushed around back and forth,
And imprisoned.
Pharaoh did not let them go,
His pride and arrogance were too great.

Verse 15
Finally, another attempt was made
By Brandenburg,[2] to ransom them,
To find out if perhaps
A better place of rest were there,
But Pharaoh's army
Never gave them any rest.

Verse 16
Wherever we attempted to flee,
The Leader of Israel spoke
Go forth from this land.
Quickly the order sounded forth:
Get up, hurry, for we all wish
To go forth out of Sodom.

Verse 17
Yes, who could believe it?
You furtive band of robbers
First robbed us of all we had,
Then drove us from our fatherland.
They wanted nothing more
Than to rob us of God and honor.

Verse 18
Just as they did in Sodom
To righteous Lot,
When he spoke of punishment:

They ridiculed him
Until upon that despised brood
Fire and sulfur rained down.

Verse 19
Previously, by God's order from above
Lot, the pious man
Also went out of Sodom
Before judgment began,
Fled to the village of Zoar
Where he, too, found his rest.

Verse 20
Just as God, from ancient times,
Led the children of Israel
And also allowed them to be led
By his mighty host of angels,
[So now] as in times of old He leads them
Happily [*glücklich*] over land and sea.

Verse 21
Ninety-two days
The journey across the sea lasted,
But their leader and traveling companion
Was their king, sovereign and Lord,
To whom, already for many years,
Wind and sea were obedient.

Verse 22
And before arriving in this land,
Already at this time
The Quakers all together
Had prepared a house for them,
Where they could enter in,
Old, young, great and small.

Verse 23
Eighteen hundred and seventeen
On the fourteenth of August
They arrived, being well
And with heart's delight, in this land,
In Old Philadelphia,
Free in North America.

Verse 24
And because they came their way
Out of such hard slavery,
From which they completely escaped,
Away from all tyranny,
All cruelty and war,
The yoke of the [slave] driver was broken.

Verse 25
Tell, where are the high councillors,
Those learned in Scripture,
Clerics who perverted the world?
Freed from legal process,
From the priests' clerical guild,
We were completely unbound and free.

Verse 26
Taxation has ended,
There is no longer any constraint,
Father, Mother and children
Are free from the Ash-Mountain[Asch-Berg] and the penitentiary,[3]
And whatever had to be hidden
Now stands in the open.

Verse 27
Freedom of conscience adorns
Those intelligent men
Who introduced freedom
With the laurel wreath
That long liberates a people
Entirely from constraint of conscience.

Verse 28
Each can now worship God
How and when and where he wishes,
So as not to burden his conscience,
Pursuing the true goal,
Entirely according to understanding of his heart,
In Pennsylvania.

Verse 29
Still, that was not yet the place
Or the determined location
Where the people were to remain

As destined by their God.
Here in the Ohio valley
Was the suitable place.

Verse 30
There was offered to them
Six thousand acres of arable land,
But naturally questions arose.
They were poor yet rich,
Their till was almost empty,
What could they show for all the years?

Verse 31
Still, Bimeler dared to try it,
Bought the entire mighty land
God gave him fortune and blessing.
Quickly, and to dissolve their debt,
He was able, from the blessing,
To hand over all that was theirs.

Verse 32
By group effort they began to build,
Laying out the little city of Zoar,
Gardens, grasslands, green meadows:
The promised Canaan
In which milk and honey flow
As promised by God to his people.

Verse 33
What God promised his people
Already many years ago
Has become evident in fullness,
The petitions and wishes:
Lead me out of danger and pain,
Into Thy peaceful Zoar.

Verse 34
There Aaron's lament is silent,
Where God's blessing flows,
Joseph's stock-rooms,
Are filled up with fruits
From the seven fat years,
Placed before his brothers.

Verse 35
May Abraham's and Jacob's blessing
Rest here upon the land of Zoar,
Given by God to his people,
Sent to His little cohort;
Jacob's blessing enriches you,
[Through] Joseph's being sold.

Verse 36
Not to be rich on this earth,
Not to be rich in this time,
Eternally rich and blessed,
You could also be in eternity
If you truly desire it with sincerity,
And follow what is taught to you.

Verse 37
O mind of a pure spirit,
You can hear eternal truth,
Words that to high choirs
And lead to eternal life,
Words full of spirit and power,
Words that create new life.

Verse 38
The Spirit leads to new life
In the land of the ancient fathers
For those who also seek God
Upon the souls' inner foundation
[Who is] their treasured Immanuel.

Verse 39
Surrounded by the Spirit's power
The sower is sent out,
And whenever he goes forth,
It is to sow the land,
And he wishes that all his seed
Will fall upon good ground.

Verse 40
Not to be trampled upon the way,
Not [to land] on rock on stone,
Not on thorns or hedges
That will choke its sprout,

[But rather] upon good land
Yielding sixty or one hundredfold.

Verse 41
So here I come to my conclusion,
My heart's beloved friend,
With thanks for the pleasure
That I enjoyed in the Community,
May God requite this pleasure,
And with that I conclude.

Daniel Hoober [Huber]
Written in Zoar, June 17, 1833
          S. B. [Perhaps Simon Beuter (1819-1907) who may have transcribed the poem]

Separatist Principles

1. We believe and confess the Trinity of God; Father, Son and Holy Ghost.
2. The fall of Adam, and of all mankind, with the loss thereby of the likeness of God in them.
3. The return through Christ to God, our proper Father.
4. The Holy Scriptures as the measure and guide of our lives, and the touchstone of truth and falsehood. All our other principles arise out of these and rule our conduct in the religious, spiritual, and natural life.
5. All ceremonies are banished from among us, and we declare them useless and injurious, and this is the chief cause of our Separation.
6. We render to no mortal, honors due to God, as to uncover the head, or to bend the knee. Also we address everyone as "thou" [*du*].
7. We separate ourselves from all ecclesiastical connections and constitutions, because true Christian life requires no sectarianism, while set forms and ceremonies cause sectarian divisions.
8. Our marriages are contracted by mutual consent, and before witnesses. They are then notified to the political authority; and we reject all intervention of priests or preachers.
9. All intercourse of the sexes, except what is necessary to the perpetuation of the species, we hold to be sinful and contrary to the order and command of God. Complete virginity or entire cessation of sexual commerce is more commendable than marriage.
10. We cannot send our children into the schools of Babylon (meaning the clerical schools of Germany), where other principles contrary to these are taught.
11. We cannot serve the state as soldiers, because a Christian cannot murder his enemy, much less his friend.
12. We regard the political government as absolutely necessary to maintain order, and to protect the good and honest and punish the wrong-doers; and no one can prove us to be untrue to the constituted authorities.

Officers of the Society of Separatists of Zoar, 1819–1898

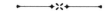

OFFICERS OF THE SOCIETY OF
SEPARATISTS OF ZOAR, 1819–1898

This appendix includes the names of the officers of the Zoar Society and the years of their service. The records are incomplete for the period between 1819 and 1832.

Johannes Breymaier	1819–1824
Joseph Georg Ackermann	1819–1830 (?)
August Huber	1819- ?
Jacob Schacher	1824- ?
Michael Sindlinger	1824- ?
Georg Grötzinger	1825- ?
Jacob Sylvan	1825–1831
Casper Fetter	1831–1834
John Miller	1831–1834
John G. Goesele	1831–1838
Jacob Ackermann	1832–1889
Christian Ruof	1834–1838
Ludwig Birk	1838–1851
Jacob Sylvan	1838–1862
John G. Grötzinger	1851–1859
John G. Ruof	1859–1889
Samuel Harr	1862–1887
Simon Beuter	1885–1890
John Sturm	1887–1893
John Bimeler	1889–1900[1]
Christian Ruof	1890–1900
Joseph Breymaier	1893–1900

STANDING COMMITTEE

Ludwig Birk	1833-1838
John G .Grötzinger	1833-1851
Joseph M. Bimeler[2]	1833-1853
Christian Meigele	1838-1847
Gottfried Kappel	1847-1876
Johann Georg Ackermann	1851-1854
Gottfried Lenz	1853-1864
John G. Ruof	1854-1859
John Breymaier	1854-1877
J. Peter Bimeler	1854-1861
Mathias Bühler	1859-1873
Martin Rauschenberger	1860-1870
Levi Bimeler	1869-1879
Simon Beuter	1870-1885
Frederick Heid	1873-1883
Franz Strobel	1877-1881
John Sturm	1877-1887
John Rieker	1879-1889
Clementz Breil	1883-1893
John Kuecherer	1885-1895
Christian Ackermann	1887-1892
Christian Ruof	1888-1890
John Bimeler	1889-1889
Jacob Rieker	1890-1900
Peter Bimeler	1892-1894
Carl Ehlers	1894-1900
Benjamin Beuter	1894-1900
Jacob Burkhart	1895-1900

CASHIER

Joseph M. Bimeler	1833-1855
Christian Wiebel	1855-1872
Jacob Ackermann	1872-1889
Louis Zimmermann	1889-1900

ARBITRATOR

Joseph M. Bimeler	1824-1833

AGENT GENERAL

Joseph M. Bimeler	1833-1853

Zoar Occupations from the US Census, 1850–1880

Occupation	1850 Census	1860 Census	1870 Census	1880 Census
Attending School				2
Baker		1*	1	3
Apprentice		1		
Blacksmith	3	1	3	2
Apprentice		3		
Boatman (canal)	2			
Brewer	1	1	1	2
Butcher			1	
Cabinetmaker	3	1	5	3
Apprentice		1		
Carpenter	1	1	1	5
Master carpenter		2		
Cobbler (Shoemaker)	5	4	6	6
Apprentice		2		
Cooper		2	2	2
Dairy		1*		2*
Doctor				1
Farmer	13		7	2
Farm laborer		13	4	
Works on farm			5	11
Female Seminary (Dormitory)	1*			
Gardener (Nurseryman)	2	2		4 + 1*

Occupation	1850 Census	1860 Census	1870 Census	1880 Census
General agent (J. M. Bimeler)	1			
Herdsman	2			
Hotel landlord	1	1	2	2
Landlady				1*
Cook				2*
Domestic servant				10*
Works at hotel				1
Barkeeper			1	
Ironworker		1		
Jeweler (watch repair?)				1
Justice of the peace			1	
Laborer	9	1	13	7
Merchant	3	2	4	1
Clerk in store		1		4 + 1*
Miller	1	5	4	3
Millwright (machinist)	2	2	3	1
Miner		2		
Painter				1
Planing Mill				2
Printer's apprentice		2		
Saddler			1	1
Sawmill				1
Schoolteacher			1	2
Seamstress				6*
Shepherd	2	1	1	2
Spinner		1	2	
Stonemason	3	3	3	1
Tailor	2	3	4	2
Tanner	2	2	3	2
Apprentice		2		
Teamster (drayer, ostler)	2	5	10	
Tinsmith		1	1	1
Trustee (overseer)		2		2
Wagonmaker (wheelwright)	1	2	2	4
Apprentice		1		
Washerwoman				2*
Woolen Mill				
Weaver	4	5	3	

Occupation	1850 Census	1860 Census	1870 Census	1880 Census
Dyer			1	1
Spooler	1			
Clothier (tailor)	1			
Carding	2			
Works in Woolen Mill			2	4

Occupations were either self-selected or ones chosen by census takers and are not consistent from census to census. The language barrier should also be taken into consideration. Some of the workers listed were hired labor, not Society members. Note that the language in this table comes directly from the censuses.

*Numbers marked with an asterisk were positions filled by women.

Articles of Agreement, 1824

1824 ARTICLES OF ASSOCIATION

The Articles of Association of the Society of Separatists of Zoar, Tuscarawas County, Ohio, adopted by its members March 18, 1824.

In the name of God the Father, and Jesus Christ the Son, and the Holy Ghost, Amen.

We, the undersigned inhabitants of Zoar and its vicinity, in Tuscarawas County and State of Ohio, being fully persuaded and intending to give more full satisfaction to our consciences in the fulfillment of the duties of Christianity and to plant, establish, and confirm the spirit of love as the bond of peace and union for ourselves and our posterity forever as a safe foundation of social order, do seek and desire, out of pure Christian love and persuasion, to unite our several personal interests into one common interest, and if possible to avoid and prevent lawsuits and contentions, or otherwise to settle and arbitrate them under the following rules, in order to avoid the disagreeable and costly course of the law as much as possible.

Therefore we unite and bind ourselves by and through this common and social contract, under the name and title of "The Separatist Society of Zoar," and we agree and bind ourselves and promise each other and all together that we will strictly hold to, observe and support all the following rules and regulations as faithfully as it ever may be possible.

In like manner, we promise to support and warrant any such new articles, amendments, or alterations, which may be in favor of the above expressed intentions, if such should be added to these articles, and obtain the consent of the several members and subscribers hereof.

ARTICLE 1

We, the undersigned members of the second class of the Society of Separatists, declare through this first article the entire renunciation and resignation of all our property, of all and every dimension, form, and shape, present and future, movable and immovable or both, for ourselves, our heirs and our posterity, with all and every right of ownership, title, claims, and privileges to the aforesaid Society of Separatists, with the express condition that from the date of the subscription of each member such property shall be forever, and also after the death of such member or members, remain the property of the said Separatist Society.

ARTICLE 2

We hereby declare that each male member at the age of twenty-one, and each female person at the age of eighteen years, being possessed with the requisite qualities and signing these articles, may become members of this Society. New members will be admitted through and by the following form, but it will be necessary for them, as well as for the first members, to resign all their property, as well for themselves as for their posterity, honestly and faithfully, and to renounce all their rights, titles, and claims entirely, and to make over the same to the directors of the Society.

ARTICLE 3

The Society elects its own directors and their successors in office, who do take and shall take all the property, as well that of the individual members as also that of the whole Society, together with all rights, titles, benefits and claims of all and every description, be the same present or future, movable and immovable, with all their authorities and powers, into their disposition, and who are hereby required to hold and manage for the general benefit of this Society and according to the prescriptions of these articles, and which they shall conscientiously apply as aforesaid to the best of their skill and understanding.

They, the said directors, shall be in duty bound to consult upon and to conduct the whole economy of the Society. They shall have power to trade, to purchase and to sell, to conclude contracts, and to dissolve them again, to allow and give orders, to which, however, they shall all have to agree and obtain the consent of the cashier thereto.

The said directors shall further conduct and regulate the laboring part of the business of the Society, and they shall have a right, whenever it may be necessary, to appoint agents or subagents for the purpose of doing or causing to be done such business as they may find suitable and necessary.

They, the said directors, shall also conduct the entire provision of all and every member in boarding, clothing, dwelling, and other necessaries of life, in such proportion as situation, time, and circumstances may require.

ARTICLE 4

We, the undersigned, promise and bind ourselves, diligently and in the most faithful manner, to obey the orders and regulations of the directors and their agents without opposition, or murmuring; we further agree to apply all our strength, good will, diligence, and skill during life to the general benefit of the Society and satisfaction of said directors.

In like manner, we do promise and agree under the same expressions and de-terminations, that our children, during the time of their minority, be subjected to all the regulations and dispositions of the aforesaid directors, not only as it regards labor and their provisions, but also to any other kind of labor, employment, or engagement, in or out of the Society, as long as they are minors or as long as said directors may find it best to do so; and the directors shall have the same power to do so as soon as they may find it suitable and more beneficial to do so, as if the parents of such children had done this themselves; for the binding of children out of the Society, however, a majority of the votes of the members must first be obtained.

ARTICLE 5

This article entitles and empowers the directors of the Society and their suc-cessors in office, in the name of the Society, to receive and take charge of all in-heritances of deceased members, together with all the rights, titles and claims in and to the same, and to ask, demand, and hold the same; in short, they shall have full right and power, as if such deceased person or persons were yet living and did themselves ask for, demand, and receipt for the same; consequently the children, friends, or relatives cannot become heirs of their parents, friends, or relatives, since all the property of the members is by them doomed to be and remain forever the property of the said Society.

The directors of said Society are further, by this fifth article, entitled and em-powered to appoint other suitable persons under them, even out of the Society, and empower them to collect, or cause others to have collected, properties, goods, or moneys belonging to members who may yet be living, as well as such who may be deceased, and to receipt or cause them to be receipted for, the same even as if the person or persons for whom it was done had collected, taken charge of, and receipted for the same themselves.

ARTICLE 6

Casual contentions or disputes between two or more members shall be made known to the directors of the Society, and shall be by them investigated and de-cided according to the majority of' their votes. Should, however, the dispute of any member or members be against more than one of the directors themselves, then the parties shall have a right to appeal; or if any of the parties should not be satisfied with the decision of two disinterested directors, then such party may proceed to an appeal, which appeal shall be and consist in the following form:

ARTICLE 7

There shall be a board of arbitration or court of appeal elected by the Society, who shall be empowered and established by this article; such board may consist in from one to three persons, and shall be elected by the Society, and through a majority of votes; said board shall be invested with the highest and concentrated power of the Society, whose organ or instrument it shall actually be.

Said board of arbitration—may it consist in one, two, or three persons—shall be bound to observe all the different branches of economy of the Society, and, whenever they may find it necessary, to give orders and instructions, to investigate accounts and plans which may have been made by the directors or their agents; in short, all transactions of importance and of the value of more than fifty dollars, shall have to obtain the consent of said board of arbitration before they shall be considered binding and valid.

The decision of said board of directors, in all kinds of litigation, without any exception, shall be treated and considered as final and conclusive. Whoever acts contrary and will not be satisfied with their judgement shall forfeit and lose all the enjoyments and rights of a member; and such further binds himself, in case he or they shall apply to any court of justice for a decision out of the Society, to pay to said Society all the damages accruing by such application, besides the costs accruing to said Society by reason of such suit in law.

Said board of arbitration shall further have power in the name of the Society, according to circumstances and when sufficient complaints have been adduced by the directors, to cross out their names and signatures, and to deprive them of all future enjoyments of the Society.

In like manner shall such arbitrators determine upon the sum or sums which such excommunicated person or persons shall have to pay to said directors for damages caused by them to said Society, for which purpose the directors of the Society shall hereby be empowered in case of a refusal or nonfulfillment of this article to take legal measures against such excommunicated and refractory members and to force them to the fulfillment of their duty and to the payment of damages as above mentioned, through the existing form of the general laws of the land.

All the judgments given by said board of arbitration, under the form and circumstances above mentioned, shall be made out in writing and entered into a book prepared for that purpose, and shall in all courts of justice be considered valid, effective, and irrevocable.

ARTICLE 8

Each person desiring to become a member of this Society must first be of full age; that is, each male person must be twenty-one and each female person must be eighteen years of age or more. Applications for admittance as members must be made to one or more of the directors, who shall investigate the reasons, grounds and capability of such applying person or persons, and if they find no direct cause of objection against such person, they shall give notice of such application to the board of arbitration and shall invite such person to appear at a certain time and place, and if then no impediment shall be found, and at least two-thirds of the Society shall vote for the reception of such person, then the applicant shall be by said board of directors admitted to sign these articles of association.

ARTICLE 9

The elections for arbitrators and directors shall be held as often as the Society may deem it suitable and necessary, and without having first determined upon any particular form for the same. There shall at all times, if possible, be three directors in office, yet, for the want of one, two shall be capable of transacting business, and each candidate for said office must have been a good member of the Society for at least five years previous, and must have proven a good moral character.

A member of the board of arbitration must have been a member of the Society for at least ten years previous, and must have lived without blemish as much as possible, if he shall be considered eligible. This shall, however, not be counted from the date of the signatures to these articles, but from the time of the reception and free exercise of the general principles of the Separatists.

Members of the board of arbitration must be members, but they may be non-subscribers. Directors, however, must be both members and subscribers to these articles. All subscribers, male and female, have a right to vote at elections, except if anyone by disorderly deportment, should have rendered himself for a time or even forever unfit for said purpose, on which the directors in office, or for want of them, the board of arbitration, shall have to decided [sic]. The officers shall be elected and established by a majority of the votes, consequently the highest power shall be and remain forever in the hands and disposition of the Society, which hereby reserves the right at pleasure to remove and establish officers or to place others in their stead; in short, to make any alterations which may be deemed best.

ARTICLE 10

The Society keeps and elects its own cashier, whose duty it shall be to manage its receipts, moneys, and expenditures, and besides him, no one shall be entitled to keep any moneys without the order of the cashier. Even the directors shall, without delay, deliver all moneys, notes, bonds, and the like, as property belonging to the Society, into the hands of the cashier. Every transgressor of this provision may be accused by any member or other person before the board of arbitration, and shall be by them treated and dealt with according to the provisions of the seventh article. The cashier is further bound to apply all moneys which may come into his hands by the order of the directors and arbitrators to the benefit of the Society, to pay its debts, and to liquidate its general wants.

ARTICLE 11

Individual demands, whether made by backsliding members or by such who, because of disorderly deportment, may have been excommunicated, may such demands consist in money, goods, or other effects, under whatever name, shall be by this article, for ourselves as well as for our posterity, forever abolished and abrogated; neither shall there ever be any demands made to the Society by anyone for any remuneration for services nor wages for any labor done for said Society. All attempts made with this intent shall be confined to the provisions of the seventh article. All deficiencies and equivocations in these bylaws shall never be explained in favor of the complainants or accusers, but shall always be translated and explained to the benefit of the Society, and be treated in the same manner.

All decisions and judgments passed by the board of arbitrators shall in every case be binding, valid, and have their full force. Disputes between directors and members or between both, shall also be decided by the board of arbitration.

ARTICLE 12

These articles made, established and adopted on the fifteenth day of April 1819, shall be treated and considered as the basis and foundation of these present articles; they shall be valid and in force until the signing of these present ones, and shall also be and remain the same to all those who signed them; and these present articles shall merely represent a more detailed explanation of the former, but in nowise shall these be considered or explained as a contradiction of the same.

This done in Zoar, Tuscarawas County and State of Ohio, this eighteenth day of March, in the year of our Lord one thousand eight hundred and twenty-four (1824).

The signatures of the members are hereby witnessed by the directors of the Society in office at the time.

Joseph Georg Ackermann

Jacob Schacker

Michael Sindlinger

Directors.

J. M. Bimeler,

Arbitrator.

Zoar Constitution, 1833

⎯⎯⎯◆⟩⟨◆⎯⎯⎯

CONSTITUTION OF THE SOCIETY
OF SEPARATISTS OF ZOAR

Pursuant to an act of the legislature of the State of Ohio, passed AD 1832, No. 126, entitled "An act to incorporate the Society of Separatists of Zoar, Tuscarawas County, Ohio," we, the undersigned members of said Society of Separatists of Zoar and its vicinity, have found it expedient to renovate our hitherto existing constitution as contained in the following articles:

In the name of God the Father and Jesus Christ the Son and the Holy Ghost. Amen.

In order furthermore to secure our consciences that satisfaction proceeding from the faithful execution of the duties which the Christian religion demands, and to plant and establish the spirit of love as the bond of peace and unity for a permanent foundation of social order for ourselves and our posterity forever, we therefore seek and desire in accordance with pure Christian principles to unite our various individual interests into one common stock; and, conformable with the example of the primitive Christians, all inequalities and distinctions of rank and fortune shall be abolished from among us and consequently to live as brothers and sisters of one common family.

Pursuant to the foregoing principles and resolutions, we voluntarily unite and bind ourselves by this joint agreement under the name of "Society of Separatists of Zoar," and we obligate ourselves each to the other, that we will hold to the following articles and rules; that we will observe and support the same to the best of our abilities, which from the day of the date hereof shall be in force and virtue in law.

ARTICLE 1

All elections for the divers necessary officers of the Society shall, agreeable with the provisions of the act of incorporation, be held on the second Tuesday of May annually, and, in accordance with the statute of the State of Ohio, be decided by ballot and majority of votes. On said election day shall annually be elected one trustee (extraordinary circumstances excepted), annually one member of the standing committee, quadrennially one cashier and an agent-general, unlimited in term so long as he possesses the confidence of the Society. The time and place, when and where the elections shall be held, also the number and kind of officers to be elected shall be made known by the trustees of the Society at least twenty days previous to the election; for which purpose the Society or any ten members thereof shall at each election appoint a committee of four persons whose duty it shall be to conduct the election in conformity with the laws of this country. The Society shall elect all the officers from amongst the members thereof; whereby special reference shall be had to the necessary and requisite qualifications, integrity, and faithfulness of the candidates.

ARTICLE 2

The Society shall elect from amongst its members three suitable directors as its directors or trustees and their successors in office who shall take charge of all the joint property of all the undersigned members; said trustees shall, as stated in the first article, be elected by a majority and agreeably to the following regulations: The majority for three years, second majority for two years, and third majority for one year, and after the expiration of one year, annually one trustee. Should the case occur that one or more candidates of one and the same office receive an equal number of votes, then the balloting shall be repeated until a legal majority shall be obtained. Each trustee may remain in office for three years unless circumstances to the contrary, such as death, sickness, absence, refusing to serve, etc., render such impossible, or in any case the misconduct of any of the trustees cause the Society to discharge one or the other, and to fill such vacancy as said Society may choose; which right of discharging and replacing the said Society reserves to itself, before the expiration of the ordinary term of three years, or even of one year; yet each trustee shall remain so long in office until his successor be chosen.

Said trustees are hereby empowered and in duty bound to take charge of all the property, real and personal, which this Society either now or in future may possess, including all property of newly accepted members, movable and immovable, of whatever name and description it may be; likewise are they authorized to receive all kinds of legacies, donations and personal claims; in fine, every species of property to which any of the members may at any time have just claim, to demand and collect the same by legal proceedings, and shall appropriate and apply the same conscientiously to the best of their knowledge and skill, in behalf and for the exclusive benefit, use, advantage of said Society. And it shall also be the duty of said trustees carefully to furnish each member, without respect to person, with board, clothing, and dwelling and other necessities alike in days of sickness and of health as good as circumstances will allow. Said trustees shall furthermore take charge of the economical affairs of' this Society; consult over and direct all the business and consequently to assign to each individual member his duty and work to be performed, to which at least the majority of said trustees, if not all, shall be agreed. Said trustees are hereby empowered to appoint subtrustees or agents as many and to whatever purpose they may see proper and necessary; and all such subtrustees or agents shall be responsible to the said trustees for all their transactions. Said trustees shall fill the various branches of economy with suitable persons, who shall conduct the same, subject to the control of said trustees and liable to like responsibility for the conduct thereof as other subtrustees or agents. But all resolutions in regard to important undertakings shall be submitted to and be subject to the approbation of the standing committee, and said trustees shall at all times be responsible for all their transactions to said standing committee. Casual discord, differences, and misunderstandings shall throughout by way of arbitration be settled amicably by the trustees of said Society; in case this cannot be accomplished by and through said trustees, then the court of appeals, cited in the subsequent articles, shall solely [be] decided. And the said trustees are by this article bound to maintain peace and order in the Society; they are furthermore hereby authorized to propose to the board of arbitration or standing committee such regulations and improvements calculated to facilitate those purposes; and if a majority of both bodies approve of the measures thus proposed as proper and necessary, they shall thereupon be recommended to be observed as such, provided that such amendment be in no way contradictory to these articles.

ARTICLE 3

In order partly to simplify, and likewise in many instances to ease the business and duties of the trustees, the Society shall elect an agent-general, who shall act for and in the name of said Society. He is hereby authorized to buy and sell, make and conclude contracts, and to discontinue and annul them again; to employ agents beyond the circle of the Society and to correspond with them; also to issue and again to accept orders; to direct and superintend, to the welfare of the Society, all its trading and commercial concerns; in fine, all affairs which in anywise appertain to the aforesaid line of business of whatever name, shape and descriptions they may be, and shall be carried on under his direction and superintendence. In like manner shall all the manufactures and similar works be under his superintending care, to the furtherance and improvement of which he shall pay due regard, and to regulate them in such a way and manner as he shall from time to time find it most conducive to the general good of said Society. The agent-general shall furthermore be entitled to appoint subagents, when and as many as he shall stand in need of, who shall be empowered to transact in his name all such business as he shall see proper to charge them with; and said subagents shall be held responsible to the agent-general for all their transactions; and the said agent-general shall, in appointing subagents, act by and with the consent of the trustees, whose concurrence shall also be necessary in all undertakings of moment and importance; and for the due administration of the powers and duties hereby committed to his care and charge, he shall be accountable to the standing committee of the Society. All deeds, mortgages, and similar instruments of writing shall be executed in the name of the trustees and be placed in the safe-keeping of the agent-general.

ARTICLE 4

By virtue of these articles the Society shall elect from amongst its members a standing committee, which shall consist of five persons, but in case a vacancy of one or two members thereof shall occur, either by death, sickness, absence or otherwise, then the three remaining members shall be capable of transacting business until the next succeeding election; this committee shall be invested with the concentrated power of the Society and shall execute all those duties which are marked out for it in this constitution; in all extraordinary cases shall this committee serve as a court of appeals, and shall, as the highest tribunal, be hereby empowered to [be] decided as such, and the judgment thereof be final and binding in all cases, provided that no complaint shall be brought before it for decision except by way of appeal; that is, in case one or both of the contending parties should be dissatisfied with the decision of the trustees. Trustees can never at the same time be members of this committee. The election of this committee shall be so regulated that annually one member to said committee shall be elected, and that each member may hold his office for five years consecutively, and are at all times eligible again as long as they possess the confidence of said Society.

ARTICLE 5

The Society shall choose a cashier or treasurer to be elected for the term of four years, and shall, after the expiration of such term, be eligible again so long as the Society entrust him with the station; said cashier shall take charge of and duly administer all its financial concerns, and besides him none of the members shall be entitled to hold any money, without order from the cashier. Even the trustees and the agent-general shall deliver up all money, notes, bonds, checks, etc., as belonging to the Society into the treasury without delay; and every transgressor of this provision shall, by any member or person whosoever, be prosecuted for the same before the trustees of the Society and shall be treated by them according to the provisions of the tenth article. It shall also be the duty of the cashier to appropriate and apply all moneys received, conformable to the directions of the trustees, the agent-general, and the standing committee, exclusively to the benefit of the Society; to pay the Society's debts, defray the general necessaries, and to credit said trustees with the surplus funds. All and every person who has charge over any one or more of the branches of economy shall hand in their accounts to the cashier at such times as he shall see proper to order the same; and the trustees are hereby entitled to request from the cashier an annual account of his transactions if they deem it necessary. The cashier shall have the right, if circumstances require it, to appoint a clerk to keep regular records of elections and of such important measures which the divers officers shall deem necessary.

ARTICLE 6

We, the undersigned members, second class of the Society of Separatists of Zoar, that all our property of all and every description, which we either now or in future may possess, movable or immovable, or both, together with all claims, titles, rights, devise, and legacies, etc., of whatever kind and name they may be, as well for ourselves as our descendants, heirs, executors, and administrators, shall be forever given up to said Society, with the express condition that such property shall from the date of the signatures of each member forever henceforth, consequently after the death of each respective member, be and remain the exclusive property of said Society; also do we promise and bind ourselves most faithfully and industriously to execute all the orders and regulations of said trustees and their subtrustees or agents, without opposition and murmuring, and we likewise agree to apply all our strength, good will, industry and skill for life to the general benefit of said Society and to the satisfaction of the trustees; likewise do we promise and agree, under the same conditions and regulations, to place our children, whilst they are in a state of minority, under the directions and regulations of said trustees, in the same manner as if they were legally bound by lawful indentures to them and their successors in office, until they shall have attained their proper age, as defined by the laws of this State.

ARTICLE 7

In accepting new members the following rule and order is to be observed: Each and every person wishing and desiring to become a member of the second class of this Society shall first of all have attained to the lawful age, that is, a male person shall be twenty-one and a female eighteen years of age; secondly, such person or persons shall have lived in and dwelled with the Society for the term of at least one year and shall have been a member of the first class of this Society, without exception if even born and educated in the Society, and provided that they have faithfully fulfilled the contract previously concluded with the trustees of' this Society at their entrance into the first class. If such person or persons can show both the aforesaid qualifications, and the resolution not being prematurely made, but who by their own free will and accord, self-convinced are so resolved, such person or persons shall make known their intention to one or more of the trustees, whose duty it shall be to hear such persons; and if after having taken the applicant's motives into due consideration, no well-founded cause for rejection or postponement be found, then said trustees shall make it known to the Society at least thirty days previous, and appoint the time and place when and where such signing shall be performed; and if during the interval no complaints or objections from the part of the Society or any of its individual members against such person or persons be made thereupon, they may be admitted to the signing of this constitution, and after signing such are thereby constituted members of the second class of the Society, and shall be considered and treated as such; provided that in case such new member shall have kept secret any of his contracted debts or other obligations foreign to the Society, such members shall have forfeited all privileges and rights of membership, in case sufficient proof be found to establish the fact.

ARTICLE 8

In accordance with this article, the Society shall keep or establish a general education institute for all the children in the community, at the head of which such male or female overseers shall be placed whose qualifications shall be found best suited for said purpose, and, agreeable to this proviso, all the parents of children in this Society bind themselves to deliver up and place their children, after having arrived at the third year of their age or sooner, to the overseers of said institution, where said children shall receive, according to their age and faculties, appropriate education and tuition. Said overseers shall be chosen and engaged by the standing committee, subject to the express duty that they shall exert their best endeavors and care to give those children placed under their care, as well in moral as in physical consideration, the best possible education, thereby having in view not only the attainment of scientific branches of knowledge, but also gradually training them to performing the divers branches of manual labor. And it is hereby made the duty of said committee to keep strict superintendence over the institution. And they shall also be authorized to place such children, as soon as their age, abilities, and bodily condition shall permit, under the control of the trustees, who shall give them such employment as they may be able to perform.

ARTICLE 9

This article entitles and empowers the trustees of the Society and their successors in office, in the name of the Society, to receive and take charge of all inheritances of deceased members, together with all the rights, titles and claims in and to the same, and to ask, demand, and hold the same; in short, they shall have full right and power, even if such deceased person or persons were yet living and did themselves ask for, demand, and receipt for the same; consequently the children, friends, or relatives cannot become heirs of their parents, friends, or relatives, since all the property of the members is by them deemed to be and remain forever the property of the said Society.

The trustees of said Society are further, by this article, entitled and empowered to appoint other suitable persons under them, even out of the Society, and empower them to collect, or cause others to have collected, properties, goods, or moneys belonging to members who may yet be living, as well as such who may be deceased, and to receipt, or cause them to be receipted for, the same even as if the person or persons for whom it was done had collected, taken charge of, and receipted for the same themselves.

ARTICLE 10

Casual contentions between two or more members, and complaints, of whatsoever kind and description they may be, shall be brought before the trustees and by them examined and settled. But in case one or the other party shall not be satisfied with the decision of said trustees, or should any one or more of the trustees themselves be involved in such contention, etc., then appeal may be had to the standing committee or court of appeal, whose decision shall in all cases be final and binding. Whosoever shall act contrary to this provision and will not be satisfied with their judgment loses and debars himself of all further enjoyment and rights of a member.

ARTICLE 11

Should any member or members find cause to secede from the Society, they shall make known their intention to one or more of the trustees, whose duty it shall be to notify the Society thereof, in order that if any complaints be existing against such member or members, they may betimes be brought forward to said trustees, who shall thenceforward act in respect to them agreeable to all the attending circumstances; but should any seceding member, unknown to the trustees, have contracted any debt or debts upon the community or have been the cause of subjecting the Society to any cost or injury, in such case said member or members shall make satisfactory restitution or otherwise render such indemnification as the said trustees shall demand, and in case such seceder or seceders should not content themselves with the judgment of said trustees and refuse to make satisfactory restitution, in that case both parties, the trustees and the seceding members, shall be entitled to an appeal to the standing committee and the decision thereof shall in all cases be binding and final. Should any person or persons, notwithstanding this provision, be dissatisfied and apply to a court of justice beyond the limits of the Society for assistance, in such cases they are also hereby bound to render due indemnification for all damages and loss of time thereby caused to and sustained by said Society. In case any seceding person should refuse to comply with the demand of the trustees in pursuance of the decision of the standing committee, the trustees shall be authorized to prosecute such person or persons and by course of law to bring them or cause them to be brought to the due fulfilment of the duty or payment, as aforesaid. Furthermore, the committee shall be authorized to act in like manner with all those who, on account of acting contrary to duty and good order, have been expelled from the Society, to expunge their names and signatures, and to excommunicate them from all further enjoyment and rights of a member of the Society. Neither the seceding members who leave the Society of their own accord nor those who are expelled therefrom can ever by virtue of their signatures and by the provisions of this article, under any pretense whatever, in wise ever or make any demand or obtain, either upon property bought to the Society or for their labor or any other service which they may have rendered to the Society, in whatever the same shall have consisted, any compensation whatever. Yet such person or persons may, if they choose, submit their pretensions to the standing committee, whose opinion shall decide whether or not, or under what condition such applicant shall be entitled to receive any indemnity. All judgments of the committee issued pursuant to the foregoing prescriptions shall be made out in writing and recorded in a book kept for that purpose, which shall in all courts of law be considered valid and incontestable. Each given judgment of said committee shall be handed over to one or more of the trustees by virtue of which he or they are authorized to execute such judgment or cause it to be executed, either on voluntary terms or by the ordinary process of law. This constitution shall never in any wise be broken or annulled by dissatisfied or seceding members.

ARTICLE 12

This Society can at any time, whenever deemed expedient and necessary, alter this constitution, or any one of the articles thereof, or add thereto, provided that such alteration or addition shall always be founded on the principles of unity and the preservation of the Society, and only then practicable if at least two-thirds of all the members be in favor of it. In no wise shall this present renewed constitution ever be viewed as declaring or presenting ineffectual or void the articles signed by the members on the fifteenth day of April 1819, and those on the eighteenth day of March AD 1824. On the contrary, said articles shall be acknowledged as the basis of the present constitution. All unintelligibleness, equivocation, or deficiency which peradventure might exist in this constitution shall always be construed and treated in favor of the Society, and never to the advantage of individual members. At least annually, at a suitable place, shall this constitution be publicly read at the place of public meeting. Written and concluded in Zoar, Tuscarawas County, and State of Ohio, the fourteenth day of May, in the year of our Lord one thousand eight hundred and thirty-three.

Contract for First Class
(Probationary) Members

We, the undersigned, members of the first class of Separatists, party of the first part, and _____, _____, and _____ trustees elect, and their successors in office, of the Separatist Society of Zoar, in the county of Tuscarawas, and State of Ohio, party of the second part, have, through confidence mutually reposed in one another, established, and by these presents do establish the following rules and principles of social compact for the better fulfillment of the duties of mankind, which we owe one another, and also for the furtherance of our spiritual and temporal welfare and happiness.

ARTICLE 1
We, the said party of the first part, do declare, that by our own free will and accord we have agreed . . . to labor obey and execute all the orders of said trustees and their successors in office; and from the day of the date hereof henceforth to use all our industry and skill in behalf of the exclusive benefit of the Separatists' Society of Zoar, and continue to do so, as long as strength and health will permit, to the entire satisfaction of the trustees and their successors in office.

ARTICLE 2
And we do also hereby agree and bind ourselves by these presents to put our minor children under the care and control of the said trustees and their successors in office, in the same manner as if they had been bound by indentures to serve and dwell with them and their successors in office, for and during the term of their minority, subject to all the duties and likewise entitled to the same rights

and protection as indentured children by law are subject and entitled to, until they shall have attained their proper age as defined by the statutes of the State of Ohio.

ARTICLE 3

And the said trustees do hereby for themselves and their successors in office, agree and bind themselves to furnish the said party of the first part with suitable dwelling, board and clothing, free of cost, the clothing to consist at any time of not less than two suits, including the clothes brought by the said party of the first part to this Society; and in case of sickness, necessary care and attendance is hereby promised to the said party of the first part; and this performance of the trustees and their successors in office shall be considered by the party of the first part a full compensation for all their labors and services, done either by themselves or their minor children, without any further claim or demands whatever.

ARTICLE 4

Good and moral behavior, such as is enjoined by strict observance of the principles of Holy Writ, are by both parties hereby promised to be observed; hence, it is clearly understood that all profane language, immoral words and acts, which may cause offense amongst the other members of this community, are not only wholly to be avoided, but, on the contrary, all are to endeavor to set good examples and to cherish general and mutual love.

ARTICLE 5

The object of this agreement being, furthermore, to preserve peace and unity, and as such can only be maintained by a general equality among its members, it is, therefore, severally understood and declared that no extra demands shall be made or allowed in respect to meat, drink, clothing, dwellings, etc., (cases of sickness excepted) but such, if any can be allowed to exist, may and shall be obtained by individuals through means of their own and never out of the common fund.

ARTICLE 6

All moneys which the said party of the first part either now possesses or hereafter may receive into his possession, shall without delay be deposited in the common fund of this Society, for which a receipt, payable on demand, is to be given; but upon the request of the said party of the first part, in order to procure extra necessaries, as the case may be, a part or the whole of said deposit shall be refunded to the owner.

ARTICLE 7

All manner of misunderstandings and differences shall be settled by way of arbitration and not otherwise; that is, by a body of three or five persons, to be chosen by both parties, and their decision shall be binding on both parties.

ARTICLE 8

All rules and regulations contained in the foregoing articles (if any there be which are not plain enough or are subject to misapprehension) shall be so understood as never to be in opposition to but always in perfect accordance with the morale, usages, principles, and regulations of the members of the second class of the Separatists' Society of Zoar.

ARTICLE 9

These articles being fully and fairly understood, to their strict and faithful performance, both parties bind themselves in the most solemn manner, jointly and severally, their children, heirs, administrators, and successors in office by the penal sum of fifty dollars, current money of the United States of America.

ARTICLE 10

If, in consequence of the foregoing, a penalty upon any one of the parties to this agreement shall be laid, then, in case of refusal or noncompliance, the party so refusing may be prosecuted for the same before any magistrate or Justice of the Peace in such township, county and state wherein the defendant may reside, and judgment shall be had agreeable to the laws of this State, and said magistrate or Justice of the Peace shall forthwith proceed to collect such penalty and pay it over to the party who by law is entitled to the same. In testimony whereof both parties have hereinto set their hands and seals this ___ day of _____, _____.

Notes

Several abbreviations have been used for the various Zoar manuscript collections (or items within them) as referenced in the notes by the following:

Adamson Papers	Adamson, Jack and Pat, Collection, 1709-1975, MS-S1276AV, Ohio History Connection, Columbus, Ohio.
Bimeler Receipt Book	Adamson Papers, MSS1276AV, Box 2, Folder 4, Ohio History Connection, Columbus, Ohio.
"Harmony Builds the House"	1832 essay about Zoar by P. F. D. Contained in the Peter Kaufmann Papers, MSS136AV, Ohio History Connection, Columbus, Ohio.
Nixon Papers	Nixon Family Papers, MSS680AV, Ohio History Connection, Columbus, Ohio.
Society Clothing Register	Zoar Papers, MSS110AV, Box 37, Ohio History Connection, Columbus, Ohio.
WRHS Papers	Society of Separatists of Zoar Papers, MSS 1663, Western Reserve Historical Society Library, Cleveland, Ohio.
Zoar Papers	Society of Separatists of Zoar Records 1811-1945, MSS110AV, Ohio History Connection, Columbus, Ohio.

INTRODUCTION

1. Today, the correct German term is a single word, *Gütergemeinschaft,* but a two-word phrase was used by the Separatists (Nixon, "Society of Separatists," 27), and thus I will do so here.

1. "AND SPEAK THE TRUTH FREELY"

1. Society of Separatists of Zoar Records 1811-1945, MSS110AV, box 93, folder 3, Ohio History Connection Library (hereafter cited as Zoar Papers). Although several verses will be quoted in this chapter and the next, the entire translated poem appears in appendix 1. My thanks to Philip Webber for his translation.

2. Fritz, "Roots of Zoar," 1:31.

3. Fritz, "From Württemberg to Zoar," 4.

4. Fritz, "Roots of Zoar," 1:34.

5. Zoar Papers, box 93, folder 3.

6. Fritz, "From Württemberg to Zoar," 5.

7. Durnbaugh, "Radical Pietist Roots," 3, 6-7.

8. MacDonald, "Roots of Zoar," 1.

9. Peters, "German Pietists," 62.

10. Nixon, "Society of Separatists," 4-5.

11. Nixon, "Society of Separatists," 6.

12. For a discussion of the tenets of the Zoar religion as espoused by Joseph Bimeler, see chapter 4.

13. This is probably a reference to the visionary Barbara Grubermann, *infra*. Though the term *Werkzeug* was used more frequently by the Inspirationists of Amana, Zoar and Amana were in contact, and the term can refer to individuals whose activity predates that of Grubermann.

14. Webber, "Sylvan's Preface," 116-17.

15. Zoar Papers, box 93, folder 3.

16. This number is taken from the Zoar Membership Database, compiled by the author; also see Fritz's two articles "Roots of Zoar," mentioned above.

17. Fritz, "Roots of Zoar," 1:29-30.

18. Fritz, "From Württemberg to Zoar," 4. Pietist assemblies were allowed, per a ducal decree of 1743, but adherents still had to attend church services.

19. Fritz, "Roots of Zoar," 1:32.

20. Fritz, "Roots of Zoar," 1:31-32.

21. Fritz, "Roots of Zoar," 1:33.

22. Fritz, "Roots of Zoar," 1:33.

23. Fritz, "From Württemberg to Zoar," 3.

24. Fritz, "From Württemberg to Zoar," 35-36.

25. Fritz, "From Württemberg to Zoar," 37, 8, 37. This song, with its forty-four verses, has been analyzed by a German historian (Helmut G. Haasis, *Stephan Huber, Ein Volck, wo Freyheits Libe brent, scheut nicht Thiranen Macht,* Paris, 1993).

26. Fritz to the author, Aug. 1998. Anna Maria Morlok emigrated to Zoar and became a member of the Zoar Society, signing the original 1819 Articles of Agreement; Fritz, "From Württemberg to Zoar," 14. Fritz speculates the stars mimicked the military "orders" worn by the king and other governmental officials; the Zoar Star is depicted on the ceiling of Zoar's Number One House, on the doorway lintels of the 1853 Meeting House, and on the cover of their Membership Book. Additional points could be added (there are twelve points to the star on the first-class Membership Book [Zoar Papers, box 1, folder 4]) to show piety.

27. Fritz, "Roots of Zoar," 2:40.

28. Morhart, *Zoar Story*, 13. Hilda Morhart recalls the story of Johannes Brey-maier (1776-1834) who, while a prisoner at the Fortress of Asperg, was brought before Napoleon Bonaparte by Württemberg's Duke Friedrich so the French emperor could see what sort of men these Separatists were. Asked by Napoleon, "Do you know who I am?" Breymaier replied, "Ein Engel des Abgrunds," an angel of the underground, or of the Abyss (Revelation 9:11). Another prisoner, Johannes Goessle (d. 1827), was also brought before the French emperor. Without bowing or removing his hat, he accused him of great sin in causing the deaths of so many. Napoleon, offended, recommended the duke punish the two prisoners for their insolence. Instead, Friedrich later told them both, "If you had shown the Emperor any more respect than you do to me, I would have had you shot."

29. Separatist Principle 6. An English translation of the principles can be found in the Adamson Collection, 1709-1975, MSS1276AV, box 10, folder 9, Ohio History Connection Library (hereafter cited as Adamson Papers) and in appendix 2.

30. Fritz, "Roots of Zoar," 1:38.

31. Separatist Principle 10; see appendix 2.

32. Fritz, "Roots of Zoar," 2:35.

33. "Barbara Grubermann's Book of Visions," a small, handwritten book (written by another) in the Nixon Family Papers, MSS680AV, box 4, folder, 1, Ohio History Connection Library (hereafter cited as Nixon Papers).

34. Morhart, *Zoar Story*, 11.

35. Fritz, "From Württemberg to Zoar," 6. Fritz says the ruler regarded the Separatists as "enemies of the state."

36. Fritz, "Roots of Zoar," 2:30.

37. Fritz, "From Württemberg to Zoar," 10. To quell Separatist activity, soldiers were also quartered in 1804 in the towns of Dettinger unter Teck and Boll.

38. Fritz, "From Württemberg to Zoar," 30-32.

39. Fritz, "From Württemberg to Zoar," 10-11. Today one can visit the grounds of Monrepos, a popular resort, but it gives a visitor pause to think of the arduous labor required to hand dig this midsize lake with islands. The grounds of the prison Hohen Asperg can also be visited. It still serves as a minimum-security prison; Fritz, "Roots of Zoar," 2:35.

40. Fritz to the author, Aug. 1998.

41. Fritz, "From Württemberg to Zoar," 14.

42. Fritz, "Roots of Zoar," 2:39.

43. Fritz, "Roots of Zoar," 2:14.

44. Fritz, "Roots of Zoar," 2:15; Selig, "Great Famine of 1817," 45-46.

45. Fritz, "From Württemberg to Zoar," 15.

46. Fritz, "From Württemberg to Zoar," 15.

47. Petition to the king, Apr. 28, 1816, Adamson Papers, box 1, folder 1. Both this and the petition to Wilhelm I were signed by Separatist Kaspar Vetter (also Fetter), a vintner of Murr.

48. Second Brandenburg Petition, Nov. 14, 1816, Adamson Papers, box 1, folder 2.

49. Second Brandenburg Petition, Nov. 14, 1816, Adamson Papers, box 1, folder 2, p. 2 of translation. "We reiterated to the departed king for the immediate support to the acceptance of our plea to Brandenburg, but our petition [was sent] back

torn, without decision, probably because of some imperfection therein." The word *reiterated* leads the author to believe that there were two petitions to Friedrich, not just one.

50. Fritz, "From Württemberg to Zoar," 15.

51. Second Brandenburg Petition, Nov. 14, 1816, Adamson Papers, box 1, folder 2.

52. Zoar Papers, box 93, folder 3.

2. "REMOVE THE WHOLE IN A BODY TO THE WEST OF THE OHIO"

1. Zoar Papers, box 93, folder 3.

2. Durnbaugh, "Strangers and Exiles," 76.

3. Specht, "Philadelphia Quakers," 98.

4. Durnbaugh, "Strangers and Exiles," 76

5. Specht, "Philadelphia Quakers," 97.

6. Nixon, "Society of Separatists," 19, from an interview with former Zoar member Mrs. Salome Beiter, July 18, 1932.

7. Durnbaugh, "Strangers and Exiles," 77.

8. Durnbaugh, "Strangers and Exiles," 76.

9. Nixon, "The Society of Separatists," 19.

10. P. F. D., "Harmony Builds the House," 9. Although not firsthand, this is the only account of the voyage I have found that explains why the ocean crossing took four months, twice the typical amount of time. Recently, a document was found (Western Reserve Historical Society Papers [hereafter cited as WRHS Papers], container 1, folder 5) that mentions Halifax and lists the family names of those who paid for bread (*brot*) at Halifax, serving to confirm the Halifax story.

11. Nixon, "Society of Separatists," 18.

12. WRHS Society Papers, container 1, box 5. Historian Eberhard Fritz ("Roots of Zoar," 2:35) says Bimeler, along with early Separatist Stephen Huber, "vanish" from the records until their joint arrival in the United States in 1817.

13. Specht, "Philadelphia Quakers," 98; Thomas Cope to Thomas Rotch, Feb. 6, 1818, Rotch/Wales Collection.

14. List of indentures, 1817, WRHS Papers, container 1, folder 4.

15. Specht, "Philadelphia Quakers," 99.

16. Dunbaugh, "Strangers and Exiles," 79

17. The lands offered lay mostly in Pennsylvania counties to the north and west of Philadelphia. Thomas Stewardson and his partners offered four thousand acres in Potter County "gratuitously" but to be held in trust. Other proposals included land in Tioga, Lycoming, Wayne, McKean, and Jefferson Counties, all of which were in northeastern Pennsylvania. The one exception came from Jeremiah Warder and Sons, who proposed a ten-thousand-acre tract in the southwest corner of Virginia along the Clinch River, where there were few slaves "that work land." Nearly all the proposals made generous terms for purchasing, and many like Stewardson offered land gratis, but much of it was second-rate and unimproved. Specht, "Philadelphia Quakers," 99. The submitted proposals can be found in the MSS Cope Collection, Quaker Collection, Haverford College.

18. Thomas Cope to Thomas Rotch, Feb. 6, 1818, Rotch/Wales Collection; Durnbaugh, "Strangers and Exiles," 80.

19. Arndt, *Indiana Decade,* 1:379–80; Fernandez, "Communal Communications," 3; Durnbaugh, "Strangers and Exiles," 81, 85.

20. Minutes of the Committee, quoted in Durnbaugh, "Strangers and Exiles," 82.

21. Nixon, "Society of Separatists," 21; Randall, *History,* 6.

22. Fernandez, "Society of Separatists of Zoar v . . . ," 106; Zoar Papers, box 3, folder 6. One historian speculates that Haga did not want to deal with multiple signatories on the deed (Landis, *Annual Report,* 173), but this doesn't account for Bimeler not transferring the land over once the Separatist Society was formed in 1819 or became a corporation in 1832.

23. Thomas Cope to Thomas Rotch, Feb. 6, 1818, Rotch/Wales Collection.

24. Durnbaugh, "Strangers and Exiles," 80–81; Nixon, "Society of Separatists," 34–35.

25. Durnbaugh, "Strangers and Exiles," 83; Fernandez, "Society of Separatists v . . . ," 110. A receipt for this amount can be found in the Zoar Papers, box 29, folder 1.

26. Specht, "Philadelphia Quakers," 100.

27. Thomas Cope to Thomas Rotch, Feb. 6, 1818, Rotch/Wales Collection.

28. Durnbaugh, "Strangers and Exiles," 87.

29. Fernandez, "The Society of Separatists of Zoar v . . . ," 106.

30. Cope to Rotch, Feb. 6, 1818, Rotch/Wales Collection.

31. Cope to Rotch, June 4, 1818, Rotch/Wales Collection.

32. James to Bimeler, Nov. 30, 1818, WRHS Zoar Papers, microfilm reel 1, folder 1.

33. Durnbaugh, "Strangers and Exiles," 88, summarizing several letters in the Rotch/Wales Collection. A letter from Zoar Society attorney C. Espich (Zoar Papers, box 1, folder 2, translation in Nixon, "Society of Separatists," 25) states he is holding the Declaration of Trust "until you and the Society decide on something else."

34. Cope to Rotch, Sept. 5, 1818, Rotch/Wales Collection; Durnbaugh, "Strangers and Exiles," 88.

35. Zoar Papers, box 1, folder 2 (translation by Philip Webber).

36. Morhart, *Zoar Story,* 14; Cope to Rotch, Feb. 6, 1818, Rotch/Wales Collection.

37. Hannah Fisher to Cope, Mar. 16, 1818, Rotch/Wales Collection.

38. Zoar Papers, box 93, folder 3.

39. Bills of Lading, Nixon Papers, box 1, folder 13.

40. Nixon, "Society of Separatists," 21.

41. Gunn, *Note-Book,* 37.

42. Gunn, *Note-Book,* 62.

43. Gunn, *Note-Book,* 62.

44. WRHS Zoar Papers, microfilm reel 1, folder 1; a bill of lading, from Philadelphia to Pittsburgh from George Schwartz, May 9, 1818, items delivered to Stephen Huber. A second receipt (on back) is dated June 12, 1818, with delivery to Sindeville (Sandyville), Zoar Papers, box 1, folder 13.

45. Nixon Papers, box 2, folder 19.

46. Bimeler to Rapp, Sept. 11, 1818, quoted in Arndt, *Indiana Decade,* 1:569.

47. Webber, "Jakob Sylvan's Preface," 120.

48. Webber, "Jakob Sylvan's Preface," 120.

49. Articles of Association 1819, Zoar Papers, box 1, folder 4.

50. Levi Bimeler, *The Nugitna,* Jan. 27, 1896, also quoted in Nixon, "Society of Separatists," 27.

51. Fritz, *Database of Württemberg Separatists.*

52. "Johannes Breymaier's Leichenwörter," Aug. 17, 1834, quoted in Nixon, "Society of Separatists," 30.

53. Articles of Association, 1819, 1824, 1833, Zoar Papers, box 1, folder 4.

3. "WHAT IS GOOD FOR ONE IS BENEFICIAL TO ALL"

1. Zoar Papers, box 3, folder 2. John Kocher made the Zoar Society heir to a note he had inherited.

2. See Kantor's *Commitment and Community* and Etizoni's *A Comparative Analysis of Complex Organizations.*

3. For a complete discussion on how Zoar fits into sociological descriptions of community, see Meyers, *A Glance of Heaven,* 53-89.

4. Pitzer, *America's Communal Utopias,* and Lockyer, "From Developmental Communalism to Transformative Utopianism," 2-5.

5. Bäumler to Rapp, Nov. 27, 1820, quoted in Arndt, *Indiana Decade,* 2:151.

6. Nixon, "Society of Separatists," 33. Christina Petermann was the first child born in Zoar, on July 14, 1819, in a cabin in what is now the central Garden.

7. Nixon, "Society of Separatists," 34.

8. The 1829 marriages were Jakob Fritz and Barbara Ackermann, Aug. 6, 1829, and Matthiaus Bühler and Magdalena Barbara Neef, Sept. 17, 1829, Tuscarawas County Probate Court Marriage Records and Zoar Papers, box 3, folder 16. The "Copulation Book" (Adamson Papers, box 1, folder 8, http://cdm16007.contentdm. oclc.org/cdm/ref/collection/p16007coll10/id/2038) does not list these first two marriages. A myth has grown up around Bimeler's marriage, that Dorothea was a maid in his household and he, for prurient reasons, ended celibacy to marry her. Dorothea may indeed have kept house for Bimeler (there are no records indicating who lived where at this time), but she was no "maid" in age: she was forty-three and he was fifty-two years old at the time of their 1830 marriage. To answer the most-asked question in Zoar, it is unknown just how many, if any, children were born during the period of celibacy, as no vital statistics of that sort were kept in Zoar until the 1834 cholera epidemic.

9. Adamson Papers, box 1, folder 6; Nixon Papers, box 1, folder 19 and Nixon, "Society of Separatists," 33.

10. Articles of Association, 1824, translation in Nixon, "Society of Separatists," 240-41.

11. Nixon, "Society of Separatists," 242.

12. Nixon, "Society of Separatists," 242.

13. This seal is on display at Zoar Village State Memorial's Number One House.

14. The 1824 Articles of Agreement and the 1833 constitution can be found in appendices 5 and 6.

15. Nixon, "Society of Separatists," 75–76. Stories handed down included having to endure a monotonous diet, having to spin an entire skein of linen thread before being allowed to go to bed at night, and sleeping in an unheated attic.

16. "Separatist Society," *Ohio Statesman*, Sept. 18, 1859.

17. Zoar Papers, box 1, folder 4. First-class membership was lower in the hierarchy than second-class membership and may be a bit confusing to today's readers.

18. Nixon Papers, box 1, folder 1.

19. Nixon Papers, box 1, folder 1.

20. Nixon Papers, box 2, folder 18.

21. Poll Book of the Society, Zoar Papers, box 1, folder 8.

22. Hinds, *American Communities*, 32. This was probably trustee Jacob Ackermann, although Nixon ("Society of Separatists," 53) says Hinds's informant was Zoar gardener Simon Beuter.

23. Nixon Papers, box 1, folder 1.

4. "HE LOVES INFLUENCE"

1. Bimeler, Application for the rights of a citizen, granted May 2, 1804. Stadtarchiv Ulm, Bürgerrechtsaufnahmen (City Archives, Ulm, Acceptance of New Citizens), A 3770 No. 6. My thanks to both Dr. Hermann Ehmer and Peter Bachteler for this document and its translation.

2. Fritz, "From Württemberg to Zoar," 11.

3. Protestant Church Archives [Landeskirchliches Archiv] (LKA) A 26 Bü 482, Questioning of Separatists Konrad Schacher and Georg Striebel by the Municipal Court of Ulm, May 1, 1806, with reference to a decree concerning Bimeler, Apr. 12, 1805. Bimeler's questioning minutes have disappeared. Quoted in Fritz, *Radikaler Pietismus*, 182–84.

4. Contributors to Brandenburg Estate, WRHS Papers, box 1, folder 6.

5. Nixon, "Society of Separatists," 18, quoting Mrs. Salome Beiter, a former Zoar member.

6. Zoar Papers, box 2, folder 1, has a letter dated 1824 with his anglicized signature, *Bimeler*. This is the earliest known instance of his anglicized name.

7. Minutes of the committee, quoted in Durnbaugh, "Strangers and Exiles," 82.

8. Historian Hermann Ehmer speculates that he adopted the first name Joseph to illustrate his leadership (see Genesis 37–46). Conversation with the author, May 27, 2016. He signs his name "Jos. Mich. Bäumler" in a letter to Frederick Rapp of the Harmony Society on Sept. 11, 1818, the earliest known use of the name "Joseph." (Joseph M. Bäumler to Frederick Rapp, Sept. 11, 1818, quoted in Arndt, *Indiana Decade*, 1:569.)

9. Nixon, "Society of Separatists," 18.

10. Knortz, *Aus der Mappe*, 44; Bimeler, *Die Wahre Separation*, 1:15–16, trans. and quoted by White, "J. M. Bimeler," 7; Webber, "Jakob Sylvan's Preface," 112, 108.

11. Bimeler, *Etwas fürs Herz!*, 2:271, trans. and quoted in White, "J. M. Bimeler," 2–3.

12. White, "J. M. Bimeler," 3.

13. Sylvan, *Introduction, Die Wahre Separation*, vii, trans. in Webber, "Jakob Sylvan's Preface," 114.

14. Webber, "Jakob Sylvan's Preface," 110.

15. White, "J. M. Bimeler," 3; Knortz, *Aus der Mappe*, 38.

16. *Die Wahre Separation*, 2:115 and 1:57-58, trans. in White, "J. M. Bimeler," 9.

17. White, "J. M. Bimeler," 9; *Die Wahre Separation*, 1:59, trans. in Webber, "Jakob Sylvan's Preface," 105.

18. Sylvan, *Introduction*, vi, trans. in Webber, "Jakob Sylvan's Preface," 113; Knortz, *Aus der Mappe*, 42.

19. White, "J. M. Bimeler," 5; *Etwas fürs Herz!*, 1:68, trans. in White, "J. M. Bimeler," 5-6.

20. Webber, "Jakob Sylvan's Preface," 116.

21. *Die Wahre Separation*, 1:100-101, trans. in White, "J. M. Bimeler," 11.

22. The journey to sanctification is also illustrated by Englishman John Bunyan's *The Pilgrim's Progress* (1678), also a favorite book of the Separatists. Many copies of *Die Pilgerreise*, as it is called in German, can be found in the Zoar State Memorial book collections.

23. *Etwas Fürs Herz!*, 1:93, trans. in White, "J. M. Bimeler," 6; Ludwig Birk and Simon Beuter to name two. Zoar Papers, various.

24. Knortz, *Aus der Mappe*, 19-20.

25. Ohio Memory: A Collaborate Project of the Ohio History Connection and the State Library of Ohio, accessed Dec. 9, 2018, http://www.ohiomemory.org/cdm/search/searchterm/Zoar!funerals/field/all!subjec/mode/all!all/conn/and!and/order/nosort/page/1.

26. Hermann Ehmer, email to the author, Jan. 7, 2018.

27. *Die Wahre Separation*, 1:82, trans. in White, "J. M. Bimeler," 12; Hermann Ehmer, email to the author, Jan. 7, 2018.

28. Sylvan, *Introduction*, v, trans. in Webber, "Jakob Sylvan's Preface," 112; Knortz, *Aus der Mappe*, 39-40; *Die Wahre Separation*, 2:247, trans. in White, "J. M. Bimeler," 14.

29. *Die Wahre Separation*, 4:345 and 3:24, trans. in White, "J. M. Bimeler," 14.

30. White, "J. M. Bimeler," 15; Nixon, "Society of Separatists" 11-12.

31. White, "J. M. Bimeler," 16.

32. Nixon Papers, box 1, folder 6; Bimeler Receipt Book, Adamson Papers, box 2, folder 4, 264, 265, 270, 272, 273, http://www.ohiomemory.org/cdm/ref/collection/p16007coll10/id/2432. Hiserich was paid twenty dollars per month.

33. Adamson Papers, box 18, folder 7.

34. Webber, "Jakob Sylvan's Preface," 103.

35. Randall, *History*, 80.

36. P. F. D, "Harmony Builds the House," 16.

37. Nixon Papers, box 1, folder 14; Bimeler Receipt Book, 31.

38. The 1850 census has him living with his wife, Dorothea, and seven other people.

39. Goesele v. Bimeler, 14 *Howard* (US 55) (1852), 606.

40. Nixon Papers, box 2, folder 6. Nixon, "Society of Separatists," 32, says the year is 1821, but the document has the later year.

41. Randall, *History,* 82; Nixon, "Society of Separatists," 18; *Die Wahre Separation,* 1:18, trans. in Webber, "Jakob Sylvan's Preface," 102.

42. [Ripley,] *New Yorker,* 279. Ripley's unsigned article originally appeared in the Transcendentalist newspaper *The Dial* earlier in 1841. It is thought the 1838 visit by her and her husband, George, to Zoar was prelude to the founding of their own community of Brook Farm and may be the reason they were disappointed that Bimeler was not "a philanthropist" who might discuss with them the philosophical reasons for Zoar's communalism.

43. Sylvan, *Introduction,* ix, trans. in Nixon, "Society of Separatists," 109.

44. Goesele v. Bimeler, 14 *Howard* (US 55) (1852), Record of Depositions, 73.

45. Zoar Papers, box 1, folder 3.

46. *Tuscarawas Advocate,* Aug. 4, 1835.

47. Bimeler Receipt Book, Expenses 1846-48, 233, 237, 238.

48. Zoar Papers, box 86, folder 6.

49. Bimeler Receipt Book is one of many other ledgers in the various collections of Zoar Papers.

50. Jacob Sylvan to Joseph C. Hance, Jan. 2, 1855, Adamson Papers, box 9, folder 8.

51. Bimeler Receipt Book, 26, 93.

52. Bimeler Receipt Book, 225 illustrates several such trips by Charles L. Mayer and Ludwig Birk.

53. Zoar Papers, box 1, folder 3.

54. Nixon Papers, box 3, folders 10, 14.

55. Will of Joseph M. Bimeler, book 3, 187, Tuscarawas County Probate Court.

56. Nixon Papers, box 1, folder 20. This parenthetical statement regarding "interlining" is included in the original document.

57. Nixon Papers, box 3, folder 14. See chapter 6 for further information on the Sandy & Beaver Canal stock.

58. Sylvan, vii, trans. in Webber, "Jakob Sylvan's Preface," 114.

5. "ENGAGED IN AGRICULTURAL PURSUITS"

1. Nixon, "Society of Separatists," 120.

2. Beuter, *Tag-Buch.*

3. Nixon, "Society of Separatists," 119.

4. Nixon, "Society of Separatists," 122, 226.

5. Gunn, *Note-Book,* Nov. 13, 1889, 9-10.

6. Gunn, *Note-Book,* Apr. 17, 1893, 71-72.

7. Nixon, "Society of Separatists," 23.

8. Morhart, *Zoar Story,* 33, 129.

9. Nixon Papers, box 1, folder 20.

10. Nixon Papers, box 1, folder 21.

11. Adamson Papers, box 6, folder 2.

12. Nixon Papers, box 3, folder 2.

13. P. F. D., "Harmony Builds the House," 7a.

14. [Bateham,] *Ohio Cultivator,* Aug. 15, 1848, 118.

15. *Canton Repository,* June 4, 1875. Farm machinery parts were purchased from the Russell Co. in 1849 and 1855. "Commercial Ledger," Zoar Papers, box 51.

16. Nixon Papers, box 1, folder 9.

17. Nixon, "Society of Separatists," 127.

18. Potts, "A Queer, Quaint People," 371.

19. *Iron Valley Reporter,* Mar. 7, 1889.

20. "Separatist Society," *Ohio Statesman,* Sept. 18, 1859.

21. Nixon, "Society of Separatists," 125.

22. Hinds, *American Communities,* 28.

23. Nixon, "Society of Separatists," 125.

24. Author's experience working at Zoar Village State Memorial, 1975-2004.

25. Society accounts 1821, quoted in Nixon, "Society of Separatists," 32.

26. P. F. D., "Harmony Builds the House," 24.

27. Morhart, *Zoar Story,* 133.

28. Potts, "A Queer, Quaint People," 314.

29. Nixon, "Society of Separatists," 128.

30. Nixon Papers, box 1, folder 20.

31. Contract with Andrew Dyer, 1861; Bimeler Receipt Book, 169. Dyer received a third of the toll of wheat and buckwheat and half of the toll of corn and screenings. The contract was renewed through 1864. Zoar Papers, box 3, folder 17.

32. Nixon, "Society of Separatists," 128.

33. "Colony of Zoar," *Penny Magazine,* 411.

34. Bimeler Receipt Book, 57, 88.

35. Bimeler Receipt Book, 209.

36. Morhart, *Zoar Story,* 46, 50.

37. Bimeler Receipt Book, 67, 164, 190, 197. In 1848 the Separatists sold 571 pounds of wool, and in 1860 they sold twenty-four pounds of hops at twenty-five cents per pound.

38. Nixon Papers, box 3, folder 11.

39. Zoar auction poster, Coll. AV9, Ohio History Connection.

40. Nixon Papers, box 2, folder 6; Fernandez, *A Singular People,* 90.

41. P. F. D., "Harmony Builds the House," 10a-12a.

42. Bimeler Receipt Book, 89, 30.

43. Morhart, *Zoar Story,* 27.

44. Adamson Papers, box 6, folder 2.

45. P. F. D., "Harmony Builds the House," 11a.

46. Nixon Papers, box 1, folder 15; [Ripley,] *New Yorker,* 279, 280. The Society purchased four dozen cowbells in 1837. The Springhouse features long water troughs filled from the Society's water system that stemmed from the springs on the hill near the 1853 church. Stored ice cut from the canal may have been added during the warm months.

47. Woolson, "The Happy Valley," 283.

48. *American Socialist,* Aug. 1, 1878, 243; Adamson Papers, box 1, folder 14, contains an 1875 draft of a contract let to John Rice of Sandy Township for the Dairy Barn, which measured 210 feet by 50 feet, with two stories and two steeples. It cost $780 to frame, build, and shingle.

49. Christine, "Zoar and the Zoarites," 37.

50. Jenkins, *Ohio Gazetteer,* 490.

51. Maximillian, *Travels,* 156.

52. Morhart, *Zoar Story,* 79.

53. Bimeler Receipt Book, canal boat *Friendship* receipts, 1842, 30.

54. P. F. D., "Harmony Builds the House," 15a.

55. *American Socialist,* Aug. 1, 1878, 243.

56. Bimeler Receipt Book, canal boat *Friendship* receipts, 1842, 30; Nixon Papers, box 1, folder 10.

57. Morhart, *Zoar Story,* 127.

58. Nixon, "Society of Separatists," 129.

59. Bimeler Receipt Book, 64, 69; Nixon Papers, box 1, folder 8. An R. J. Black of Fairfield Co., Ohio, on Jan. 8, 1857, asks for a couple of grafts of the Zoar Beauty Pear, "as described by Mr. Elliott in his Western Fruit Book." He says it was formerly known as the Zoar Seedling Pear. Christian Wiebel replies the grafts will be sent when "frost is out of the trees."

60. Nixon Papers, box 2, folder 6, quoted in Nixon, "Society of Separatists," 130.

61. Hayward, "Journal," 278-79. This is the first contemporary mention of the Zoar Garden or greenhouse.

62. Quinby, *Diary,* Oct. 12, 1831.

63. Nixon, "Society of Separatists," 33.

64. Beuter, *Tag-Buch,* as quoted in Nixon, "Society of Separatists," 130.

65. Morhart, *Zoar Story,* 83.

66. Morhart, *Zoar Story,* 77.

67. Bimeler Receipt Book, 214.

68. Morhart, *Zoar Story,* 127.

69. P. F. D., "Harmony Builds the House," 15a; notes for 1850 Census, Nixon Papers, box 3, folder 11.

6. "THE WEALTH THEY HAVE ACCUMULATED IS ENORMOUS"

1. "Colony of Zoar," *Penny Magazine,* 411.

2. Nixon, "Society of Separatists," 36.

3. P. F. D., "Harmony Builds the House," 27a.

4. P. F. D., "Harmony Builds the House," 28a.

5. Hilda Morhart tells the story that a canal surveyor traveling through town made the offer to the trustees to dig this section. After deliberation, the trustees called a town meeting and the decision to participate was made. Morhart, *Zoar Story,* 33.

6. Landis, *Annual Report,* 176.

7. Nixon, "Society of Separatists," 36.

8. *Annual Report,* Ohio Canal Commission, 1833, Nixon Papers, box 3, folder 14.

9. Bimeler Receipt Book, 47 (1844) and 130 (1857). In 1863, during the Civil War, Christian Wiebel had to ask Levi Sargent of Newcomerstown, a member of the Ohio Board of Public Works, for a fifty-dollar partial payment of this yearly repair bill. Nixon Papers, box 1, folder 9.

10. Bimeler Receipt Book, 21, shows freight hauled by the boat *Industry* in 1841.

11. "Boat Friendship will, in all probability, not be in Cleveland this spring, having no produce to ship." Christian Wiebel to N. C. Winslow, Apr. 17, 1855, Nixon Papers, box 3, folder 10.

12. Nixon Papers, box 3, folder 10.

13. Bimeler Receipt Book, 238, 98; Nixon Papers, box 1, folder 6.

14. Bimeler Receipt Book, 44 and 294 (Brunny); 78 (Petermann).

15. Morhart, *Zoar Story,* 25.

16. Nixon Papers, box 1, folder 14.

17. In fact, Bimeler called himself the "master" of the *Industry* in a document dated June 9, 1835. Nixon Papers, box 3, folder 14.

18. Nixon Papers, box 3, folder 10.

19. Bimeler Receipt Book, 32 (1844); 77 (1849). These are some of the cities mentioned in the canal boat accounts for 1842 (30) and 1843 (31).

20. Zoar Papers, quoted in Nixon, "Society of Separatists," 145.

21. Nixon Papers, box 3, folder 14.

22. Bimeler Receipt Book, 26.

23. Bimeler Receipt Book, 40.

24. Nixon Papers, box 3, folder 10.

25. Gieck, *Ohio's Canal Era,* 202.

26. Nixon Papers, box 3, folder 10.

27. Bimeler Receipt Book, 25 and 66, and Zoar Papers, box 3, folder 1.

28. Zoar Papers, box 3, folder 1.

29. Zoar Papers, box 3, folder 1; Ledger 1833-53, box 4.

30. Nixon Papers, box 3, folder 14.

31. Nixon Papers, box 1, folder 10. Zoar was still shipping freight by canal in 1865.

32. Bimeler Receipt Book, 242.

33. Nixon Papers, box 1, folder 8. N. C. Winslow and Co. was known in 1849 as R. Winslow and Co. (Commercial Ledger, Zoar Papers, box 51, 3).

34. Nixon Papers, box 1, folder 8.

35. Bimeler Receipt Book, 198.

36. Morhart, *Zoar Story,* 58.

37. Potts, "A Queer, Quaint People," 431.

38. Bimeler Receipt Book, 233.

39. Nixon, "Society of Separatists," 119.

40. Nixon Papers, box 1, folder 18.

41. Zoar Papers, box 20.

42. Bimeler Receipt Book, 64, 72, 225, 228, 231, 236, all list buying trips to New York in 1842-51 by either Ludwig Birk, Charles L. Mayer, or Christian Zimmermann. Later, in 1867, David L. Silvan made a trip east on Oct, 14; he took with him $1,353 in currency and $2,460.87 and $6,966.08 in drafts and ended up buying goods worth $9,888.50 at Philadelphia and $1,233.28 at Pittsburgh. Zoar Papers, box 66, "Cash Book No. 27," 38 and 41.

43. Nixon Papers, box 1, folder 21. Zimmermann (see above note) was a Society member and went frequently on eastern buying trips. Stoerl, never a member, also

went on an earlier buying trip in 1850 (Bimeler Receipt Book, 241), but nothing else is known about him or why he was chosen to go on these buying trips.

44. Zoar Papers, box 4.

45. Commercial Ledger, Zoar Papers, box 51, 176.

46. Bimeler Receipt Book, 329, 191.

47. Adamson Papers, box 1, folder 13.

48. Nixon Papers, box 2, folder 6.

49. To learn about the vagaries of midcentury banking, the Society subscribed to the *Journal of Finance and Bank Reporter.* Nixon Papers, box 1, folders 8 and 9. They used the broker Drexel and Co. of Philadelphia, Bimeler Receipt Book, 329.

50. Nixon Papers, box 3, folders 13 and 15.

51. Adamson Papers, box 6, folder 1.

52. Bimeler Receipt Book, 155, 162, 351-55.

53. "Bills Payable" ledger, Zoar Papers, box 56.

54. "Bills Payable" ledger, Zoar Papers, box 56; box 6, folder 7. The interest paid declines to 3.5 percent by 1882.

55. Christine, "Zoar and the Zoarites," 33-34.

56. Jenkins, *Ohio Gazetteer,* 491.

57. Fritz to author, Aug. 19, 1998, provides biographical data on some of the early Separatists.

58. Nixon, "Society of Separatists," 120.

59. Bimeler Receipt Book, 85, shows Georg Grötzinger sold furniture; p. 68 shows "G. Cass" had a pair of pantaloons repaired at the Sewing (*Näh*) House, and p. 108 shows Jacob Fritz was paid to repair a piano.

60. An entire folder of contracts for the use of patent machinery, dating from 1828 to 1849, can be found in the WRHS Papers, microfilm roll 4.

61. Christine, "Zoar and the Zoarites," 38.

62. Nordhoff, *Communistic Societies,* 110.

63. *Tuscarawas Advocate,* July 28, 1835; Bognar, "Blast Furnaces," 508.

64. Zoar Papers, box 4, and Bimeler Receipt Book, 80.

65. Nixon Papers, box 2, folder 1. The terms were extended; the note was not paid off until 1847. Zoar Papers, box 4, 80. Nixon gives an earlier date of 1845; Nixon, "Society of Separatists," 138.

66. Bognar, "Blast Furnaces," 508, 510.

67. *Republican Advocate,* May 6 and Nov. 1, 1837. Both were advertisements for the store operated by William Childs.

68. Nixon, "Society of Separatists," 139-40; Nixon Papers, box 2, folders 9, 10.

69. Nixon Papers, box 2, folder 10.

70. Nixon Papers, box 2, folder 10.

71. Bimeler Receipt Book, 42 (Zoar Furnace) and 43 (Fairfield Furnace).

72. "Inventory of Zoar Fnace Establmt, Januar [*sic*] 1, 1844," Zoar Papers, box 4.

73. Smith's name was originally Schmidt; he was probably a German speaker from Austria-Hungary.

74. Randall, *History of the Zoar Society,* 43, among others.

75. Nixon Papers, box 1, folder 1.

76. Bimeler to Daniel Keller, Apr. 8, 1850, Nixon Papers, box 1, folder 6.

77. Bimeler Receipt Book, 96; Nixon Papers, box 2, folder 11; Zoar Papers, box 3, folder 2; Bimeler Receipt Book, 278; Zoar Papers, box 4; Nixon Papers, box 3, folder 18. Zoar attorney Joseph C. Hance was paid five dollars for writing the purchase contract with William Green of the Dover Iron Co. and another fifty dollars for "correcting the title of lands" purchased from Christmas, Hazlett & Co.—that is, Fairfield Furnace.

78. Nixon Papers, box 1, folder 7.

79. Morhart, *Zoar Story,* 41. This building, still standing, is where Hilda Morhart was born in 1899.

80. Bimeler Receipt Book, 100, 157, 158, 192; Nixon, "Society of Separatists," 141. The Commercial Ledger, 171 (Zoar Papers, box 51), shows they were selling ore to Jacob Burton of Massillon from 1868 to 1871 and getting pig metal in return. A list of taxable items for 1868 includes five hundred dollars' worth of castings, Bimeler Receipt Book, 214.

81. Nixon, "Society of Separatists," 142.

82. P. F. D., "Harmony Builds the House," 21–23.

83. Zoar Papers, box 86, folder 6.

84. "Colony of Zoar," *Penny Magazine,* 411; Bimeler Receipt Book, 190; Nixon Papers, box 1, folder 9.

85. Morhart, *Zoar Story,* 65. Merklingen in Württemberg, Bimeler's hometown, was noted for its fine linen (its town seal even today features a linen bleaching field). Bimeler, who began his adult life as a master weaver there (see chapter 4), is thought to have woven linen.

86. Morhart, *Zoar Story,* 65.

87. Nixon Papers, box 3, folder 12.

88. Adamson Papers, box 9, folder 36. Some of the coverlets in the Zoar museum collection are labeled "G[ottfried] Kappel & Co., Zoar 1845." It is presumed this "company," named for the head of the Woolen Mill, was created to sell the coverlets to outsiders. No direct documentation on such a company has yet been discovered in the Zoar manuscripts.

89. Nixon Papers, box 1, folder 18. The Woolen Mill record book (Adamson Papers, box 7, folder 3) shows the Society sold $712.78½ worth of custom work just for the month of January 1833.

90. Old Economy Village Archives. Unsure if this was processed or unprocessed woad.

91. Nixon Papers, box 3, folder 12.

92. Bimeler Receipt Book, 217 (beginning of year) and 214 (end of year).

93. *Iron Valley Reporter,* Nov. 27, 1890.

94. Bimeler Receipt Book, 87, 136, 145, 168.

95. Bimeler Receipt Book, 39.

96. Bimeler Receipt Book, 88; Nixon Papers, box 1, folder 10.

7. "WE ALL GREET ALL THOSE WHO HEARTILY WISH IT"

1. Reibel, *A Guide to Old Economy*, 5.

2. *The Community of True Inspiration* quoted in Nixon, "Society of Separatists" 150-51.

3. Nixon, "Society of Separatists," 151.

4. Arndt, *Indiana Decade*, 2:153; Bimeler to Frederick Rapp, June 30, 1818, quoted in Arndt, 1:544; Bimeler to Frederick Rapp, Nov. 27, 1820, quoted in Arndt, 2:151.

5. Rike and C. Zellerin to their Godmother in the Harmony, Aug. 25, 1817, quoted in Arndt, 1:379-80.

6. Bimeler to Rapp, June 30, 1818, quoted in Arndt, 2:544.

7. Boller and Solms to Rapp, Oct. 21, 1817, quoted in Arndt, 2:411.

8. George Rapp to Frederick Rapp, Sept. 30, 1817, quoted in Arndt, 1:399.

9. Boller and Solms to Frederick Rapp, Jan. 20, 1818, pp. 454-55; Boller to Frederick Rapp, Nov. 4, 1818; Boller to Frederick Rapp, Dec. 7, 1818; all quoted in Arndt, vol. 1. See chap. 2.

10. Arndt, *George Rapp's Harmony Society*, 76.

11. Durnbaugh, "Strangers and Exiles," 82.

12. Haga to George Rapp, Dec. 24, 1819, quoted in Arndt, 1:795.

13. Bimeler to Frederick Rapp, June 30, 1818, quoted in Arndt, 1:545.

14. Bimeler to Frederick Rapp, Sept. 11, 1818, in Arndt, 1:568-69.

15. Bimeler to Frederick Rapp, Nov. 27, 1820, quoted in Arndt, 1:151-52.

16. Bimeler to Frederick Rapp, Sept. 11, 1818, quoted in Arndt, 1:569.

17. Sylvan to Baker, June 24, 1859, quoted in Nixon, "Society of Separatists," 155.

18. Baker to Jacob Sylvan, Dec. 7, 1859, quoted in Nixon, "Society of Separatists," 157.

19. Bimeler to Frederick Rapp, Nov. 27, 1820, quoted in Arndt, 2:152.

20. Nixon, "Society of Separatists" 190-200. See chap. 9 for more on the court cases.

21. Report of the Standing Committee, quoted in Nixon, "Society of Separatists," 190.

22. Sylvan to Baker, Feb. 9, 1855, Harmony Society Papers, Old Economy Village.

23. Baker to Sylvan, Mar. 24, 1853, and June 18, 1853, Nixon Papers, box 2, folder 12.

24. Duss, *The Harmonists*, 95-96.

25. Baker to Sylvan, Jan. 23, 1857, Zoar Papers, box 86, folder 1.

26. Duss to L. Zimmerman, Apr. 27, 1896, Zoar Papers, box 86, folder 1.

27. Jacob Ackermann to Baker, Feb. 2, 1863, Zoar Papers, box 86, folder 1; Louis Heid to Economy trustees, Sept. 1, 1863, Zoar Papers, box 86, folder 1; David Sylvan to Baker, Nov. 3, 1863, Zoar Papers, box 86, folder 1; Bill to Economy, June 27, 1857, Nixon Papers, box 2, folder 12; June 19, 1883, Harmony Society Papers, Incoming Correspondence Files, Harrisburg, PA.

28. Bill for "Milch Cows," Mar. 5, 1856, Harmony Society Papers, Old Economy Village; Bimeler, order to Economy, Sept. 8, 1830, Harmony Society Papers, Old Economy Village; Bimeler to Frederick Rapp, Apr. 18, 1832, Harmony Society Papers, Old Economy Village.

29. Bimeler to George Rapp, Mar. 2, 1846, Harmony Society Papers, microfilm reel 76.

30. Kappel to Baker, May 16, 1866, Zoar Papers, box 4, folder 6.

31. Zoar trustees to Baker, Feb. 21, 1867, and Zoar trustees to Baker and Henrici, Mar. 20, 1867, Harmony Society Papers, Incoming Correspondence Files.

32. Sylvan to Baker, Oct. 30, 1854, Zoar Papers, box 86, folder 1; Nixon, "Society of Separatists," 154; Sylvan to Baker, Oct. 31, 1856, Zoar Papers, box 86, folder 1.

33. Zoar Trustees to Economy Society, May 28, 1863, Zoar Papers, box 86, folder 1; Jacob Ackermann to Lenz, Sept. 14, 1878, Harmony Society Papers, Incoming Correspondence Files; Jacob Ackermann to Henrici and Lenz, Oct. 23, 1882, Harmony Society Papers, Incoming Correspondence Files; Jacob Ackermann to Baker, Aug. 16, 1865, Harmony Society Papers, microfilm reel 105.

34. Bimeler to Baker, Aug. 18, 1845, Zoar Papers, box 86, folder 1; Nixon, "Society of Separatists," 134; Bimeler to George Rapp, Mar. 2, 1846, Harmony Society Papers, microfilm reel 76.

35. Zoar Store to Harmony Society, Sept. 1, 1847, Nixon Family Papers, box 2, folder 12.

36. Ackermann, Ruof, and Harr to Baker and Henrici, Aug. 4, 1863, Zoar Papers, box 86, folder 1; Jacob Sylvan to Henrici, Dec. 27, 1855, Harmony Society Papers, Old Economy Village.

37. Louis Heid to Economy Trustees, Sept. 1, 1863, Zoar Papers, box 86, folder 1; Zoar to Economy, undated, Zoar Papers, box 9, folder 1; Jacob Sylvan to Baker, Aug. 5, 1856, Zoar Papers, box 86, folder 1.

38. Accounts of Zimmerman, Nixon Papers, box 1, folder 17.

39. Sylvan to Baker, Apr. 13, 1859, Zoar Papers, box 86, folder 1.

40. See notes 28 and 32.

41. Zimmerman to Baker, Apr. 18, 1856, and Sylvan to Baker, Nov. 14, 1856, Zoar Papers, box 86, folder 1.

42. Sylvan to Baker, Oct. 31, 1856, Zoar Papers, box 86, folder 1.

43. Gunn, *Note-Book,* 39.

44. The program is in the Adamson Papers, box 10, folder 10. Nixon, "Society of Separatists," 157, says the date is 1896, but his source is descendant Salome Beiter, who may have been mistaken about the date, or there may have been visits by the band on consecutive years.

45. Schillinger to Haug, Feb. 1823, 541; Schillinger to Haug, June 18, 1823, 632; Bimeler to Rapp and Haug, Sept. 11, 1823; Schillinger to Haug, Dec. 10, 1823, p. 745; all quoted in Arndt, *Documentary History,* vol. 2.

46. Sylvan to Baker, Dec. 2, 1853, Zoar Papers, box 86, folder 1.

47. Sylvan to Baker, Feb. 9, 1855, Harmony Society Papers, Old Economy Village.

48. David Sylvan to Henrici and Lenz, Jan. 11, 1869, Zoar Papers, box 86, folder 1; Bimeler to Frederick Rapp, Nov. 27, 1820, quoted in Arndt, *Documentary History,* 2:152.

49. Beuter to Henrici, June 20, 1868, Zoar Papers, box 86, folder 1, quoted in Nixon, "Society of Separatists," 186.

50. Beuter to Henrici and Lenz, Apr. 22, 1878, Zoar Papers, box 86, folder 1.

51. Nixon, "Society of Separatists," 90-91.

52. Nixon, "Society of Separatists," 90-91.

53. Miller to Baker, Sept. 8, 1861, Zoar Papers, box 86, folder 1; Beuter to Lenz, Oct. 26, 1877, Zoar Papers, box 86, folder 1.

54. Sylvan to Baker, Jan. 3, 1861, and Apr. 11, 1862, Zoar Papers, box 86, folder 1.

55. Mayer and G. A. Weber to Lewis F. Birk, Jan. 20, 1844, Zoar Papers, box 2, folder 4.

56. Hinds, *American Communities,* 275.

57. Testimony of Christian Metz, Sammlung 18, no. 18, p. 97, Zoar, Apr. 22, 1843, Amana Society Papers.

58. Testimony of Christian Metz.

59. Metz, *Historische Beschreibung,* quoted in Nixon, 108.

60. Bill to Zoar Society from Ebenezer Society, 1846, Nixon Papers, box 1, folder 16.

61. Mayer to Sylvan, May 25, 1857; Zoar Society to Mayer, Apr. 12, 1859; John Beyer to Zoar trustees, Jan. 26, 1872; all Nixon Papers, box 2, folder 1.

62. Keilman to Sylvan, May 27, 1853, Nixon Papers, box 2, folder 1.

63. Zimmer to Zoar, Mar. 10, 1858, Nixon Papers, box 2, folder 1.

64. F. Moerschel to D. L. Sylvan, June 6, 1863, and Mar. 22, 1866, Nixon Papers, box 2, folder 1.

65. Zoar trustees to Mayer, June 29, 1858; C. Wiebel to Mayer, Sept. 8, 1858; Zoar to Mayer, Apr. 12, 1859; F. Moerschel to C. Wiebel, Jan. 30, 1862; F. Moerschel to D. L. Sylvan, June 6, 1863; F. Moerschel to D. L. Sylvan, June 27, 1863; all Nixon Papers, box 2, folder 1.

66. Zoar Papers, box 51; the date was June 21, 1850.

67. J. P. Trautman to Zoar, Sept. 24, 1881, Nixon Papers, box 2, folder 1.

68. Deed, Zoar Papers, box 4, folder 9.

69. Metz, *Historische Beschreibung,* quoted in Nixon, "Society of Separatists," 159.

70. Zimmer to Zoar, Mar. 10, 1858, quoted in Nixon, "Society of Separatists," 160.

71. Contract between Bimeler and Mayer, 1837, Nixon Papers, box 1, folder 20.

72. Nixon, "Society of Separatists," 158.

73. Metz, *Historische Beschreibung,* quoted in Nixon, "Society of Separatists," 158.

74. Mayer to Metz, July 9, 1843, Amana Society Papers.

75. Metz, *Historische Beschreibung,* quoted in Nixon, "Society of Separatists," 159.

76. Zimmer to Zoar, Mar. 10, 1858, quoted in Nixon, "Society of Separatists," 160.

77. Nixon Papers, box 2, folder 20; Wittke, "Ora et Labora," 131.

78. Wittke, "Ora et Labora," 135.

79. Nixon Papers, box 2, folder 20, as quoted in Nixon, "Society of Separatists," 162.

80. Wittke, "Ora et Labora," 146.

81. Nixon, "Society of Separatists," 162.

82. Nixon, "Society of Separatists," 162.

83. Andrews Shaker Collection, folder 1048.

84. Andrews Shaker Collection, folder 1048.

85. Hinds, *American Communities,* 30.

86. "Life and Experiences of Issachar Bates," 25.

87. "Life and Experiences of Issachar Bates," 26.

88. Hinds, *American Communities,* 31. In an interview with a trustee, probably Jacob Ackerman (Nixon says it was Simon Beuter), the trustee identifies a person,

presumably Blodget, as "a native of New Hampshire" and as the oldest member at age ninety-five. "He lived with the Shakers from 1830 to 1841, since then with us." This interview presumably occurred before Blodget's death in 1877; Hinds's book was published in 1878.

89. Zoar Membership Database, author's collection, and Zoar Membership Book, Zoar Papers, box 1, folder 4. Interestingly, it looks as if Blodget may have served in the War of 1812, probably before he joined the Shakers at Enfield, as a military pension is listed in a Zoar ledger under "Domestic [i.e., Society members'] Bills Payable." From all appearances, it seems Blodget never drew upon these funds and they were "assigned to the Society" upon his death. Zoar Papers, box 53.

8. "A LIFE FREE FROM CARE"

1. Sylvan, *Die Wahre Separation,* 1:ix, quoted in Nixon, "Society of Separatists," 109.

2. Nixon, "Society of Separatists," 84.

3. Nixon, "Society of Separatists," 65. Nixon says the horn blast included four ascending notes to which the Zoarites put words *Auf-der-Ar-beit* (on to work).

4. Randall, *History,* 12.

5. "Colony of Zoar," *Penny Magazine,* 412.

6. See appendix 4 for a list of occupations listed by the census.

7. Nixon Papers, box 1, folder 20. The farmer was paid a third in cash and two-thirds in trade at the store.

8. Nixon, "Society of Separatists," 124.

9. Hinds, *American Communities,* 28. Although tobacco use was regarded as sinful, one prominent member, Gottfried Kappel Sr., the head weaver, apparently started using tobacco and snuff in Aug. 1849. Society Clothing Register, 154.

10. Nixon Papers, box 1, folder 19. Mary Ann Short Beiter died in 1905.

11. Nixon Papers, box 1, folder 19. Several sources (below and *Cleveland, Ohio: Pictorial and Biographical Deluxe Supplement*), give Bührer's age as seventeen when he departed Zoar for Cleveland. However, the Society Clothing Register, 151, shows him receiving many items of clothing from 1843 to Jan. 1845, which suggests he left Zoar at age nineteen, not seventeen. Bührer was born Dec. 25, 1825.

12. Case Western Reserve University, "Bührer, Stephen," https://case.edu/ech/articles/b/buhrer-stephen.

13. Zoar Papers, boxes 51, 85, 249, 265.

14. Nixon, "Society of Separatists," 186.

15. Nixon Papers, box 3, folder 7.

16. Morhart, *Zoar Story,* 51–52. Bread cloths were sold to outsiders as well, Society Clothing Register, 114, account of outsider Jethro Macy. The cost was twenty-eight cents. It's not known if the Macy family used their bread cloth to obtain bread at the Zoar Bakery.

17. Nixon, "Society of Separatists," 164.

18. Zoar Papers, box 86, folder 10; Nixon, "Society of Separatists," 39.

19. Birth and Death Book, Nixon Papers, box 4, folder 6.

20. Mitchener, *Ohio Annals,* 326–27.

21. Morhart, *Zoar Story,* 75.

22. Zoar Papers, box 2, folder 70.

23. Zoar Papers, box 2, folder 63; Nixon Papers, box 3, folder 15.

24. Hinds, *American Communities,* 27-28.

25. "Separatist Society," *Ohio Statesman,* Sept. 18, 1859.

26. Quinby, *Diary.*

27. Randall, *History,* 47.

28. P. F. D., "Harmony Builds the House," 18.

29. Owen, "Foodways," 13-14.

30. Morhart, *Zoar Story,* 63.

31. Owen, "Foodways," 28-30.

32. P. F. D., "Harmony Builds the House," 19-20.

33. Owen, "Foodways," 28; Nixon, "Society of Separatists," 71.

34. Morhart, *Zoar Story,* 27.

35. Nixon, "Society of Separatists," 72.

36. Nixon, "Society of Separatists," 121.

37. Morhart, *Zoar Story,* 47, 69.

38. Nixon, "Society of Separatists," 72; Morhart, *Zoar Story,* 47.

39. P. F. D., "Harmony Builds the House," 19.

40. Bimeler Receipt Book, 5-6.

41. Morhart, *Zoar Story,* 52.

42. Bimeler Receipt Book, 5-6.

43. Nixon, "Society of Separatists," 70; Morhart, *Zoar Story,* 52.

44. Morhart, *From Field to Table,* 51; Morhart, *Zoar Story,* 52; Nixon, "Society of Separatists," 77. The author has used this recipe to make whole-wheat bread, and it does work but takes quite a long time to rise.

45. Nixon, "Society of Separatists," 77.

46. Morhart, *Zoar Story,* 116.

47. Hinds, *American Communities,* 25.

48. Morhart, *Zoar Story,* 82.

49. Nixon, "Society of Separatists," 73.

50. Nixon, "Society of Separatists," 72, 73.

51. Notes for 1850 census, Nixon Papers, box 3, folder 11.

52. Both the 1860 and 1880 census lists Elizabeth Mock as heading the Dairy. Morhart, *Zoar Story,* 70, lists Jacobina Roth Dischinger, Mary Rieker Rouf, and Charlotte Breymaier.

53. "Separatist Society," *Ohio Statesman,* Sept. 18, 1859.

54. An example of such a cushion or "head pad" can be seen today on display at Number One House.

55. P. F. D., "Harmony Builds the House, 20.

56. *The American Socialist,* Dec. 12, 1878; Christine, "Zoar and the Zoarites," 36; P. F. D., "Harmony Builds the House," 20.

57. "Separatist Society," *Ohio Statesman,* Sept. 18, 1859.

58. Morhart, *Zoar Story,* 71. The "Working Book for Masons" [Adamson Papers, box 2, folder 4] lists innumerable instances of whitewashing.

59. Nixon, "Society of Separatists," 79.

60. P. F. D., "Harmony Builds the House," 20-21.

61. Zoar Papers, box 1, folder 5; the purchase of use of a patent for a washing machine in 1831 can be found in WRHS Papers, microfilm reel 4.

62. Bimeler Receipt Book, 87.

63. P. F. D., "Harmony Builds the House," 21. Outsiders did sometimes pay for clothing repair (ten cents for repairing G. Cass's "pantafons" [pantaloons] at the "Näh" [Sewing] Haus in 1848) and shoes (sold in 1858, 1859, 1861). Bimeler Receipt Book, 58, 136, 145, 168.

64. J. B. L., "The 'Zoar-ites' or Separatists," *Summit Beacon,* July 12, 1862.

65. [Ripley,] *The New Yorker,* 279; Howe, *Historical Collections,* 700.

66. Woolson, "The Happy Valley," 283; [Ripley,] *New Yorker,* 279.

67. Morhart, *Zoar Story,* 89. The Bible verse is 1 Timothy 2:9: "In like manner that the women adorn themselves in modest apparel, with shamefacedness and sobriety; not with braided hair, and gold or pearls or costly raiment."

68. Morhart, *Zoar Story,* 66, the memories of descendant Helen Burkhart.

69. P. F. D., "Harmony Builds the House," 17.

70. Nixon, "Society of Separatists," 67.

71. Mrs. Helena Beuter (Jacob) Class, interview with the author, ca. 1975. Mrs. Class was born in 1889.

72. Maximillian, *Travels,* 156.

73. Morhart, *Zoar Story,* 67.

74. Collection of the Western Reserve Historical Society, catalog no. 42.531 *et seq.* Some of these items, borrowed from Western Reserve, were on display at Zoar's Number One House in 2018.

75. Nixon, "Society of Separatists," 68.

76. Society Clothing Register, 97, lists a credit of $135.44 from Christian Leins of Ulm on J. Peter Bimeler's (Joseph Bimeler's son and a second-class [or full] member) account page.

77. Nixon, "Society of Separatists," 77; P. F. D., "Harmony Builds the House," 18a.

78. Nixon Papers, box 3, folder 7. In Oct. 1837 thirty-two females and twenty-six males attended the Zoar School, called Lawrence Twp. School District No. 1.

79. Bimeler Receipt Book, 92. Simon Beuter received $152 in 1854 for his "school teaching wage," which was turned over to the Society coffers.

80. Thomas White school contract, Nixon Papers, box 3, folder 7; Nixon, "Society of Separatists," 96.

81. *Tuscarawas Advocate,* Sept. 11, 1884.

82. P. F. D., "Harmony Builds the House," 21a

83. Nixon Papers, box 3, folder 7. These "outside scholars" paid one dollar per year for tuition and books.

84. Nixon Papers, box 1, folder 17.

85. Nixon, "Society of Separatists," 98.

86. Nixon Papers, box 1, folder 6.

87. Morhart, *Zoar Story,* 108. The word *Spazierengehen,* used by Morhart, may be Zoar dialect. A more correct German word is *Spaziergang.*

88. Ott to Feucht, Sept. 11, 1866, in Arndt, *Rapp's Re-Established Harmony Society* (subsequent translation by Hilda Kring), 813–14.

89. Adamson Papers, box 9, folder 35.

90. Nixon Papers, box 1, folder 9.

91. Nixon, "Society of Separatists," 83.

92. Adamson Papers, box 9, folder 15.

93. Potts, "A Queer, Quaint People," 430.

94. Ott to Feucht, Sept. 3, 1865, in Arndt, *Rapp's Re-Established Harmony Society,* 767-68. Ott married Zoar member Joseph Roth on Nov. 11, 1866, a little more than a year after writing this.

95. Zoar Membership Database. At least fourteen illegitimate births with the father listed as "unknown" occurred to women in Zoar families during the Society period.

96. Ott to Feucht, Sept. 11, 1866, in Arndt, *George Re-Established Harmony Society,* 814. Salome Rauschenberger Heid's son, Eugene, was born Dec. 14, 1866, just three months after this letter.

97. Nixon, "Society of Separatists," 83; Ludwig Birk, a member who acted as Society business manager, was appointed one in 1849. Society of Separatists of Zoar Papers 1839-57, MSS 984, folder 11.

98. Adamson Papers, box 12, folder 8. Marriage records are available for view at the Tuscarawas County Probate Court. The "Copulation Book" starts in 1830 and does not record the first two marriages in 1829, but the county records have that information. These first two marriages are also found in Zoar Papers, box 3, folder 16.

99. Zoar Membership Database. The death records in the database were obtained from the Birth and Death Book (1834-1907), Nixon Papers, box 4, folder 6.

100. Nixon, "Society of Separatists," 84; Nixon Papers, box 1, folder 14. Birk gave justice of the peace fees back to the Society coffers. He earned $68.42½in 1834.

101. Bimeler Receipt Book, 85; Nixon, "Society of Separatists," 203.

102. Nixon Papers, box 1, folder 3.

103. Nixon, "Society of Separatists," 204.

104. Beuter, *Tag-Buch,* quoted in Nixon, "Society of Separatists," 205.

105. *Iron Valley Reporter,* June 25, 1896.

106. Nixon, "Society of Separatists," 205.

107. Nixon, "Society of Separatists," 94.

108. "Leading Causes of Death at Zoar 1834-1905," list in possession of the author.

109. The Society Clothing Register lists and monetizes the services of a number of outside doctors. Treatments listed included purges (178) and vaccinations (221) at twenty-five cents each.

110. Adamson Papers, box 7, folders 15 and 1; box 6, folder 1.

111. "Register of Births 1851-1882," Nixon Papers, box 4, folder 6; Bimeler Receipt Book, 151.

112. Shackleton, "In Quaint Old Zoar," 517.

113. Adamson Papers, box 1, folder 20.

114. Nixon, "Society of Separatists," 106.

115. Morhart, *Zoar Story,* 104; Nixon, "Society of Separatists," 84.

116. Morhart, *Zoar Story,* 104; Nixon, "Society of Separatists," 84.

117. Morhart, *Zoar Story,* 103.

118. Quoted in Nixon, "Society of Separatists," 84.

119. Morhart has a detailed description of making apple butter, *Zoar Story,* 42.

120. Morhart, *Zoar Story,* 50.

121. Nixon, "Society of Separatists," 86, 87.

122. Morhart, *Zoar Story,* 101.

123. Potts, "A Queer, Quaint People," 372.

124. Adamson Papers, box 18, folder 26; Nixon, "Society of Separatists," 87.

125. Nixon, "Society of Separatists," 88.

126. Bimeler Receipt Book, 257, 252.

127. Nixon Papers, box 1, folder 17; Nixon, "Society of Separatists," 89. This 1845 bill for "piano forte wire" may be for the strings of one of Fritz's first pianos.

128. Nixon Papers, box 3, folder 2.

129. Zoar Papers, box 86, folder 5, and Nixon Papers, box 2, folder 7, include minutes and officers' lists.

130. Adamson Papers, box 9, folder 36.

131. Morhart, *Zoar Story,* 29.

132. Except for Mathias Schmidt, who set fire to the Zoar Furnace Coal House in 1835. See chap. 6.

133. Morhart, *Zoar Story,* 110, 113.

134. P. F. D., "Harmony Builds the House," 17a.

135. Nixon, "Society of Separatists," 94. A price list for this company was on display at the Zoar Town Hall in 2018.

136. Bimeler Receipt Book, 99, 149; Nixon Papers, box 1, folder 16; Bimeler Receipt Book, 86, 103.

137. Morhart, *Zoar Story,* 102; Fernandez, "The Zoar Artist." Unlike others, Maier signed his last name in the Articles of Association with a fraktur style *M.*

138. Christian Wiebel to Joseph Fetter, Oct. 29, 1863, Nixon Papers, box 1, folder 5.

139. Fernandez, *A Singular People,* 103. The date is written on the back of the photo, found in the Properties Collection, P365AV, Ohio History Connection.

140. Bimeler Receipt Book, 95, gives the cash amounts and Nixon Papers, box 1, folder 17, gives the list of articles sold, enumerated by Simon Beuter. Beuter's total of $51.70 does not agree with the $47.31 that Jacob Ackermann entered into the Receipt Book (done after Bimeler's 1853 death). I am using the Receipt Book total.

141. Morhart, *Zoar Story,* 82.

142. Nixon Papers, box 1, folder 16.

143. Adamson Papers, box 6, folder 2.

144. *Boehringer et al.* Petition, 1845. Zoar Papers, box 3, folder 9.

145. Post Office Records 1852–71. Zoar Papers, box 84.

146. *Iron Valley Reporter,* Feb. 11, 1882.

147. Colpetzer, "Regional Social Context," 46.

148. Howe, *Historical Collections,* 483.

149. Mansfield, *Tuscarawas County,* 565–67.

150. Colpetzer, "Regional Social Context," 50.

151. Nixon, "Society of Separatists," 24.

152. Colpetzer, "Regional Social Context," 83. For a more comprehensive look at the attitude of the local community toward the Zoarites, see Colpetzer.

9. "TO ENJOY THE ADVANTAGES COMMON TO ALL"

1. Record of Depositions, Goesele et al v. Bimeler et al, 14 Howard (U. S. 55), 114–22.

2. Record of Depositions, 124.

3. Record of Depositions, 126, 117, 124, 126.

4. "An Act to Incorporate the Society of Separatists of Zoar, Tuscarawas County, Ohio, No. 126," Zoar Papers, box 1, folder 7.

5. Zoar Constitution, 1833, Zoar Papers, box 1, folder 4.

6. Zoar Membership Database.

7. Sieber, quoted in Nixon, "Society of Separatists," 188–90.

8. Sieber, quoted in Nixon, "Society of Separatists," 188.

9. Bimeler Receipt Book, 253, Adamson Papers, box 2, folder 4, and Zoar Papers, box 3, folder 9. Schande's account in the Society Clothing Register (Zoar Papers, box 37, p. 61) ends in Dec. 1842 and lists him as having "died in the poor house." After the adjudication of the Supreme Court case, Weizhaar was granted an annuity of ten dollars per month until his death on May 9, 1856.

10. The correct German spelling is *Gössele;* it is referred to as *Gasely* in most of the court cases, *Gaseley* in the document expelling him from the Society (Zoar Papers, box 3, folder 8), and *Goesele* in the US Circuit and Supreme Court cases (10 Federal Cases 533 and 14 Howard [US 55]).

11. Fritz to author, Aug. 1998.

12. The actual birthdates and death dates of Johannes Jr. and his wife, Anna Maria, are unknown. Male members could join the Society at age twenty-one.

13. "Proceedings Against Gaseley," Zoar Papers, box 3, folder 8.

14. Used as precedent in cases from the Amana Society, Oneida Community, and the Harmony Society, "Rose's Notes," 679–80, contained in *Supreme Court Decisions.* The Amana case centered on the validity of its religious corporation; the Harmony Society and Oneida cases concerned whether their membership contracts were valid.

15. Testimonies of William Ehlers and George Ackermann, Jan. 15, 1845, Zoar Papers, box 3, folder 8.

16. Testimonies of Ehlers and Mary Short, Jan. 15, 1845, Zoar Papers, box 3, folder 8.

17. Testimony of John Bronney [Brunny], Jan. 15, 1845, Zoar Papers, box 3, folder 8.

18. Testimony of Peter Bimeler, Jan. 15, 1845, Zoar Papers, box 3, folder 8.

19. Testimony of Valentine Bieger, Jan. 15, 1845, Zoar Papers, box 3, folder 8.

20. Goesele to trustees, Jan. 16, 1845, Zoar Papers, box 3, folder 8.

21. "Notice to John Gasely from Zoar Trustees," Mar. 4, 1845, Zoar Papers, box 3, folder 8.

22. Zoar Clothing Register, 197. Interestingly, Heilman was still receiving clothing from the Society until Jan. 1846, after the suit was filed.

23. Boehringer Petition, Zoar Papers, box 3, folder 9.

24. Boehringer Petition, Zoar Papers, box 3, folder 9.

25. Goesele v. Bimeler, Tuscarawas County Court Records, bk. 7, 208.

26. Gasely v. Bimeler, 14 Howard 55 US 589 (1852), transcript in Nixon Family Papers, box 3, folder 16.

27. The parties in the first Goesele case became defendants on Jan. 10, 1849, Jans and Weizhaar on Apr. 30, 1849. Schedule, US Supreme Court Records, brief 309, 158, typescript in Nixon Papers, box 3, folder 16.

28. Gasely v. Bimeler, Case 2980, US Supreme Court Transcript, quoted in Kerr, "Dissident Movements"; Zoar Membership Database. Weizhaar left the Society on Jan. 23, 1843.

29. Testimonies of Caspari and Heilman, brief 209, case 2980, Transcript, US Supreme Court Law Library, 75–76, 95. Typescript in Nixon Papers, box 3, folder 16.

30. Nixon, "Society of Separatists," 193.

31. Zoar Papers, box 3, folder 9. The statement about "coverd heads" is in reference to Johannes Goesele Sr., who reportedly kept his hat on in an audience before Württemberg's Duke Frederick and Emperor Napoleon Bonaparte. See Morhart, *Zoar Story*, 13.

32. Zoar Papers, box 3, folder 9.

33. Zoar Papers, box 3, folder 9. Quinn later placed an advertisement in the *Ohio Democrat* in Oct. 1849: "Bimeler is merely their trustee, and suit is now pending to try his right. David Quinn, Atty.," Zoar Papers, box 84, folder 2.

34. Nixon Papers, box 3, folder 13. My grateful thanks to my friend and colleague Philip Webber for translating this document for me.

35. Marshall, *Courts and Lawyers of Ohio*, 4:270–71, 4:278–79.

36. Bimeler Receipt Book, 232, 237, 243. Stanberry also represented the Society in the Anna Maria Goesele case.

37. Shnayerson, *History of the Supreme Court*, 60–61.

38. Marshall, *Courts and Lawyers of Ohio*, 3:811–13.

39. *Ohio Federal Cases*, 533, 528 et seq.

40. Zoar Papers, box 3, folder 10.

41. Zoar Papers, box 3, folder 10.

42. Zoar Papers, box 3, folder 10.

43. Zoar Papers, box 3, folder 10.

44. Zoar Papers, box 3, folder 10.

45. Zoar Papers, box 3, folder 10.

46. R. L. Baker to Jacob Sylvan, Mar. 24, 1853, Nixon Papers, box 2, folder 12. The Harmonists' case was the Nachtreib case, also settled by the US Supreme Court in 1857. (See Duss, *The Harmonists*, 95–96.)

47. A fact misunderstood by other historians, including Nixon, "Society of Separatists," 195. The similar names make these cases very easily confused.

48. Copy of receipt of goods "furnished by the Society of Separatists of Zoar for John Gasely and family at Canal Dover by John J. Ruof," dated July 8, 1853, "barrel of flour, dried apples, 3 loaves bread, 4 lb. cheese, total $5.98"; furnished on Sept. 30, 1853 by Ruof: "flannel, jean, woolen yarn, barrel flour, 10 lb. beef, dried apples, cheese, green apples, more flannel, muslin, total $14.01½", Zoar Papers, box 3, folder 13.

49. John Gasely and Anna Maria Gasely v. The Society of Separatists of Zoar, Tuscarawas County Court of Common Pleas; copy of complaint in Zoar Papers, box 3, folder 13.

50. Zoar Papers, box 3, folder 8.

51. Zoar Papers, box 3, folder 13

52. Critchfield, *Cases Argued,* 13:155, 145.

53. Zoar Papers, box 3, folder 7.

10. "TESTED THE CONVICTION"

1. Nixon, "Society of Separatists," 14.

2. Fritz, "Roots of Zoar," 2:31; Zoar Separatists Matthias and Jakob Schacher, Jakob and Michael Gemmi and Jakob Walz all spent time in the Fortress Asperg for refusing to serve as soldiers before their emigration. See Eberhard Fritz's list of Separatists at http://eberhardfritz.de.tl/Separatisten-Wohnorte-H.htm.

3. Webber, *Civil War,* 9-10. I am grateful to my friend Philip Webber for these and many other translations that appear in this work.

4. Jan. 3, 1861, Zoar Papers, box 86, folder 1.

5. Webber, *Civil War,* 10-11.

6. Webber, *Civil War,* 11.

7. Webber, *Civil War,* 11.

8. Zoar Papers, box 86, folder 1.

9. Webber, *Civil War,* 14; Zoar Membership Database.

10. Adamson Papers, box 9, folder 15. This unsigned essay is in the writing style of Eugene B. Wright.

11. Adamson Papers, box 9, folder 15.

12. Morhart, *Zoar Story,* 117.

13. Webber, *Civil War,* 19, 22. I am indebted to Philip Webber for this list of names.

14. Nixon Papers, box 2, folder 2.

15. Adamson Papers, box 11, folder 3. The German version is in folder 2.

16. Title translation is in Webber, *Civil War,* 25.

17. Zoar Papers, box 64, Cash Book 20.

18. Adamson Papers, box 9, folder 15. The letter is unsigned.

19. Nixon Papers, box 2, folder 2.

20. Zoar Papers, box 96, folder 1.

21. Zoar Papers, box 64, Cash Book 20.

22. Adamson Papers, box 18, folder 7.

23. Adamson Papers, box 11, folder 4.

24. From Wright's "Autobiography," Adamson Papers, box 18, folder 7; Webber, *Civil War,* 41.

25. Adamson Papers, box 18, folder 7.

26. Adamson Papers, box 9, folder 14.

27. Zoar Papers, box 96, folder 1.

28. Adamson Papers, box 9, folder 14.

29. Adamson Papers, box 11, folder 7.

30. Webber, *Civil War,* 54.

31. Adamson Papers, box 9, folder 14.

32. Adamson Papers, box 9, folder 14.

33. Adamson Papers, box 9, folder 14.

34. Morhart, *Zoar Story*, 119; Zoar Papers, box 96, folder 1.

35. Zoar Papers, box 96, folder 1.

36. Adamson Papers, box 11, folder 11.

37. Zoar Papers, box 96, folder 1.

38. Quoted in Webber, *Civil War,* 33.

39. Adamson Papers, box 11, folder 10.

40. Morhart, *Zoar Story,* 119.

41. Zoar Papers, box 96, folder 1. The letter is dated 1864, but its contents point to 1863, as Rieker was released back to service on Oct. 6, 1864 (Webber, *Civil War,* 79).

42. Morhart, *Zoar Story,* 117.

43. Zoar Papers, box 96, folder 2; Nixon Papers, box 2, folder 2; WRHS Papers, container 2, folder 20.

44. *Ohio Democrat,* Nov. 13, 1863; Bimeler Receipt Book, 292-94; Adamson Papers, box 1, folder 6.

45. Zoar Papers, box 96, folder 1.

46. Zoar Papers, box 96, folder 1.

47. Zoar Papers, box 96, folder 1.

48. Adamson Papers, box 9, folder 8.

49. Adamson Papers, box 9, folder 36.

50. Adamson Papers, box 9, folder 36.

51. Webber, *Civil War,* 38-39.

52. Adamson Papers, box 9, folder 19.

53. Zoar Papers, box 65, Cash Book 23.

54. Zoar Membership Database; Zoar Papers, box 96, folder 1.

55. Zoar Papers, box 65, Cash Book 24. Ansbacher was not a member of the Society, but a Mag[dalena], age sixty-five, and a John, age twenty-one, are listed in the 1870 census, and perhaps are his mother (or grandmother) and brother. Neither of these were Society members.

56. Zoar Papers, box 56.

11. "APPLICANTS OF GOOD CHARACTER"

1. George F. Biggars to Ackermann, undated, Adamson Papers, box 9, folder 36.

2. Probationary Membership Contracts, Zoar Papers, box 2, folders 1-51

3. Zoar Constitution, 1833, Article 7, Zoar Papers, box 1, folder 4.

4. First Class Constitution reprinted in Nordhoff, *Communistic Societies,* 105, and appendix 7.

5. Hinds, *American Communities,* 26. Hinds in 1878 reported there were fifty-four members in the second class and seventy-five in the first class.

6. Hinds, *American Communities,* 27.

7. Zoar Membership Database. For instance, Carolina Ruof joined the first class in 1871, Regina Breymaier in 1878, Mary Breil in 1880, Carolina Kuemmerle in 1862; none of them joined the second class until 1898.

8. Nixon, "Applicants," 343; Hinds, *American Communities,* 26.

9. Hinds, *American Communities,* 30.

10. See the Sylvan-Seyfang correspondence in the Adamson Papers, box 9.

11. Hinds, *American Communities,* 30.

12. Nixon, "Applicants," 344.

13. Sanborn, "Communistic Societies of the United States," 27.

14. Karl Gustav Andler, Apr. 22, 1875, Nixon Papers, box 2, folder 17.

15. Nordhoff, *Communistic Societies,* 109, 110.

16. Zoar Papers, box 2, folder 58.

17. Ulmer, Mar. 1877, Nixon Papers, box 2, folder 17.

18. Rose, July 14, 1877, Nixon Papers, box 2, folder 17.

19. Johann Rossman, June 26, 1875, Nixon Papers, box 2, folder 17; Hoffman, Oct. 5, 1876, as quoted in Nixon, "Applicants," 245; Codman (his mark), Oct. 5, 1875, Nixon Papers, box 2, folder 17; Carter, Sept. 1 and Oct. 9, 1876, as quoted in Nixon, "Applicants," 346.

20. Biggars, July 29, (no year), as quoted in Nixon, "Applicants," 346.

21. Archut, Apr. 25, 1876, Nixon Papers, box 2, folder 17.

22. Edwins, June 29, 1876, Nixon Papers, box 2, folder 17; Flynn, ca. 1880, Nixon Papers, box 2, folder 17.

23. Melchior Vogt, Jan. 10, 1876, and Friedrich Simon, Feb. 24, 1876, Nixon Papers, box 2, folder 17.

24. Roesstle, National Soldiers' Home, Mar. 12, 1873, quoted in Nixon, "Applicants," 349.

25. Schmidt, National Soldiers' Home, Oct. 18, 1880, as quoted in Nixon, "Applicants," 346.

26. Birkbeck, Nov. 9, 1876. Nixon Papers, box 2, folder 17.

27. Brewer, June 19, 1876, Nixon Papers, box 2, folder 17.

28. Andler, Aug. 20, 1875, Nixon Papers, box 2, folder 17.

29. Dotterer, Aug. 30, 1875, Nixon Papers, box 2, folder 17.

30. Nordhoff, *Communistic Societies,* 112.

31. Zoar Society to J. Turner, Gettysburg, PA, June 10, 1859, Nixon Papers, box 2, folder 16, quoted in Nixon, "Society of Separatists," 181.

32. Zoar Society to Louisa W. (?) Speidel, Sidney, Ohio, July 28, 1859, Nixon Papers, box 2, folder 16.

33. A. W. Birkbeck, Nixon Papers, box 2, folder 17.

34. Nixon, "Applicants," 350.

35. Simon Beuter to Henrici and Lenz, Economy, PA, Apr. 22, 1878, quoted in Nixon, "Applicants," 348.

12. "THY DELIGHTS, ENCHANTING ZOAR"

1. Hayward, "Journal," 278–79.

2. Quinby, *Diary,* Oct. 18, 1831. Note that the errors in spelling and punctuation and the strike-throughs are in the original.

3. "Colony of Zoar," *Penny Magazine,* 411.

4. [Ripley,] *New Yorker,* 279.

5. Jenkins, *Ohio Gazetteer,* 491.

6. Bimeler Receipt Book, 15. Some of these funds may have come from non-member boarders who worked in the Society's iron furnaces and other enterprises; the record does not show where the funds came from or from whom.

7. P. F. D., "Harmony Builds the House," 1a–2a.

8. Nixon Papers, box 2, folder 13.

9. *Tuscarawas Advocate,* June 23, 1835.

10. Nixon, "Society of Separatists," 146.

11. Nixon, "Society of Separatists," 146.

12. *Iron Valley Reporter,* June 20, 1874.

13. *Iron Valley Reporter,* June 30, 1883; *Tuscarawas Advocate,* June 26, 1884.

14. Nixon Papers, box 1, folder 11.

15. Zoar Properties Collection, P369AV, Ohio History Connection.

16. Nixon Papers, box 2, folder 13.

17. Nixon Papers, box 2, folder 6; Moore, *Woolson,* 19.

18. Nixon Papers, box 2, folder 14.

19. Nixon Papers, box 2, folder 2.

20. Adamson Papers, box 9, folder 16.

21. Woolson to Christian Ruof (Woolson mistakenly spelled it as *Rouf*), Sept. 21, 1863, Adamson Papers, box 9, folder 16. A second letter on the same subject was written on Oct. 8, 1863.

22. Zoar Papers, box 51, Society Ledger, 144. Unlike other hotel guests, Woolson was such a good customer he had his own page of transactions in the ledger.

23. Adamson Papers, box 9, folder 16.

24. Nixon Papers, box 2, folder 13.

25. Moore, *Woolson,* 144.

26. Woolson, "The Happy Valley," 284, 285.

27. Woolson, "The Happy Valley," 285.

28. Adamson Papers, box 9, folder 25.

29. Woolson, "Wilhelmina," 296, 277.

30. *Tuscarawas Advocate,* Jan. 1, 1875.

31. *Tuscarawas Advocate,* Jan. 22, 1875.

32. *Tuscarawas Advocate,* Jan. 22, 1875.

33. Moore, *Woolson,* 48–49.

34. Moore, *Woolson,* 48.

35. Moore, *Woolson,* 49.

36. Moore, *Woolson,* 41, 141.

37. *Ohio Democrat,* June 12, 1874.

38. Potts, "A Queer, Quaint People," 372.

39. Potts, "A Queer, Quaint People," 373, 428, 431.

40. *Tuscarawas Advocate,* Oct. 26, 1882.

41. Knortz, *Aus der Mappe,* 27.

42. Heald, *Stark County Story,* 562.

43. Morhart, *Zoar Story,* 37.

44. *Encyclopedia of Cleveland History,* "George Worthington Co.," https://case.edu/ech/articles/g/george-worthington-co/.

45. Gunn, *Note-Book,* Nov. 12, 1889, 8.

46. Gunn, *Note-Book,* June 25, 1892, 51; Huntington, "Gunn of the Zoarites," 510; *Dictionary of American Biography* (1936), s.v. "William C. Whitney."

47. Gunn, *Note-Book,* Nov. 12, 1889, 7.

48. Gunn, *Note-Book,* June 4, 1892, 46.

49. Gunn, *Note-Book,* May 21, 1898, 237; Gunn, 255-61, lists all the varieties of roses and trees.

50. Huntington, "Gunn of the Zoarites," 506.

51. Nixon, "Society of Separatists," 212-13.

52. Nixon, "Society of Separatists," 214, 207.

53. Zoar Papers, box 1, folder 9.

54. Gunn, *Note-Book,* 44, 48.

55. *Iron Valley Reporter,* July 14, 1892. The same newspaper even included an engraving of the proposed new structure (May 5, 1892). Such an original engraving was an expensive and rare occurrence in a weekly newspaper of the time and shows the regard the local community had for Zoar and its tourist trade.

56. Morhart, *Zoar Story,* 120-21.

57. *Tuscarawas Advocate,* June 3, 1897.

58. Morhart, *Zoar Story,* 115.

59. *Iron Valley Reporter,* May 24, 1896.

60. See Waldman and Adams, "Zoar Art Colony," *Timeline Magazine,* 2-21, for a comprehensive illustrated discussion of Zoar as an artists' mecca in the late nineteenth and early twentieth centuries.

13. "VANISH LIKE A LIGHT MORNING MIST"

1. Knortz, *Aus der Mappe,* 28.

2. Shackleton, "In Quaint Old Zoar," 515.

3. Landis, *Annual Report,* 186-87.

4. Gunn, *Note-Book,* July 23, 1892, 54.

5. Nixon, "Society of Separatists," 220.

6. Nixon, "Society of Separatists," 217.

7. Adamson Papers, box 9, folder 14.

8. Beuter, *Tag-Buch,* trans. and quoted in Nixon, "Society of Separatists," 216.

9. Simon Beuter to John Duss, June 17, 1892, Economy-Zoar Correspondence, Old Economy Village.

10. Gunn, *Note-Book,* Apr. 2, 1897, 216.

11. *Iron Valley Reporter,* May 14, 1896.

12. Nixon, "Society of Separatists," 220.

13. Nixon, "Society of Separatists," 217-18.

14. Adamson Papers, box 7, folder 4. The profit for the Woolen Mill in 1897 was just $355.09.

15. Gunn, *Note-Book,* July 20, 1893, 80.

16. Nixon, "Society of Separatists," 218-19.

17. Nixon, "Society of Separatists," 219-20.

18. Nixon, "Society of Separatists," 223.

19. *The Nugitna,* 1, no. 1 (Dec. 30, 1895). The original *Nugitna* copies are at the Ohio History Connection Library, Vault 284.1, N896. All issues are reproduced in their entirety in Randall, *History,* 55-68.

20. *The Nugitna* 1, no. 2 (Jan. 27, 1896).

21. *The Nugitna* 1, no. 3 (Feb. 24, 1896).

22. Nixon, "Society of Separatists," 224.

23. *The Nugitna* 1, no. 4 (Mar. 23, 1896; issue never published).

24. Nixon, "Society of Separatists," 225.

25. Zoar Papers, box 1, folder 10.

26. Nixon, "Society of Separatists," 136. This was part of a long-standing idea to use the clay deposits on this land. In 1891 the trustees, searching for new income, tried to entice investors to exploit these resources. It was not until 1911 that the Zoar Fire Clay Company, which operated under different names through the 1990s, was formed.

27. Zoar Papers, box 3, folder 5.

28. Nixon, "Society of Separatists," 226.

29. Nixon, "Society of Separatists," 216-17.

30. Gunn, *Note-Book,* May 21, 1898, 238.

31. Gunn, *Note-Book,* May 21, 1898, 238; May 24, 1898, 239.

32. Randall, *History,* 47.

33. Randall, *History,* 48.

34. Gunn, *Note-Book,* Oct. 5, 1898, 243-44.

35. Nixon, "Society of Separatists," 224.

36. *Iron Valley Reporter,* Sept. 29, 1898.

37. Nixon, "Society of Separatists," 227.

38. "The Dissolution of the Separatists," *Plain Dealer,* Mar. 27, 1898.

39. Editorial, *Iron Valley Reporter,* Mar. 10, 1898.

40. *Iron Valley Reporter,* Aug. 4, 1898 and Aug. 18, 1898.

41. *Iron Valley Reporter,* Oct. 13, 1898.

42. Randall, *History,* 75-76.

43. Gunn, *Note-Book,* Jan. 13, 1899, 245.

44. *Iron Valley Reporter,* Sept. 14, 1899.

45. *The Chronicler,* Spring 2002, Tuscarawas County Historical Society. Nixon says ("Society of Separatists," 229) the first pastor was a Reverend Bittner, but Fred Miller, director of the Historical Society, in his article on the Zoar dissolution, checked the record book of Bolivar St. John's United Church of Christ (then the Reformed Church) to confirm the first pastor was Dr. Merten.

46. Nixon, "Society of Separatists," 229.

47. Beuter, *Tag-Buch,* trans. and quoted in Nixon, "Society of Separatists," 229.

48. Morhart, *Zoar Story,* 135.

14. "POSSESSES NATIONAL SIGNIFICANCE"

1. Sarbaugh, "A Brief History of Zoar."

2. Randall, *History,* 73.

3. The author was told by several descendants that, especially as they entered their teen years at school in Bolivar, they were teased by their "outsider" peers for their clothes and accents. Many born after the dissolution, like Hilda Morhart and Hildegard Mead, learned German as their first language and spoke English with an accent for the rest of their lives.

4. Hodgdon, *Little Town,* 13.

5. Electric bill, Zoar Village State Memorial files.1902. This generator is in the Ohio History Connection collection.

6. Randall, *History,* 74.

7. "Lake Zoar" brochure (1923), Adamson Papers, folder 19, box 11; "Fire Levels Hall at Zoar," *Daily Reporter,* Jan. 24, 1959.

8. Adamson Papers, box 19, folder 10.

9. A "Zoar Mineral Springs Water" poster can be seen at the Zoar Town Hall museum.

10. "Towpath Trail Guide."

11. "Zoar Bicentennial Celebration," *The Chronicler,* Winter 2016, 3.

12. Adamson Papers, box 19, folder 11.

13. Hodgdon, *Little Town,* 16.

14. The Zoar drawings and photos can be found online at http://www.loc.gov/pictures/related/?q=Ohio--Tuscarawas%20County--Zoar&fi=places&co=hh. To find images from the Index of American Design, now housed at the National Gallery of Art, Washington, DC, go to https://www.nga.gov/content/ngaweb/Collection/collection-search.html. Paintings of Zoar buildings done by the Art Project can be seen today at Zoar Village State Memorial.

15. "Our plans will permit preservation and development of the village in line with the wishes of state and national historical societies," A. D. Taylor, consulting engineer for the War Department, quoted in the story "How Zoar Will Benefit by Muskingum Plan," *Plain Dealer,* Nov. 14, 1934.

16. US Army Corps of Engineers, "Zoar Levee Study," 9.

17. Hodgdon, *Little Town,* 24-31. Additionally, in 1974, Hilda Morhart wrote a cookbook "From Field to Table" (1974), illustrated by Edna Leuking and containing many traditional Zoar recipes.

18. Hodgdon, *Little Town,* 31.

19. National Park Service, "The Route to Prosperity."

20. US Army Corps of Engineers, "Zoar Levee Study," 12.

21. US Army Corps of Engineers, "Zoar Levee Study," 12.

22. "Zoar's Bimeler House," *Timeline Magazine,* 12.

APPENDIX 1

1. This may refer to Napoleon's incorporating Württemberg into the French Empire, or some other political or religious event where the clergy would lose special privilege.

2. This refers to the aborted purchase of the estate of Brandenburg, not the northern German state. See chapter 1.

3. Huber is making a play on words in reference to the Fortress Hohen Asperg, where he and many other Separatists were imprisoned.

APPENDIX 3

These records are from Nixon, "Society of Separatists," 251-52.

1. The Zoar Society corporation was not officially dissolved until 1900, and the trustees and Standing Committee remained in office to complete the work of the division. Note that the Standing Committee and the office of cashier were established with the 1833 Constitution; the office of arbiter was established with the 1824 Articles of Agreement and its powers transferred to the office of agent general with the 1833 Constitution. Joseph Bimeler was the only person to hold the office of agent general, which remained unfilled after his 1853 death.

2. For an unknown reason, Edgar Nixon referred to Joseph Michael Bimeler as "John" Bimeler throughout his dissertation. The first name has been corrected here.

Bibliography

BOOKS

Arndt, Karl J. R. *A Documentary History of the Indiana Decade of the Harmony Society 1814-1824.* 2 vols. Indianapolis: Indiana Historical Society, 1975.

——. *George Rapp's Harmony Society (1785-1847).* Philadelphia: Univ. of Pennsylvania Press, 1965.

——. *George Rapp's Re-Established Harmony Society, 1848-1868.* New York: Peter Lang, 1993.

Bimeler, Joseph Michael. *Die Wahre Separation, oder die Wiedergeburt.* Zoar, OH, 1856.

——. *Etwas fürs Herz! Oder Geistliche Brosamen von des Herrn Tisch gefallen.* Zoar, OH, 1860.

Brown, Dale W. *Understanding Pietism.* Rev. ed. Nappanee, IN: Evangel Publishing House, 1995.

Cleveland, Ohio: Pictorial and Biographical Deluxe Supplement. Vol. 2. Chicago: S. J. Clarke, 1910.

Critchfield, Leander J. *Reports of Cases Argued and Determined in the Supreme Court of Ohio.* Vol. 13. Cincinnati: Robert Clarke & Co., 1874.

Dictionary of American Biography. Vol. 10. New York: Charles Scribner & Sons, 1936.

Duss, John S. *The Harmonists.* Ambridge, PA: Harmonie Associates, 1970.

Etizoni, Amatai. *A Comparative Analysis of Complex Organizations.* New York: Free Press, 1975.

Fernandez, Kathleen M. *A Singular People: Images of Zoar.* Kent, OH: Kent State Univ. Press, 2003.

Fritz, Eberhard. *Radikaler Pietismus in Württemberg.* Epfendorf: Bibliotheca Academica, 2003.

Gieck, Jack. *A Photo Album of Ohio's Canal Era 1825-1913.* Kent, OH: Kent State Univ. Press, 1988.

Gunn, Alexander. *Hermitage-Zoar Note-Book and Journal of Travel.* New York: privately printed, 1902.

Heald, E. T. *The Stark County Story.* Vol. 2. *The McKinley Era.* Canton, OH: Stark County Historical Society, 1950.

Hinds, William Alfred. *American Communities.* Rev. ed. Chicago: Charles H. Kerr and Co., 1902. First published Oneida, NY, 1878.

Hodgdon, Dorothy Nixon. *Zoar: The Little Town that Thought It Could,* privately published, 2017. First published 1993.

Howe, Henry. *Historical Collections of Ohio.* Vol. 2. Cincinnati: C. J. Krebiel and Co., 1908. First published 1847.

Jenkins, Warren. *Ohio Gazetteer and Travellers Guide.* Columbus, OH: Isaac N. Whitney, 1841.

Kantor, Rosabeth. *Commitment and Community.* Cambridge, MA: Harvard Univ. Press, 1972.

Knortz, Karl. *Aus der Mappe eines Deutsch-Amerikaners, Frommes und Gottleses.* Bamberg, 1893.

Mansfield, John B. *History of Tuscarawas County.* Chicago: Warner, Beers & Co., 1884.

Marshall, Carrington T. *Courts and Lawyers of Ohio.* Vols. 3 and 4. New York: American Historical Society, 1934.

Maximillian, Prince of Wied. *Travels in the Interior of North America.* Vol. 3, contained in *Early Western Travels,* bk. 24. Edited by Reuben Gold Thwaites. Cleveland: Arthur Clark Co., 1905.

Metz, Christian. *Historische Beschreibung der wahren Inspirations-Gemeinschaft, wie sie bestanden und sich fortgephlanzt hat, vom Jahr 1714 bis zum Jahr 1845.* Buffalo, NY, 1863.

Mitchner, C[harles] H. *Ohio Annals, Historic Events in the Tuscarawas and Muskingum Alleys, and in Other Portions of the State of Ohio.* Dayton, OH: T. W. Odell, 1876.

Morhart, Hilda Dischinger. *The Zoar Story.* Dover, OH: Seibert Printing Co., 1967.

———. *From Field to Table: A Collection of Original Zoar Recipes.* Zoar, OH: privately printed, 1974.

Meyers, David. *A Glance of Heaven: The Design and Operation of the Separatist Society of Zoar.* Lexington, KY: Exploding Stove Media, 2015.

Moore, Rayburn S. *Constance Fenimore Woolson.* New York: Twayne Publications, 1963.

National Park Service. *A Route to Prosperity.* Omaha, NE: National Park Service, 1993.

Nordhoff, Charles. *Communistic Societies of the United States.* New York: Dover Publications, 1966. First published 1875.

Ohio Federal Cases. Vol. 3. Norwalk, OH: Laning Printing Co., 1900.

Pitzer, Donald E., ed. *America's Communal Utopias.* Chapel Hill, NC: Univ. of North Carolina Press, 1997.

Randall, E. O. *History of the Zoar Society from its Commencement to its Conclusion: A Sociological Study of Communism.* 3rd ed. Columbus, OH: Press of Fred J. Heer, 1904. First printed as an article in the *Ohio Archaeological and Historical Society Quarterly,* 1899.

Reibel, Daniel B. *A Guide to Old Economy.* Harrisburg, PA: Pennsylvania Historical and Museum Commission, 1972.

Shambaugh, Bertha A. *The Community of True Inspiration.* Iowa City: State Histori-
cal Society of Iowa, 1908.
Shnayerson, Robert. *A History of the Supreme Court.* New York: Abrams, 1986.
Supreme Court Decisions, 13-16 Howard. Vol. 14. Lawyers Edition. Rochester, NY:
Lawyers Cooperative Publishing Co., 1918.
Webber, Philip E. *Zoar in the Civil War.* Kent, OH: Kent State Univ. Press, 2007.
Woolson, Constance F. "Wilhelmina" and "Solomon," *Castle Nowhere: Lake-Country
Sketches.* Boston: James R. Osgood & Co., 1875.

PAMPHLETS

"Ohio & Erie Canal Towpath Trail Guide." Tuscarawas County Canal Lands Development Committee, 2002.
Sarbaugh, Howard A. "A Brief History of Zoar." Zoar, OH: Zoar Historical Society,
1931.
US Army Corps of Engineers. "Zoar Levee and Diversion Dam Safety Modifica-
tion Study," 2013.

NEWSPAPERS

American Socialist (Oneida, NY)
Canton (Ohio) Repository
Daily Reporter (Dover, OH)
Elmira (New York) Telegram
Iron Valley Reporter (Dover, OH)
The Nugitna (Zoar, OH) [Vault 284.91 N896, Ohio History Connection Archives
and Library]
Ohio Democrat (New Philadelphia, OH)
(Columbus) Ohio Statesman
Plain Dealer (Cleveland, OH)
Republican Advocate (Wooster, OH)
Summit Beacon (Akron, OH)
Tuscarawas Advocate (New Philadelphia, OH)

JOURNAL AND MAGAZINE ARTICLES

[Bateham, M. B.] *Ohio Cultivator* 4 (Aug. 15, 1848): 118.
Bognar, E. J. "Blast Furnaces Operated by the Separatist Society of Zoar, Ohio."
Ohio Archaeological and Historical Society Quarterly 39 (1930): 503-13.
Case Western Reserve University. Encyclopedia of Cleveland History. https://case
.edu/ech/.
Christine, Geoffrey Williston. "Zoar and the Zoarites." *Peterson's Magazine* 95, no.
1 (Jan. 1889): 33-39.

The Chronicler. Newsletter (Tuscarawas County Historical Society) 15, no. 2 (Spring 2002): 3-12; 29, no. 6 (Winter 2016): 1-3.

"The Colony of Zoar." *Penny Magazine* 6 (Oct. 26, 1837): 411-12.

Durnbaugh, Donald F. "'Strangers and Exiles': Assistance Given by the Religious Society of Friends to the Separatists Society of Zoar in 1817-1818." *Ohio History* 106 (Winter/Summer 2000): 71-92.

Fernandez, Kathleen. "A Separatist Song: A Newly Discovered Poem About Zoar's Beginnings." *Communal Societies* 38, no. 1 (2018): 81-108.

———. "The Society of Separatists of Zoar v . . ." *Communal Societies* 26, no. 1 (2006): 105-15.

Fritz, Eberhard. "Roots of Zoar, Ohio, in Early 19th Century Württemberg: The Separatist Group in Rottenacker and Its Circle." Pts. 1 and 2. *Communal Societies* 22 (2001): 27-44; 23 (2002): 29-44.

Huntington, Webster P. "Gunn of the Zoarites." *Ohio Magazine* 1 (1906): 499-510.

Landis, George. "The Society of Separatists of Zoar, Ohio." *Annual Report of the American Historical Association* (1899): 165-220.

"Life and Experiences of Issachar Bates." *Shaker Quarterly* 2 (Spring 1962): 24-27.

Lockyer, Joshua. "From Developmental Communalism to Transformative Utopianism." *Communal Societies* 29, no. 1 (2009): 2-5.

Nixon, Edgar B. "The Zoar Society Applicants for Membership." *Ohio Archaeological and Historical Society Quarterly* 45, no. 4 (1936): 341-50.

Peters, Victor. "The German Pietists: Spiritual Mentors of the German Communal Settlements in America." *Communal Societies* 1 (1981): 55-66.

Potts, Pipsey [Rosella Rice]. "A Queer, Quaint People." Pts. 1, 2, and 3. *Arthur's Home Magazine* (May 1882): 312-14; (June 1882): 371-74; (July 1882): 428-31.

[Ripley, Sophia Dana]. "A Western Community." *New Yorker,* July 17, 1841. Originally published in *The Dial,* July 1841.

Sanborn, Franklin. "The Communistic Societies of the United States." *North American Review* 12, no. 246 (1875): 227.

Selig, Robert. "O Gieb Mir Brod Mit Hungert: The Great Famine of 1817." *German Life* (Dec. 2015-Jan. 2016): 44-46.

Shackleton, Robert. "In Quaint Old Zoar." *Godey's Magazine* 83, no. 797 (1896): 514-17.

Specht, Neva Jean. "'Constrained to Afford Them Countenance and Protection': The Role of the Philadelphia Quakers in the Settlement of the Society of Separatists of Zoar." *Communal Societies* 24 (2003): 95-108.

Waldman, Lawrence, and Henry Adams. "Zoar Art Colony." *Timeline Magazine* 34, no. 3 (July-Sept. 2017): 2-21.

Webber, Philip E. "Jakob Sylvan's Preface to *Die Wahre Separation oder die Widergeburt,* as an Introduction to Un(der)studied Separatist Principles." *Communal Societies* 19 (1999): 101-28.

———. "Simon Beuter's Journal as a Primary Source for Zoar History: Illustrated by Passages Dealing with the Passing of Zoar's Founding Leader, Joseph M. Bäumeler." *Communal Societies* 26 (2006): 117-34.

Wittke, Carl. "Ora et Labora: A German Methodist Utopia." *Ohio History* 67, no. 2 (Apr. 1958): 129-40.

Woolson, Constance Fenimore. "The Happy Valley." *Harper's New Monthly Magazine* 41, no. 242 (July 1870): 282-85.
"Zoar's Bimeler House." *Timeline Magazine* 34, no. 2 (Apr.-June 2017): 10-13.

UNPUBLISHED PAPERS

Durnbaugh, Donald W. "Radical Pietist Roots." Unpublished paper presented at Zoar's 175th anniversary, Zoar, OH, Nov. 1992.
Fernandez, Kathleen. "Communal Communications: Zoar's Letters to Harmony and Amana." Unpublished paper presented at the Communal Studies Association, Amana, IA, 1984.
———. "The Zoar Artist." Unpublished paper presented at the Communal Studies Association, Oneida, NY, 1994.
Fritz, Eberhard. "From Württemberg to Zoar: Origins of a Separatist Community." Unpublished paper presented at the Communal Studies Association, Zoar, OH, Oct. 6, 2017.
Kerr, Jonathan. "Dissident Movements within the Separatist Society of Zoar." Unpublished paper, 1975, Zoar Village State Memorial Library.
MacDonald, Gerald. "The Roots of Zoar in Radical Pietism." Unpublished paper presented at the Communal Studies Association, Zoar, OH, Oct. 2017.
Owen, Cheryl A. "Zoar's German Foodways, 1835-1860." Unpublished paper, 1992, Zoar Village State Memorial Library.
White, Elizabeth S. "J. M. Bimeler: Religious Leader of the Zoarites." Unpublished paper presented at Zoar's 175th anniversary, Nov. 1992.

MANUSCRIPT COLLECTIONS

Adamson, Jack and Pat, Collection, 1709-1975, MSS1276AV, Ohio History Connection Library, Columbus, OH.
Amana Society Papers, Amana Heritage Society, Amana, IA.
Andrews Shaker Collection, folder 1048, Union Village to New Lebanon, June 7, 1824, Winterthur Library, Wilmington, DE.
Beuter, Simon. *Tag-Buch,* MIC 70, Ohio History Connection Library.
Bimeler Receipt Book, Adamson Papers, MSS1276 AV, box 2, folder 4. http://www.ohiomemory.org/cdm/ref/collection/p16007coll10/id/2432.
Harmonist-Zoar Correspondence, Old Economy Village Archives, Ambridge, PA.
Harmony Society Papers, MSS 185, Pennsylvania State Archives, Harrisburg, PA, Incoming Correspondence Files and microfilm reels 76 and 105.
Hayward, George Washington. "Journal of a Trip to Ohio," (Sept. 26, 1829), 278-79, Ohio History Connection Library.
Nixon Family Papers, MSS680AV, Ohio History Connection Library, Columbus, OH.
P. F. D., "Harmony Builds the House," 1832 essay about Zoar. Contained in the Peter

Kaufmann Papers, MSS136AV, Ohio History Connection Library, Columbus, OH. (Translation by Wolfgang Fleishhauer in author's possession.)

Quinby, Moses. *Diary,* Oct. 12-13, 1831. MSS 217, Cornell University Library, Ithaca, NY.

Rotch/Wales Collection, Massillon (OH) Library. http://www.ohiomemory.org /cdm/compoundobject/collection/p267401coll36/id/21249/rec/3.

Society Clothing Register, Zoar Papers, MSS110AV, box 37, Ohio History Connection Library, Columbus, OH. http://www.ohiomemory.org/cdm/ref/collection /p16007coll10/id/3692.

Society of Separatists of Zoar Papers 1839-1857, MSS984AV, Ohio History Connection, Columbus, OH.

Society of Separatists of Zoar Papers, MSS 1663. Western Reserve Historical Society Library, Cleveland, OH.

Society of Separatists of Zoar Records 1811-1945, MSS110AV. Ohio History Connection Library, Columbus, OH.

DISSERTATIONS AND THESES

Colpetzer, Susan E. "The Society of Separatists of Zoar: A Study of a Communal Society within a Regional Social Context, Focusing on the Years 1870-1898." MA thesis, Ohio State University, 1985.

Nixon, Edgar. "The Society of Separatists of Zoar." PhD diss., Ohio State University, 1933. http://rave.ohiolink.edu/etdc/view?acc_num=osu1141932248.

DATABASES

Fernandez, Kathleen. *Zoar Membership Database,* in possession of the author.

Fritz, Eberhard. *Database of Württemberg Separatists.* http://eberhardfritz.de.tl /Separatisten-Wohnorte-H.htm.

Index

＋✕＋

Page numbers in italics refer to illustrations.

Ackermann, Christina, 128
Ackermann, Jacob, 133, 156-57, 188
Ackermann, Joseph Georg, 25, 33-34, 36, 52, 75, 116
Adamson, Jack, 215
Adamson, Pat, 215
advertising: auction of Zoar, 61, *201*, 202; for canal contracts, 48-49; by farm equipment maker, 56; for tourism to Zoar, 177, 185, 186, 190; by Zoar iron industry, 83, 85-86, 91
agriculture, 54-67; agricultural transactions and Zoar finances, 91; apple orchards and products, 33, 64-67, *65*, 115; Canal Mill, 59, 62, 79, 175, 199; Cider Mill, 67, 98-99, 116-17; contractors and hired labor, 55-56, 58-60; dairy operations and transactions, 60-63, 92; Garden House, 178, 210; grapes, 67, 117; land used for, 22, 54-55; livestock, 29-30, 51, 60-64; methods of, 56-57, *57*; mills for, 58-60, *59;* tenant farmers, 55-56, 110; trustee in charge of, 29, 50-51; and Zoar dissolution, 202-3; Zoar Garden, 65-66, 177, *177,* 208-9, *209. See also* animals; dairy
alcohol production and use: Brewery, 67, 104, 116, 207; Canal Tavern, 69, 72, 97, 139-41, 146-47; Cider Mill, 67, 98-99, 116-17; grapes for wine, 67, 117; Number One House as wine dispensary,
117; and tourism to Zoar, 177-78, 186, 187, 190
Alexander I, Czar, 12
Allen, William, 16
Amana Society, 94, 139. *See also* Inspirationists
American Communities (Hinds), 165-67, 170-71
American Historical Association, 193
American Socialist (newspaper), on communal living, 171
Andler, Karl Gustav, 172
animals: dog breeding, 133; horses used by tourists, 179, 181; livestock, 29-30, 51, 60-64; and Zoar dissolution, 207
Ansbacher, William, 164
appearance of Zoar members. *See* clothing and appearance
Archut, Carl, 171
Arndt, Karl J. R., 95
art: artists' studios at Zoar, 190-91; Zoar "antique" interest, 210; Zoar Artist, *44,* 129, 133. *See also* music
Arthur's Home Magazinei, on lifestyle, 124
Articles of Agreement: amending, 37; Constitution (1833), 26, 31-32, 37, 166; creation of society (1819), 20; first Articles (1819), 26-27, 29-30; lawsuit about, 141-47; original signers of, 25-26; second Articles (1824), 26, 31; signatures by illiterate members, 134; on "true Christian love," 24